SOVIET PRISON CAMP SPEECH:

A Survivor's Glossary

SOVIET PRISON CAMP SPEECH

A Survivor's Glossary

SUPPLEMENTED BY TERMS FROM THE WORKS
OF A. I. SOLŽENICYN

COMPILED BY

Meyer Galler

AND

Harlan E. Marquess

The University of Wisconsin Press

Published 1972
The University of Wisconsin Press
Box 1379, Madison, Wisconsin 53701

The University of Wisconsin Press, Ltd.
70 Great Russell Street, London

First printing

Printed in the United States of America

ISBN 0-299-06080-2; LC 75-176411

To Ewel and Tamara Galler, my parents,
and to Estera Galler, my wife,
all of whom perished in Auschwitz in 1943

M. G.

Contents

ACKNOWLEDGMENTS

It is a pleasure for us to acknowledge the valuable assistance of those who have contributed to the Glossary in various ways. We are indebted to several present and former members of the Slavic Department of the University of Wisconsin—to Lawrence L. Thomas for suggestions for handling certain technical problems, to J. Thomas Shaw and Victor Terras for reading an early draft of the manuscript and making many valuable suggestions, and to all three for their interest and encouragement. For helping us to understand nuances of Russian words and expressions and to find suitable English slang equivalents, our obligations extend to colleagues, Russian acquaintances, and students who were often not even aware of the assistance they were providing. Special thanks are due Gleb P. Struve, who has encouraged our project from the very beginning, who has read all drafts of the manuscript, and who has been unstintingly generous with his time and most valuable advice. Needless to say, the responsibility for the final product is ours alone.

M. G.
Hayward, California

H. E. M.
Madison, Wisconsin

Origin of the Glossary

The idea of compiling a glossary of Soviet labor camp and prison jargon, based on my own experiences in Stalin's camps and prisons, came to me in 1964 while reading the reminiscences of Maksimov, Krasnov, Margolin, and other former prisoners. It seemed to me that such a glossary would be of great interest to many people: to historians, social scientists, and students of the Russian language, and to the general reader as well, particularly in the free world. This special jargon, which appears in the reminiscences of former prisoners published since the end of World War II (and even earlier), became most widely known, perhaps, after the publication in 1962 of Aleksandr Solženicyn's *One Day in the Life of Ivan Denisovič*. But, despite numerous occurrences of the jargon in a variety of publications, no extensive glossary has appeared until now.

Let me give some brief biographical data to demonstrate my association with Soviet prison and camp life for almost seventeen years. With the German invasion of Poland in 1939, I was caught up in the whirlwind of World War II. August, 1941, found me in the Alma-Ata district of Kazax SSR, where I was employed till May, 1942. On May 22, 1942, I was asked to report to the Special Section of the organization where I was working. There, after a few questions, two secret agents of the NKVD politely "extended an invitation" to visit the Alma-Ata NKVD office to clarify certain matters. My visit with the organs of the secret police lasted exactly ten years.

Following my arrest, I was placed in solitary confinement in the inner prison at Alma-Ata for the six months of my investi-

11

gation. At the end of this period, after exhaustive daily and nightly interrogations, I signed a statement of all charges against me, and thereupon was transferred to a common cell to await trial.

A year later (in 1943), I was finally presented with an administrative decision of the Special Commission of the NKVD which, on the basis of my alleged "counter-revolutionary activities," sentenced me without trial to ten years of corrective labor camps. Up to that moment I did not even know that my fate would be decided by this notorious agency. Refusing to sign this document only resulted in my being confined in a cold, windowless dungeon, where I soon realized that I could survive only by signing it.

Soon after this I was transferred to the Jangijul' transit camp near Taškent, the capital of Uzbek SSR. This was a three-day trip in a very crowded Stolypin railroad car, the first of several I was to take. I remained at Jangijul' for several weeks digging construction foundations, and in August, 1943, I was transferred to the Aktjubinsk labor camp in Kazax SSR. There at different times I worked in the housing zone for free employees, in a brickmaking camp, in an agricultural area, and in a penalty lime camp, as well as in the main compound. At the beginning of 1945 I was reassigned to the infamous old Karaganda camps, or Karlag. On the way, the shipment was delayed for several months in the Sol'-Ileck transit prison. In the spring of 1945 we continued our journey in Stolypin railroad cars, going by way of Nižnij Tagil. It is still a mystery to me why, in order to reach Karaganda, we travelled to Nižnij Tagil, but it is one of the many mysteries of Soviet prisoner shipments. At this enormous labor camp, called by Solženicyn "a kingdom bigger than France," I passed through the Karabas transit camp, the gateway for me to Čurubaj-Nura, Sarepta, Dolinka, Saranstroj, and to numerous sub-sections of these districts of the Karaganda camp system.

My release occurred exactly on the tenth anniversary of my arrest. A passport with the thirty-ninth provision was issued to me, restricting me to small towns and villages in the Asian part of the Soviet Union. Due to this limited choice, I selected the Irkutsk area near Lake Bajkal, also an area with numerous corrective labor camps, and considered to be a region of severe climate, but superior to Karaganda. Initially I settled in Kitoj and, afterwards, in Angarsk, where I worked as a "free" employee alongside prisoners till 1956. Angarsk, a new settlement built around a huge industrial complex, was settled mainly by ex-prisoners. At the time I left, the population had reached about 150,000 residents. There, along with thousands of prisoners and ex-prisoners like myself, I participated as a laborer in the construction of Angarsk and its huge chemical factory. Because of the restrictions of the thirty-ninth provision, I was unable to work in my field (chemistry).

At the end of 1953, having observed the changes which were occurring in Soviet Russia after Stalin's death, I decided that the time was right to request the Soviet judicial authorities to review my case. I emphasized that I did not feel, and had never felt, that I had committed any crime, even according to Soviet law. Previously, numerous such requests resulted in a standard laconic answer, "the case has been reviewed and upheld." I must admit that I was luckier than many of my peers because my request did not result in an additional sentence. In 1956 I was rehabilitated upon the order of the chief military prosecutor of the USSR. I assume that my rehabilitation at that time was the result of my personal appeal, and not of a general rehabilitation of ex-prisoners after de-Stalinization, because two of my co-defendants, who did not appeal, were not rehabilitated until a year later. Upon the order of the chief military prosecutor, the camp office where I completed my sentence issued a statement to the effect that I had worked ten years as an agro-technician in POB R-246, a section of the Karaganda camp system. This was the last but one of the countless jobs performed by me during the ten years of my imprisonment. Such statements were issued only to rehabilitated prisoners who were entitled to include the imprisonment period in their total length of service. Without full rehabilitation, an ex-prisoner lost continuity of service (which is very important in the Soviet Union, where all employment is with the government). It may be of interest to the reader to learn that, according to Soviet law, I received two months' salary as compensation for my ten years of imprisonment after my rehabilitation.

In 1957, before leaving the Soviet Union, I returned to Karaganda for personal and economic reasons. There I had the opportunity to observe the changes which had occurred after the de-Stalinization period. I remained there till the end of 1958, when I was permitted to leave Russia under the terms of the Polish–Soviet Union treaty.

M. G.

Introduction

A distinctive Russian idiom, spawned by and spoken in Soviet prisons and labor camps, has recently come to the attention of readers of "concentration camp" literature. This substandard variety of Russian, which I shall designate prison camp speech, is essentially Russian, but "tainted" by legal and administrative jargon, borrowings from non-Russian Soviet nationalities, criminal argot, obscenities, and, frequently, by elements of un-educated peasant speech. Literature containing prison camp speech typically circulates "underground" in the Soviet Union and eventually makes its way to the West, where it is published, although the most famous example, Aleksandr Solženicyn's Один день Ивана Денисовича (*One Day in the Life of Ivan Denisovič*), was first published in the Soviet Union.[1] In this short novel, which created a sensation when it appeared in 1962, not only do most of the characters use prison camp speech, but the narrator and main character does as well. But, although this novel is most striking in the amount of prison camp speech used, it is by no means unique, and it is more than likely that other works containing this speech will continue to appear in the years ahead.

1. The system of transliteration used throughout is that designated System III in J. Thomas Shaw, *The Transliteration of Modern Russian for English-Language Publications* (Madison, 1967). Russian titles cited in the text of the Introduction and in the notes will be followed in parentheses either by a translation or by the corresponding English title (which occasionally will not be a literal translation of the Russian). References in square brackets are to the List of References, where complete biblio-graphical information may be found.

Prison camp speech first began to appear in print soon after the Russian Revolution and long before the appearance of Solženicyn's novel. Early examples of it can be found in the 1920s in the accounts of prisoners who had been released or who managed to escape and subsequently find their way to the West [e.g., Malsagoff 1926, Bessonov 1928].[2] The 1930s, particularly the period of the purges (1934–37), evoked a rather large number of works by former prisoners, some of which are only now being published. Nearly all contain some prison camp speech. A recent example is Evgenija Semenovna Ginzburg's Крутой маршрут (*Journey Into the Whirlwind*) [Гинзбург 1967]. An earlier, very interesting example is R. V. Ivanov-Razumnik's Тюрьмы и ссылки (*The Memoirs of Ivanov-Razumnik*) [Иванов-Разумник 1953]. This work describes the author's experiences in prisons not only during the 1930s, but during the early 1920s and in 1901 under the tsarist regime as well.

A third group of reminiscences deals with World War II and the postwar period. Many of these accounts were written by Poles, who were deported to camps in 1939–40 and released in 1941–42 to join the Polish troops being formed in the Soviet Union to fight the Nazis. Representative works include Gustav Herling's *A World Apart* [Herling 1951] and Jerzy Gliksman's *Tell the West* [Gliksman 1948].[3] Many of these Polish nationals, however, such as Julij Margolin, author of Путешествие в страну зэ-ка (*Journey to the Land of the Z-k*) [Марголин 1952], and the co-author of this Glossary, Meyer Galler, were obliged to serve out their sentences, in the words of the prisoners themselves, от звонка до звонка 'from the first bell to the last.' The post-World War II period is represented most notably by the fiction of Aleksandr Solženicyn. Besides his famous first novel, two others containing prison camp speech have been published in the West, Раковый корпус (*The Cancer Ward*) and В круге первом (*The First Circle*) [Солженицын 1968, 1969a]. Also published only in the West and containing much prison camp

---

2. A bibliography containing many memoirs of former prisoners from the twenties and thirties is to be found in Dallin and Nicolaevsky 1947 pp. 309–319.

3. Although some prison camp speech is necessarily lost or obscured in works published in non-Russian languages, many forms "survive" the transition from Russian as transliterations.

speech is his play, Олень и шалашовка (*The Love-Girl and the Innocent*) [Солженицын 1969b].[4]

And finally, one might mention Anatolij Marčenko's Мои показания (*My Testimony*) [Марченко 1969], a work which may be the first of a new wave of reminiscences, one dealing with the post-Stalin penal system. It is sometimes thought that the lot of Soviet prisoners has greatly improved since Stalin's death. Marčenko's account reveals that, while political imprisonment may be less common today, in many ways the conditions in camps and especially in prisons are just as grim as ever.

The origin of prison camp speech, then, can be traced back to the first years after the Revolution. The number of speakers in the USSR who understand and use it is, presumably, quite large, given the fact that vast numbers of persons have had firsthand exposure to prison camp speech, and millions more have been closely associated with someone who has. Since, so far as is known, there are no published Soviet studies of prison camp speech (as opposed to studies of criminal argot), the extent of its intelligibility among the populace can only be surmised. In the opinion of Meyer Galler and others who have left the Soviet Union more recently, it is widely used, and some evidence, admittedly sparse, can be garnered in support of this contention. For example, in 1956 Thomas F. Magner noted in the speech of the *stiljagi* 'hepcats, flashy dressers' he chanced casually to meet in the streets of Moscow, a number of slang words and expressions current at that time [Magner 1957]. Included among the 36 items he recorded in an article on the subject are шухер 'danger,' бочата 'a watch,' and ботать по-фени 'to speak *stiljaga* slang,' all of which, according to Galler, are also known and used in prison camps (where the last item means, rather, 'to speak in criminal argot'). These forms might very easily have been picked up by young people from former prisoners, but since they are known to be of prerevolutionary criminal argot origin (whence they entered camp speech), it is also possible that they long ago directly entered colloquial Russian speech.

4. The novel, Архипелаг ГУЛАГ (*The GULAG Archipelago*), which should contain substantial amounts of prison camp speech, has reportedly found its way to the West, but has not yet appeared either in Russian or in translation.

Additional evidence is provided by a small dictionary of Russian slang recently compiled by M. M. and B. P. Krestinskij [Крестинский 1965]. Roughly 9 percent of its 400-plus entries are either labeled "criminal argot," or their definitions refer to prisoners and camp life and can thus be assumed to be of prison camp origin. Since additional items of criminal argot origin contained in the dictionary have not been labeled by the authors (i.e., items which have been previously recorded in dictionaries of argot), the percentage is actually higher.

Such meager evidence cannot, of course, indicate how extensively prison camp speech is used in colloquial, or slang, speech, but it does show that it definitely is a component, and perhaps a significant one. And if, as seems likely, prison camp speech is almost universally understood, then it is natural and inevitable that it will make its appearance in more and more literary works in the future, literary works, to be sure, from the Soviet underground. It is not to be expected, of course, that all such works will utilize prison camp speech in the same way and to the same degree. Many writers, such as E. S. Ginzburg, make only very discreet use of such speech, introducing it into the text for stylistic reasons and usually carefully explaining it for the benefit of the reader. In such instances, no special glossary such as this one is required for understanding. But a Solženicyn can make such extensive use of prison camp speech as to pose a formidable obstacle to understanding, not only for the non-Soviet native speaker, but particularly for the nonnative speaker who has learned his Russian from studying the nineteenth-century Russian classics. A thorough knowledge of the language of Turgenev and Čexov is no preparation for tackling *One Day in the Life of Ivan Denisovič* in the original.[5]

This being so, it is imperative that a glossary of prison camp

---

5. To illustrate how the unwary can be misled by prison camp speech, one might cite the example of a translator of Solženicyn's В круге первом (*The First Circle*) who translated пахан, a name commonly given Stalin by prisoners, as "Plowman," construing the term as a derivative of пахать 'to plow.' The word, which actually means "father" or "boss, chief," could have been found correctly defined only in a rather obscure article [Стратен 1931] and in the Krestinskij dictionary [Крестинский 1965]. Šiljaev's article [Шиляев 1969], which also contains the correct definition, appeared in print after the translation.

speech be available. But there is another reason for such a glossary: prison camp speech exists, and science and scholarship require that it be recognized and recorded. A glossary of this type, however, is not to be expected from the Soviet Union, where the very existence of prison camp speech is officially ignored. Publication of substandard or even obscene forms, particularly in dictionaries and in scholarly articles, does not, as the Soviets seem to think, either put the stamp of respectability on them or recommend their adoption. Dictionaries of this type have existed for English and other languages for many years, with no observable harmful effect on the languages.

The reader of prison camp literature seeking help must, at present, turn to western sources, and these are by no means plentiful. There are several more-or-less useful published lists scattered about in various sources, but the reader's success in finding them will depend largely on luck, since their titles usually give no hint of the presence in them of a glossary of prison camp speech. Two such glossaries have been published by the Institute for the Study of the History and Culture of the USSR in Munich. One of these is contained in B. Jakovlev's Концентрационные лагери СССР (*Concentration Camps in the USSR*) [Яковлев 1955]. It contains a short list of 31 entries of prison camp speech and a separate list of 24 items of criminal argot. The other glossary, consisting of a list of 70 abbreviations, a list of 25 words relating to the guarding of prisoners, and a list of 159 items of criminal argot, is contained in Vjačeslav P. Artem'ev's Режим и охрана исправительно-трудовых лагерей МВД (*Living Conditions and Policing of MVD Corrective Labor Camps*) [Артемьев 1956]. A recent article by Evgenij Šiljaev, "« Лагерный язык » по произведениям А. И. Солженицына," ("'Prison Camp Language' in the Works of A. I. Solženicyn") is also useful [Шиляев 1969]. This article defines some 50 or 60 words and expressions and provides a brief characterization of prison camp speech. The Krestinskij dictionary also contains some examples of such speech. None of these works, however, is so comprehensive as is needed, and none is a bilingual (i.e., Russian-English) glossary.

This Glossary of prison camp speech does not pretend to be complete and exhaustive. Its scope has been deliberately limited by the compilers to the speech observed by the co-author,

Galler, in the camps where he was a prisoner or in exile in the years 1942–57.[6] Since the Soviet writer, A. I. Solženicyn, was also a prisoner in the same area at roughly the same time (1945–53), it is not inappropriate to add some 65 words taken from those works of his which deal with prison camp life.[7] These additions have been made in order to make the Glossary as useful as possible to the reader.

Speech, particularly vocabulary, changes in time, and not all the words and expressions current at one time will be found at a later period. This rather obvious truth is easily demonstrated: the now quite common inflected masculine noun, зэк 'prisoner,' derives from an original uninflected abbreviation, з/к (from заключенный, pronounced [ze-ká]). Galler remembers hearing this form only as an abbreviation, and it is so recorded in the Glossary; on the other hand, Anatolij Marčenko, who was imprisoned during most of the 1960s, records only зэк in his *My Testimony*, published in 1969. Similarly, a number of terms common in Soviet prisons during the 1930s, such as тетка,

6. Though he was born in Poland, in Bialystok (Belostok), then occupied by Russia, Galler's native language is Russian. He spoke Russian at home and during the early years of elementary school until it was supplanted by Polish following the establishment of the independent Polish State (ca. 1921). He was obliged to read a considerable amount of Russian technical literature in doing research for his thesis in 1936, and was required to take advanced, formal courses in Russian at the Lvov Polytechnic Institute in 1939. He first began Polish in elementary school, and was fluent in that language by the time of the outbreak of hostilities. He also claims a lesser knowledge of Latin, Yiddish, and Ukrainian.

Except for a meeting of about three days in the early stages of the writing and another of about a day towards the end, our actual work of collaboration had to be done by correspondence. Galler provided, in written form, entries and definitions, as well as illustrative sentences and translations into English. These entries were checked against earlier sources, were edited for style, and every effort was made to find roughly equivalent English slang and obscenity for the definitions and the translations of the illustrative sentences. The entries were then returned to Galler to ascertain whether or not the meanings had been altered by the editing, or his intentions otherwise misconstrued.

7. Additional words were culled from the novels, Один день Ивана Денисовича (*One Day in the Life of Ivan Denisovič*), В круге первом (*The First Circle*), Раковый корпус (*The Cancer Ward*), and from the play, Олень и шалашовка (*The Love-Girl and the Innocent*).

тетушка, тетенька 'auntie,' nicknames for the GPU, were, according to Galler, no longer used in the 1940s and 1950s.[8] Given the fact that vocabularies do change, it seems desirable to limit the scope of the Glossary as we have. Eventually, a more comprehensive glossary of prison camp speech may well take into account the changes that have occurred in the word stock. Such a glossary can best be made on the basis of individual, synchronic records such as this one.

Despite the inevitable changes that have taken place in prison camp speech over the years, the bulk of its vocabulary has remained, on the whole, remarkably constant. Furthermore, although the Glossary contains prison camp speech used in a specific geographical area (i.e., in the camps where Galler was imprisoned), it seems to be universally understood everywhere. If, for example, one examines the memoirs of Julij B. Margolin, one will find few forms not also included in this Glossary. Yet, Margolin's "journey" took place in northern Russia, while Galler's experience was in Central Asia and Siberia. A perusal of the other works containing prison camp speech, both literary and official, and including both the most recent and the earliest, reveals the same thing: prison camp speech has been and remains remarkably homogeneous. For this reason the Glossary, despite the intentional limitation in its scope, can be considered an adequate aid for the reader of Soviet prison camp literature, whenever it was written.

CHARACTERIZATION OF PRISON CAMP SPEECH

It should be emphasized that prison camp speech is not a special language distinct from Russian, nor is it even a special regional or social dialect of Russian. It is, rather, a special vocabulary which can be readily incorporated into the speech of any user of Russian. A prisoner arrives in camp with his linguistic habits already formed, and these habits are unlikely to change significantly. A college-trained person continues to use a spoken variety of standard Russian, and an uneducated farm worker,

---

8. The terms are recorded by Иванов-Разумник 1953.

for example, continues to use the dialect of his village. Both, however, can easily incorporate into their speech the special vocabulary used in labor camps and prisons. This situation has its parallel in the ability of the languages of primitive societies to absorb new technical vocabulary along with new technology.

Since the basic linguistic structure of a prisoner's speech remains unchanged, and since both standard Russian and many of its dialects have frequently been studied in the past, there is little need to subject prison camp speech to formal linguistic analysis, to attempt a study of its phonology, morphology, and syntax. In any case, because the material contained herein is not transcribed from actual utterances, but is recorded with the standard orthography, it is unsuitable for linguistic analysis, particularly a phonological study. Presumably, phonetic differences would be minor, reflecting, in certain words, only minor deviations from the standard pronunciation. For example, the word одежда 'clothing' is pronounced either with a stressed medial *o* vowel or with a stressed *e* vowel. The former pronunciation is influenced by the colloquial form одежа, which has the same meaning and same vowel; the latter pronunciation is the prescribed standard form. In morphology, too, and in syntax, little can be found here that differs from standard Russian. One will find an occasional form that is proscribed in standard Russian, such as the genitive plural бубней for бубен 'diamonds,' and the forms чечен, чеченов for чеченец, чеченцев 'Chechens,' but such forms are merely archaic or obsolescent. And syntactic constructions of the type что-то находилось в двадцать километров от ... 'something was located 20 kilometers from . . .' instead of the prescribed что-то находилось в двадцати километрах от ... are not unknown in prison camp speech. Such deviations from the norms are minor, however, and alter the overall structure of the language scarcely at all.

We are left, thus, with the lexicon, and the remarks to follow concerning the characteristics of prison camp speech are primarily lexical in nature. They are, furthermore, not meant to be exhaustive, but rather to indicate some of the more striking, or more numerous, kinds of entries to be found here. These remarks may be conveniently directed to five main topics: proverbs and sayings, abbreviations, criminal argot, obscenities, and a residue of forms that do not fit into the first four categories.

Proverbs and sayings. Prison camp speech, like Russian speech in general, is rather rich in proverbs, maxims, and similar sayings. Since they frequently refer to such basic concerns as hunger, beatings, and dealings with the established higher authorities, and since it is precisely these concerns that preoccupy the prisoners, they are very popular in labor camps and prisons. Proverbs also provide us with a revealing picture of the intangible aspects of prison camp life, particularly the morality of and the personal code followed by the prisoners. As one might expect, the morality developed in the extremely hard conditions is a mockery of what one normally understands by the term, yet it is difficult to judge too severely the prisoner who knows that не украдешь, не проживешь 'if you don't steal, you won't make it.' It is but one of the many tragic aspects of his situation that his "making it" contributes to his fellow prisoners' not "making it." Закон — тайга 'The taiga is the law,' the prisoners say of life in the camps, and a number of proverbs reported by Galler illustrate this law: Кто кого сможет, тот того и гложет 'He who can will swallow you'; Привыкнешь! а не привыкнешь, подохнешь 'You'll get used to it; if not, you've had it!'; and Подохни ты сегодня, а я завтра 'Croak today if you wish, but I'll wait till tomorrow.'

Among the approximately fifty proverbs and sayings recorded by Galler, about a dozen are well-known old ones not restricted to use by prisoners and about ten more seem clearly to be modeled on, or inspired by, older proverbs. Most of the remainder may have originated among the prisoners, although, in a few instances, their prison camp origin may be questioned. If a proverb was found either in V. P. Žukov's recent Словарь русских пословиц и поговорок (*Dictionary of Russian Proverbs and Sayings*) [Жуков 1966] or in Vladimir Dal''s much larger Пословицы русского народа (*Proverbs of the Russian People*) [Даль 1862], or in both, this was taken as prima facie evidence for its not being of prison camp origin. Since the latter work is enormous and lacks an index, it is possible that a few proverbs were overlooked.

The well-known old proverbs and sayings are, in most cases, extremely apt for describing the conditions the prisoners find themselves in: Дуракам закон не писан 'The law is not written for fools' [i.e., fools will do as they please]; От тюрьмы и от сумы не зарекайся (in some sources, ... не отрекайя) 'One can escape neither prison nor begging'; Вошь на аркане (in Dal', В одном кармане вошь на аркане, в другом блоха на цепи 'In one pocket a louse on a leash, in the other, a flea on a chain,' a frequent, jocular response to a guard's question); Это только цветочки, а ягодки впереди 'These are only flowerets, the (little) berries lie ahead' [i.e., the worst is still to come]; and Кто кого сможет, тот того и гложет 'He who can will swallow you.'

The proverb, Была бы шея, а ярмо найдется (in Dal', ... а хомут найдем, same meaning) 'If you have a neck, a yoke will be found for it,' is a frequent, ironic response to new arrivals in camp who express concern about the work that they will be assigned. In camps, the common expression, Век живи, дураком помрешь 'Though you live to be a hundred, you will die a fool,' implies that even the most astute camp inmates cannot rely on their experience. To describe the great physical and mental resistance of female prisoners to the rigors of camp life, the expression, живучая, как кошка 'having nine lives, like a cat' is often used. Also popular are Дорога ложка к обеду 'A spoon is valuable at dinner time,' implying that in camp the value of a thing is determined by its usefulness, rather than by its intrinsic worth; Куда Макар телят не гонял 'Where Makar did not drive his calves,' a designation for the far-northern camps; and Москва слезам не верит 'Moscow does not heed tears,' an expression of the futility of judicial appeals to the capital.

Москва слезам не верит is an example of a proverb which had lost its original significance and fallen into disuse when the capital of the country was moved to St. Petersburg. In the Soviet period, with the return of the capital to Moscow, and when the overturning of a sentence became almost unheard of, the proverb was "revived" and became quite popular once more.

The opposite tendency may also be noted, that is, the eclipse of a formerly quite popular proverb because of the changed historical and social conditions following the Revolution. The proverb, Закон, что дышло: куда повернул, туда и вышло 'The law is like a wagon tongue: it goes wherever you direct it, is listed by Žukov, Dal', and by V. F. Traxtenberg in his pre-revolutionary dictionary of criminal argot [Трахтенберг 1908].

(Some versions of the proverb substitute (за)хочешь or (по)-
вернешь for повернул, and воротишь for вышло, but the
meaning remains essentially the same.) The proverb has apparently undergone an *official* eclipse in the Soviet period (Žukov
labels it "obsolescent"), obviously because, unlike in tsarist
times, laws are supposed no longer to be administered capri-
ciously. The political prisoner, however, knew (and knows)
better. The proverb is not only alive, but, with the addition
of the adjective Советский 'Soviet,' is thriving in labor camps
and prisons.

Other modified versions of old proverbs may be found in the
Glossary. In some cases the antecedent proverb is quite clear.
The proverb, Дурак работу любит, и работа дурака любит
'A fool likes work, and work likes a fool,' is an expanded version
of Работа дураков любит, cited by Žukov. The implication of
the prison camp version is that work must be avoided in order
to survive. The prison camp proverb, Чему бы дитя ни радо-
валось, лишь бы работало 'Anything to keep the child happy,
so long as it [the child] works,' is an obvious play on the well-
known Чем бы дитя ни тешилось, лишь бы не плакало
'Anything to keep the child amused, so long as it doesn't cry.'
The proverb, Хоть горшком назови, только корми 'Call me
a chamber pot if you wish, but feed me' may be a combination
of Хоть чертом зови, да хлебом корми! 'Call me devil if you
wish, but feed me bread!' (cited in Dal') and Хоть горшком
назови, только в печь не станови 'Call me a (cooking) pot if
you wish, only don't put me in the oven' (cited in Graf 1960).
By the word горшок in the prison camp proverb, according to
Galler, the prisoner means "a chamber pot," rather than the
"cooking pot" obviously meant in the latter proverb.

There is somewhat less certainty with regard to the following
proverbs, but there are at least possible precedents nevertheless.
The proverb, Не падай духом, а брюхом 'Don't lose your
spirit, but your belly' may be a prison camp version of Постись
духом, а не брюхом! 'Keep the fast in spirit, and not in the
belly!' The proverb, Подохни ты сегодня, а я завтра 'Croak
today if you wish, but I'll wait till tomorrow,' at least expresses
similar sentiment to Дай Бог умереть хоть сегодня, только не
нам 'God grant that someone else die (even) today, only not us.'
And Вода мельницы ломает 'Water wears down mills' is quite

similar to Вода камень точит 'Water wears away stone.' The prison camp proverb refers to the harmful effect on the human organism of consuming large quantities of watery camp soup without any caloric value.

Many prison camp proverbs, rather than being inspired by a specific older proverb, may simply be following what might be called a standard formula for proverb making. This formula can be represented Был бы А, а В будет (or найдется), where A and B represent nouns which determine the gender and number of the verbs. The formula might be translated, "Provided we have A, B will be found" (or "If there is A, B will be found"). The proverb Была бы шея, а хомут найдется, mentioned earlier, follows this formula. It would seem to be a relatively simple matter to use such a formula to construct proverbs on almost any subject. But the inspiration of specific old proverbs cannot be disregarded. The proverb Была бы кость, а шкура нарастет 'If the bone is left, the hide will grow back' may be based on Были бы кости, (а на костях) мясо будет 'If the bones are left, the flesh will grow back (on the bones).' The camp proverb, of course, emphasizes the skin, rather than the flesh: one could not expect to have much flesh under labor camp conditions. And Был бы человек, а дело найдется 'Provided we've got the man, we can find a charge for him' may be inspired by Была бы спина, найдется и вина 'Provided we've got the man (lit., back), we can find out what he's guilty of.' The camp proverb, Человек должен только существовать, а преступление найдется 'You need only exist, and a crime will be found,' may also be inspired by this old proverb.

The remaining proverbs and sayings appear to be of recent prison camp origin, although several of them, such as От работы лошади дохнут 'Work has killed many a horse,' Дай, Боже, завтра тоже 'May God give us a tomorrow,' and Не украдешь, не проживешь 'If you don't steal, you won't make it,' echo sentiments which are applicable as well outside camps as within, and may well be old. They were not found in Dal''s collection of proverbs, but, as noted above, they might have been overlooked. The others are: Чем добру пропадать, лучше пусть пузо лопнет 'Rather than waste the good, better let the belly burst'; Лучше кашки не доложь, но работой не тревожь 'Better not to increase the rations (lit., cereal), than to bother us

with work'; Прокурор медведь, а хозяин черпак 'The prosecutor is a bear, but the ladle is your master'; Все дураки
подохли, одни умные остались 'All the fools croaked; only
the smart ones made it'; Где раньше была совесть, там пизда
выросла 'Where I once had a conscience now a cunt has grown';
and Первых пять лет трудновато, а потом привыкнешь 'The
first five years are rather hard, but then you get used to it.'

Abbreviations. A rather large part of the Glossary, perhaps
10 percent, consists of various kinds of abbreviations. These
abbreviations can be conveniently divided into five main types,
with a small residue of anomalous forms. The most numerous
(Type A, 45 items) consists of letter abbreviations, composed of
the initial letters of the words represented. In the overwhelming
majority of cases, the initial letters themselves are pronounced
consecutively, with the stress falling on the name of the last
letter. Such abbreviations are indeclinable. So, for example,
ЖВН '*ж*ена *в*рага *н*арода' (wife of an enemy of the people), is
pronounced [že-ve-én]. Although such abbreviations in the
standard language normally are of the same gender as the head
word in their resolved forms, there is a tendency, especially in
speech, for them to take on their own gender.[9] This tendency is
reflected in the speech recorded in the Glossary, the gender
selected, in most cases, being neuter. For example, the abbreviation КВЧ [ka-ve-čé] '*к*ультурно-*в*оспитательная *ч*асть'
(culture and education section), whose head word часть is of
feminine gender, nevertheless is treated as neuter: КВЧ при-
везло [neut.] кинокартину. 'The KVČ brought in a movie.'
If a letter abbreviation happens to contain a medial vowel so
that it can be pronounced as a word, as in БУР [búr] '*б*арак
*у*силенного *р*ежима' (strict discipline barracks), or СЛОН
[slón] '*с*еверные *л*агеря *о*собого *н*азначения' (northern camps
of special designation), it takes the gender (usually masculine) of
the noun class it resembles and is inflected accordingly. In a
single instance, ВТеК [fték] '*в*неочередная *т*рудовая *к*омиссия'
(special commission to determine working ability), the vowel *e*
is inserted in order to make the form pronounceable as a word.
It is treated as masculine, although its main word комиссия is

9. Корицкий 1963, pp. 18–19.

feminine. As was noted above, the abbreviation for prisoner, з/к [ze-ká] 'заключенный,' was eventually to be treated this way, and to be inflected as an ordinary masculine noun, зэк.[10] Originally, however, and other writers agree with Galler in this respect, the form was treated as an indeclinable abbreviation. Compare the title of Julij Margolin's memoir, Путешествие в страну зэ-ка, published in 1952, with the usage in the novels of Solženicyn.

Type B contains 39 abbreviations in which an abbreviated adjective is prefixed to a whole noun which determines the gender and inflection of the entire form, as, for example, санчасть 'санитарная часть' (central medical office). The abbreviated portion of the adjective nearly always consists of a single syllable, although in two instances, надзор- 'надзорный' (supervisory) and опер- 'оперативный' (operations, adj.), we find di-syllabic abbreviated portions. The form гужрабсила (рабгужсила, according to Margolin) contains the abbreviated portions of two adjectives before the noun: гуж- 'гужевой' (tractive) and раб- 'рабочий' (work, adj.). In вагонзак 'вагон заключенных' (Stolypin car), the abbreviated adjective (here used as a substantive) follows, rather than precedes, the noun.

Type C contains only 11 abbreviations composed entirely of syllabic portions, such as начкар 'начальник караула' (chief of camp guards) and сексот 'секретный сотрудник' (collaborator). These abbreviations are all pronounceable as words and inflect as ordinary nouns.

Type D contains 10 abbreviations made up of mixed letters and syllabic portions, such as ГУЛАГ 'Главное управление лагерей' (main administration of camps) and СМЕРШ 'Смерть шпионам' (Death to spies). As is true of the letter abbreviations of Type A, the forms in Type D inflect provided they correspond to the shape of normal inflected words. It should be noted in this connection that stress seems to play a role in those Type D forms which resemble nouns terminating in a vowel: шизó 'штрафной изолятор' (special penalty isolator), ОСÓ 'Особое совещание' (Special Commission), САНÓ 'санитарный отдел'

10. Or, perhaps more likely, the form was simply reconstrued as a masculine noun from the pronunciation of the abbreviation, which already contained the vowel: [ze-ká] became [zek.]

(main medical office), and губчека́ '*гу*бернская *ч*резвычайная *к*омиссия' (provincial Cheka), with final stress, do not inflect, while врйдло '*вр*еменно *и*сполняющий *д*олжность *ло*шади' (human tractive power) and во́хра '*в*оенизированная *охр*ана' (camp garrison), with initial stress, do. The form вохра, listed in the Glossary as an inflecting feminine noun, is recorded by some writers (e.g., Margolin and Solženicyn) as an inflecting masculine noun, вохр. It might also be noted that губчека (as well as ЧК [če-ká] '*Ч*резвычайная *к*омиссия' [Cheka], usually represented orthographically as Чека), although indeclinable in the prison camp usage recorded by Galler, is not infrequently inflected in colloquial Russian.[11]

The syllabic portion, лаг, for лагерь 'camp' or лагерный 'camp, adj.' may be a component of abbreviations of Types B, C, or D. In Type B, for example, we have лагпункт '*лаг*ерный *пункт*' (prison camp section), in Type C, особлаг '*особ*ый *лаг*ерь' (camp of special designation), and in Type D, ГУЛАГ. Not listed in the Glossary, but constituting a large number of abbreviations of Type C, are abbreviations for specific prison camp clusters. Examples are Карлаг '*Кар*агандинский *лаг*ерь' (in Kazax SSR), Сиблаг '*Сиб*ирский *лаг*ерь' (Novosibirsk region), and Краслаг '*Крас*ноярский *лаг*ерь' (Krasnojarsk region), to name only a few.

These four types of abbreviations are also to be found in standard literary Russian. The fifth type, however, does not appear to be typical of the literary language and may, therefore, be peculiar to prison camp usage and probably to colloquial usage in general. Abbreviations in this group are resolvable into adjective plus noun as, for example, гарантийка '*гарантий*ная пайка' (guaranteed ration). They are formed by the addition of a suffix -к-а to the truncated adjective, with the noun not being represented in the abbreviation at all, probably because the main semantic burden is borne by the adjective. In this type, the adjective portion may be longer than it is in Type B. Attested are the monosyllabic выш- '*высш*ий' (highest), the di-syllabic солов- '*солов*ецкий' (Solovetsk), запрет- '*запрет*ный' (forbidden), внезап- '*внезап*ный' (sudden), внутрян- '*внутрен*ний'

---

11. Губчека and Чека are marked "indeclinable" in Корицкий 1963, thus agreeing with the prison camp usage recorded by Galler.

(inner), транзит- '*транзит*ный' (transit, adj.), бутыр- '*бутыр-ский*' (pert. to Butyrka), and the tri-syllabic гарантий- '*гарантий*ный' (guaranteed), концентрац- '*концентрац*ионный' (concentration), обвини- '*обвини*тельный' (indictment, adj.), одиноч- '*одиноч*ный' (solitary), принуди- '*принуди*тельный' (forced), пересыл- '*пересыл*ьный' (transit, adj.), and слабосил- '*слабосил*ьный' (weak). When the suffix is attached to концентрац-, a mutation of ц to ш occurs. The extended suffix -ловк-а is added to the truncated adjectives принуди- and обвини-, the only ones in this corpus which end in a vowel. The evidence, thus, is too sparse to attempt any generalizations as to the distribution of the suffixes (such as, for example, -ловк-а appears after vowels; -к-а, after consonants). Of the 14 abbreviations of this type attested in the Glossary, Соловки 'Соловецкие острова' (Solovetsk Islands) occurs only in the plural, and Бутырка 'Бутырская тюрьма' (Butyrka prison) seems to fluctuate between singular and plural. Galler at first used the form in the plural (Я год просидел в Бутырках 'I served a year at Butyrka'), but on a subsequent occasion he employed the singular form (в Бутырке). The form is used in the singular by the writer Ivanov-Razumnik, and is recorded in the plural in P. Fabričnyj's short glossary of argot [Фабричный 1923]. V. F. Traxtenberg, in his dictionary, cites the form in both the singular and the plural.[12] The same uncertainty with regard to this abbreviation is shown by other writers.

The residue consists of a handful of forms which, for one reason or another, do not belong to any of the above types. The abbreviations КТР [ka-te-ér] and з/к (see above) differ from the letter abbreviations in Type A in that they derive their constituent letters not from the initials of three (or two) words, but from a single word in each case: *катор*жанин 'prisoner at hard labor' and *за*к*лю*ченный 'prisoner.' The abbreviation в/н [ve-én], for *вольно*наемный 'free employee,' may be another example, although вольнонаемный is itself composed of two words, вольный and наемный.

Three abbreviations are back clippings of longer forms: опер from the Type B abbreviation *опер*уполномоченный (from

---

12. Compare his entry "Кича," where it is cited in the plural, with his entry "Милосердная."

*опера*тивный *уполномоченный* 'security officer'), винт from *винт*овка 'rifle,' and контра from *контр*революционеры 'counter-revolutionaries.' The last form, labeled "coarse and popular" by the four-volume dictionary of the Academy of Sciences and defined there as "a counter-revolutionary," is used as a collective in the speech recorded in this Glossary.[13] The term for an individual counter-revolutionary is контрик, formed by the addition of the suffix -ик-ϕ to the abbreviation. Other derivations from abbreviations are formed with the nominal or adjectival suffixes -овец-ϕ, -овк-а, and -овск-ий. Examples are ИТРовец [i-te-éraɣic], ИТРовский and АТПеровец, АТПеровский (the latter two with the suffixes -ровец-ϕ, -ровск-ий), meaning, respectively, "*инженерно-т*ехнический *р*аботник" (engineering technical worker) and "*административно-т*ехнический *п*ерсонал" (administrative-technical staff worker). Note also КТРовец, КТРовка [ka-te-éraɣic, ka-te-érafka] 'male, female prisoner at hard labor,' вохровец 'a (male) member of the camp garrison,' and ЧСИРовка [če-se-írafka] 'a female member of a traitor's family.'

Criminal argot. The special jargon employed by criminals as a means of communication constitutes an important component of prison camp speech. Soviet prisoners can be conveniently divided into political prisoners and criminals, a division observed not only by the camp authorities, but by the prisoners themselves. The vast majority of the prisoner population consists of political prisoners. They and the nonprofessional criminals are regarded as outsiders by the smaller, tightly organized professional criminal group (урки, блатные) and are called by them фрайера 'pigeons.' Besides their distinctive jargon, the criminals have their own code and customs and, because they are trusted by the Soviet authorities more than the political prisoners, they usually have power and privileges far out of proportion to their limited numbers. Criminals are customarily given the easiest jobs in camp, are assigned to positions of authority over the political prisoners, and they make use of their advantageous position to terrorize and generally to victimize the

13. Словарь 1957–61. This dictionary will be cited hereafter as Academy Dictionary.

latter. Since political prisoners were, from the beginning, confined together with criminals, the special jargon of the criminals soon became the common property of both. Thus, in its earliest form, prison camp speech consisted almost entirely of the prerevolutionary jargon of criminals. But new words and expressions, devised to reflect new conditions in the camps and in Soviet free life, were gradually added to this initial stock of words until eventually they came to outnumber the criminal component.

This special jargon of criminals will be referred to here as criminal argot, or, simply, argot, to distinguish it from prison camp speech as a whole.[14] In Russian, corresponding terms are воровское арго or воровской жаргон, the latter being slightly more pejorative [Ахманова 1966]. The terms блатной язык and блат, also used for argot, are even more pejorative than воровской жаргон. In prerevolutionary Russia, the criminals' own designation for their argot was блатная музыка 'thieves' cant'; more recently, it is феня, presumably from an earlier афеня, офеня 'peddler' and афенская, офенская речь 'peddlers' speech.'[15] A survey of the rather extensive published work on Russian jargons and Russian criminal argot is given in the following section.

More than a hundred of the items recorded in the Glossary can be positively identified as being of criminal argot origin, and the number is probably higher. It is not always possible to decide whether a given word or expression is argot, or a prison camp term invented during the Soviet period. Since, however, a number of scholarly articles and dictionaries of argot were compiled and published during the first three decades of the present century, we have labeled as argot all terms in this Glossary which were also found to be listed in them. A reference to one of these sources, then, indicates that the word is of argot origin. It should be remembered, however, that some words may have been missed by the compilers of these works, and also that new words have surely been added to the argot word

14. This distinction is made by Stuart Berg Flexner in Wentworth and Flexner 1967, pp. vi–vii.
15. The terms афеня, офеня and афенская, офенская речь appear in Даль 1903–9.

stock by criminals in the more than thirty years since the last compilation was made. For these reasons, it is likely that words of argot origin are included in the Glossary which have not been so labeled.

Obscenities. Obscenities, vulgarities, and curses, not surprisingly, constitute a prominent feature of prison camp speech, although, of course, they are not peculiar to this speech alone. Vulgar, abusive speech is extensively used by many groups of male (and female) speakers, by soldiers, students, and workers, to mention only a few, and it is doubtful that it is more widely used in labor camps and prisons. But certainly the animal-like life the prisoners lead, with its grim struggle for survival in the face of terrible conditions, does nothing to inhibit its use. Moreover, the use of abusive speech is the only form of rebellion to camp conditions open to the prisoners. The speech of the authorities, according to the testimony of witnesses such as Ivanov-Razumnik, Galler, and others, is no less abusive. Indeed, foul, abusive speech is sometimes deliberately employed by interrogators as a device (among others) for breaking the spirit of the prisoner and forcing him to confess to his "crimes." The constant use of abusive speech by overseers and guards seems to be part of a deliberate design to vilify and dehumanize the victims.

The most useful dictionary for obscenities now available is that of Vladimir Dal' in the third or fourth editions edited by Baudouin de Courtenay [Даль 1903–1909]. There the reader will find such standard, but taboo, words as манда, пизда 'cunt,' хуй 'prick,' жопа 'ass,' говно 'shit,' and ебать 'to fuck.'[16] When the Soviets reprinted Dal''s dictionary in 1955, however, they utilized the second edition, which lacks these (and other) additions of Baudouin. The third edition, in a reprint published in Paris, is currently available, but is rather expensive and less likely than the Soviet edition to be in the average reader's library. Max Vasmer's *Russisches etymologisches Wörterbuch* [Vasmer 1953–1957] also lists the standard obscene words,

16. The form ебать is a re-formation by analogy with the nonpast stem еб-. Даль 1903–9 gives the infinitive as ети, and does not mention the form ебать at all.

but this rather specialized dictionary is no more likely to be on the average reader's bookshelf. It is interesting to note that the Soviet translation of Vasmer now being done (two volumes, so far, of a projected four) includes some of the obscenities, such as говно, жопа, and манда, but deletes ебать [Фасмер 1964–1967]. Perhaps this indicates that Soviet publishers are becoming somewhat less prudish and that we may one day expect them to treat obscenities frankly and openly.

None of the obscenities contained in this Glossary, as far as I know, originated in Soviet camps and prisons, and none of them deal exclusively with aspects of camp and prison life, the two main principles followed for inclusion. Indeed, most of them can only be regarded as standard Russian obscenities. But, since the dictionaries most likely to be available to the reader of prison camp literature do not contain such terms, they have been included in the Glossary.

Residue. The largest portion of the Glossary is made up of forms which do not fit any of the categories mentioned above; that is, they are neither proverbs, nor abbreviations, nor argot, nor obscenities. As noted above, a few terms may be criminal argot, either of recent origin, or older forms simply not recorded heretofore in the dictionaries of argot. But most of this category consists of entirely new formations for persons, events, institutions, or procedures relating to Soviet camp and prison life. These terms are derived in ways no different from those used in the standard language, primarily from new combinations of Slavic roots and affixes, but also from changing the meanings of old words. There appears to be no special word-derivational device for prison camp speech distinct from those used in the standard language, as, indeed, if this speech is not a distinct language, none would be expected.

It does not seem possible to characterize this residue in any meaningful, formal, linguistic way. Evgenij Šiljaev has noted that nouns formed with the suffixes -ag-a and -ug-a are quite common in the works of Solženicyn, but only a handful appears in this Glossary.[17] They are работяга 'hard worker,' ворюга 'thief,' блатяга 'criminal,' тюряга 'prison,' честняга 'criminal,'

17. Шиляев 1969, p. 241.

шпаняга, шпанюга 'young thug,' доходяга 'goner,' and
вольняга 'free employee.'[18] These few examples neither prove
nor disprove Šiljaev's statement. The most common suffixes are
-к-а (about 115 items) and -ик-ф, -ник-ф (about 60), but little
can be made of this fact, since these suffixes are also very
common in the standard language.

It seems possible, therefore, to characterize prison camp
speech only as to its vocabulary. A number of investigators of
jargons, such as D. S. Lixačev, have noted that the special
vocabularies they contain embrace only the relatively few areas
of concern to the jargon-using groups in question, and that the
vocabulary of the standard language is used elsewhere.[19] The
numerous glossaries prepared in the nineteenth century for a
variety of Russian jargon-using groups were examined by
Russian scholars and found to contain a large common stock of
words covering only a few areas of meaning.[20] The same conclusion can be reached on the basis of a study of the terms
appearing in this Glossary. The approximately 656 substantives
contained in the Glossary (for the purposes of this study,
abbreviations and substantives from the argot and obscene
categories were included along with the residual items) were
assigned to such rough semantic categories as "Names for fellow
prisoners," "The arrest, investigation, sentence," "Sections of
prisons and camps," "Food and drink," and the like. Substantives were selected because they constitute a large and easily
defined group and because it was thought that few, or no,
additional areas of meaning would be uncovered by including
the entire lexicon. No attempt was made here to be mathemat-
ically precise; the percentage figures in the following chart are
intended merely to present a rough idea of the distribution of
the words among the various semantic areas. In cases where
there was any doubt or uncertainty as to the appropriate category,

---

18. Derived from вольнонаемный. A secondary derivative, вольня-
жка, is more frequently used by prisoners for "free employee." Although it seems clear that, on etymological grounds, this form should
be represented orthographically as above, it should be noted that it
usually (or always) appears in print as вольняшка. See, *inter alia*, the
Paris YMCA-Press edition of Solženicyn's В круге первом.
19. Лихачев 1964, p. 316.
20. One of the better such studies is Стратен 1931.

the word was simply regarded as "Unclassifiable" (6 percent, or 40 items).

Names for fellow prisoners	15 %	94 items
The arrest, investigation	14	88
Sections of prisons and camps	11	72
Abusive, derisive terms	11	70
Officials and functionaries	8	51
Crimes, specialties, weapons	7	48
Labor	7	48
Specific camps and prisons	5	34
Food and drink	4	27
Health	3	24
Camp and prison routine	3	23
Wearing apparel	2	15
Parts of the human body	2	14
Tobacco	1	5
Cards	1	3
Unclassifiable	6	40
	100 %	656 items

A study of this table reveals how the chief concern of the prisoners in labor camps and prisons—survival—is reflected in their speech. Survival under the difficult conditions, amply documented in "concentration camp literature" as well as in this Glossary, means finding enough food, enough clothing to protect oneself from the elements, and, above all, avoiding the extremely difficult work. If we combine under the rubric "Survival" the totals for "Labor," "Food and drink," "Wearing apparel," and "Health," we get a group containing 16 percent (114 items) of the total number of forms being considered here. Another major area of concern for the prisoners is represented by the 88 items (14 percent of the total) under the rubric "The arrest, investigation." This is not surprising, since, again to judge by the reports of prisoners, the investigation represents such a painful and harrowing experience that a sentence to prison camps is frequently accepted with relief and gratitude at having escaped death.

Two more rather large groups can be established in the

same way. "Specific camps and prisons" and "Sections of prisons and camps" can be grouped under the rubric "Locale," containing about 16 percent of the forms (106 items). And, under the rubric "Social," made up of "Names for fellow prisoners" and "Officials and functionaries," we have a group (145 items, 23 percent) containing the names of persons with whom the prisoners come in contact in their daily lives. One might also add to this group the large number of items under 'Abusive, derisive terms" (11 percent) as indicative of the manner in which the social contacts were conducted.

It is interesting to observe, in passing, the very small number of words having to do with cards and gambling (only 1 percent). An outstanding characteristic of criminals, we are told, is their passion for gambling, and this fact seems to be supported by the evidence of V. F. Traxtenberg's dictionary, where some 13 percent of the 510 nouns it contains are gambling terms [Трахтенберг 1908]. This discrepancy may result from Galler's stated lack of interest in cards, or it may be that most political prisoners either do not share the criminals' vice or lack the time and resources to gamble.

These four groups of forms, then, the "Locale" (16 percent), "Social" (34 percent), "Survival" (16 percent), and "The arrest, investigation" (14 percent), constitute 80 percent of the areas of meaning, and cover nearly all aspects of the prisoners' day-to-day existence.

In order to conclude this brief characterization of prison camp speech on a brighter note, a few observations may be made about humorous elements it contains. It soon becomes clear, upon perusing this Glossary, that regardless of how grim and hopeless the situation the prisoner finds himself in, his sense of humor does not fail him. True, the humor is often not very lighthearted. But even gallows humor must serve to make the lot of the prisoners understandable and endurable, if only as a joke. In fact, it has been said that one of the main functions of humor in general is to reconcile man to the painful, unacceptable, and tragic aspects of his condition. If so, then a great deal of humor might be expected in Stalin's labor camps and prisons.

The forms which humor can take are varied. One tempting target for the prisoners' wit is the Communist slogan, so much a part of the daily lives of the prisoner and the free Soviet citizen as well. Such officially displayed slogans as Догнать и перегнать капиталистические страны 'Overtake and surpass the capitalistic countries,' Труд — дело чести и совести 'Labor is a matter of honor and conscience,' and Дал слово — сдержи; взял обязательство — выполни 'You gave your word—keep it; you accepted an obligation—fulfill it,' sometimes emblazoned on the walls of the barracks and other camp buildings, are the last things seen at night, and the first things seen in the morning. Tampering with such slogans is a dangerous thing to do, since even in camp a prisoner can be given an additional sentence and the prisoners are nearly always infiltrated by informers for the secret police. Many prisoners have been convicted for a much less serious "crime." But perhaps the risk only adds spice to the wit. One of the more amusing examples of parodying such slogans is Социалистическая бздительность 'Socialistic farting' for Социалистическая бдительность 'Socialistic vigilance,' based on the close phonetic similarity of the nouns. Similarity, we find Битье (instead of Бытие) определяет сознание 'Beating (instead of 'Being') determines consciousness.' The first example may be an example of light-hearted humor, although it had special implications in camps (compare also the expression пердячим паром 'by farting steam,' a not-so-oblique reference both to heavy labor and to cold temperatures); the second is more grim in its connotations.

Ironic encouragement to newcomers is contained in such expressions as Не падай духом, а брюхом 'Don't lose your spirit, but your belly,' and by reference to that soon-to-be-lost belly as соцнакопление 'socialistic accumulation.' Well-meant warnings to prisoners who attempt to still hunger pangs by drinking water are contained in the proverb Вода мельницы ломает 'Water wears down mills,' and in the ungrammatical (not to mention taboo) Пей вода, ешь вода, ебать не захочешь никогда 'Drink water, eat water, and you'll never feel like fucking.' The ungrammaticalness of this last refrain, it could be argued, is determined by the rime, that is, ... ешь водá, ... никогдá, rather than the grammatically correct ... ешь вóду, ... никогдá. By its use of the nominative case of вода for the accusative, however, it is also reminiscent of the common Russian imitation of non-Russian usage.

The camp newcomer who is apprehensive as to the kind of work he will be doing might be reassured by Не бойся, здесь дадут тебе двадцатикилограммовый карандаш, и пиши по карьеру 'Don't worry, here they'll give you a twenty kilogram "pencil" [i.e., a crowbar] and you can "write" in the quarry.' Irony is to be found also in the term земляк (from земля 'earth'), normally a term for a fellow-countryman. It is popular and especially apt in camps because so many of the prisoners are employed at digging in the earth. The same occupation evokes the prisoners' reinterpretation of the abbreviation, КР as "Dig and chop" (копай и руби). Normally, the abbreviation, a reference to article 58 of the Soviet Criminal Code of 1926, stands for "counter-revolutionary" (контрреволюционный or контрреволюционер). The prisoners' wit is also frequently directed at the institutions of Soviet justice. A defense attorney, for example, is called помощник прокурора 'prosecutor's assistant,' since he generally aids the prosecution more than the defendant. And the prisoners' opinion of what they consider to be a really trifling sentence (of five years or less) is that it can be served on the latrine pail (на параше сидеть). The verb сидеть, which by itself can mean "to serve a prison term," is in this phrase used simultaneously in its basic meaning of "to sit."

Given the fact of the prisoners' constant struggle for enough to eat, it would be surprising if there were not some witticisms concerned with food. Certainly hunger is a painful aspect of their condition much in need of the relief that humor might provide. The prisoners' attitude, their whole philosophy even, might be summed up in the following refrain: Подъем будет, не буди, / Развод будет, не буди, / Обед будет, два раза буди 'Reveille will come, don't wake me, / Time to work will come, don't wake me, / When it's dinner time, wake me twice.'

SURVEY OF WORKS ON RUSSIAN ARGOT

Jargons of various kinds have been recognized for hundreds of years, and they have been studied by scholars since at least the fifteenth century. First to be noticed, apparently, were the jargons of those groups located on the fringes of respectable society, such as vagabonds, gypsies, and thieves, and interest in these groups has persisted down to the present day. The earliest examples so far discovered are of the jargon of vagrants (*Rotwelsch*), which appeared in the thirteenth century in Germany [Krapp and Bradley 1930]. In France, the earliest examples are contained in the well-known fifteenth-century "Ballades" of François Villon [Schöne 1887, Vitu 1883]. Examples of "cant," "St. Giles Greek," "rogues' language," and "peddlers' French" are recorded in England in such works as Robert Copland's *The Hye Way to the Spyttell Hous* (1517), John Awdelay's *Fraternitye of Vacabondes* (1561), and Thomas Harman's *Caueat for Commen Cursetors, vulgarely called vagabones* (1567).[21] Better known is William Harrison's description of Britain and the speech of her inhabitants, prefixed to Raphael Holinshed's (d. ca. 1582) *Chronicles of England, Scotland, and Ireland.* Jargon is also reflected in the literature of the Elizabethan period, notably in the work of Shakespeare, Ben Jonson, and others.

Scholarly work began in Germany about 1490 with an attempt at a jargon dictionary by a Gerold Edilbach; a similar dictionary, *Liber vagatorum*, appeared in 1510 [Krapp and Bradley 1930].[22] Numerous other dictionaries and studies followed, particularly in the nineteenth and twentieth centuries [Kluge 1901, Dauzat 1929]. Continuing interest, particularly in the argot of thieves and criminals, is evidenced by the large number of articles, both of a popular and scholarly nature, that have appeared in the last fifty years or so. The bibliography in Wentworth and Flexner's *Dictionary of American Slang* lists dozens of such articles. Interest is also manifested by the publication of a number of dictionaries devoted to argot, of which probably the best known is *A Dictionary of the Underworld* by Eric Partridge. This dictionary of British and American underworld argot appeared in 1949, with a second edition in 1961 [Partridge 1961]. A similar dictionary, *Dictionary of American Underworld Lingo*, contains American criminal argot [Goldin 1950]. One of the best dictionaries, however, one which embraces all slang (and

21. Harman's work and the 1575 edition of Awdelay are contained in Viles and Furnivall 1869.

22. The 1529 edition of this dictionary contains a preface by Martin Luther.

not only argot), is that of Wentworth and Flexner. The work is
interesting, not only because of the slang itself, but because of
the scholarly material added by Stuart Flexner. Flexner's attempt at achieving rigorous definitions for the terms slang, cant,
jargon, and argot is especially valuable, and his discussion of
derivational devices of American slang, with accompanying
word lists, even more so.

The earliest Russian materials now available date from the
eighteenth century, and are rather meager. They consist of some
examples of argot contained in an autobiography of a certain
Van'ka Kain, some hundred or so words from the speech of
peddlers contained in P. S. Pallas's comparative dictionary, and
a 1786 manuscript of Andrej Mejer describing an allegedly
secret Belorussian dialect of Kričev [Каин 1793, Паллас 1786–
1789, Мейер 1786]. The pertinent vocabulary items contained
in the Mejer manuscript are listed in an appendix to Traxtenberg's dictionary.[23]

The best and, to this day most nearly complete bibliography
of works dealing with Russian jargons is to be found in "Черты
первобытного примитивизма воровской речи" ("Traits of
Primordial Primitivism in the Speech of Criminals"), an article
on criminal argot by the Soviet scholar, D. S. Lixačev [Лихачев
1935]. (See p. 47.) Examination of this bibliography reveals a
wealth of nineteenth-century materials, beginning in 1820 with
a volume published by the Society of Lovers of Russian Literature [Труды 1820]. This volume contains lists of words, compiled by various correspondents of the Society, from allegedly
secret, or unknown jargons, or from trade jargons employed in
regions north and east of Moscow. Lixačev's bibliography lists
approximately 100 items published in the nineteenth century,
including 7 works of literature, such as Dostoevskij's Записки из
мертвого дома (*Notes from the House of the Dead*) and Vsevolod
V. Krestovskij's melodramatic novel Петербургские трущобы
(*The Dens of St. Petersburg*). A dictionary of the words and
expressions of criminal origin found in the latter work was
compiled by N. Smirnov in 1899 [Смирнов 1899]. Some 18 of
the items in the bibliography are general studies of jargons,
about 15 record the jargon of a specific city or region (Černigov,

23. The Mejer manuscript itself is described in Артемьев 1884.

Tula, Galič, Brjansk), and the largest group (about 47 items) treats various trade or professional jargons (such as criminals, beggars, lyrists, cattle merchants, tailors, and peddlers). Of these "professional" groups, criminals are treated 6 times and peddlers 24 times.

In the twentieth century the attention of scholars began to be directed more and more to the speech of criminals, and less to regional and urban groups, a fact clearly reflected by the titles in Lixačev's bibliography. In the whole of the nineteenth century only 6 titles having to do with criminal argot appear; in the first three decades of the twentieth century, by contrast, we find 31 titles. On the other hand, in the nineteenth century about 56 titles treat various regional, urban, and professional jargons, while in the twentieth century we find fewer than 10.

In the early years of the twentieth century scholarly work consisted almost entirely of the compilation of word lists and dictionaries, such as V. F. Traxtenberg's Блатная музыка (« Жаргон » тюрьмы) (*Thieves' Cant* [*Prison "Jargon"*]) the first major product of the awakened interest in argot at the turn of the century and in many ways still the best dictionary of Russian argot [Трахтенберг 1908]. Based on materials gathered in prisons in Warsaw, Vilna, St. Petersburg, Moscow, Kiev, and Odessa, it is a well-executed work of some 754 entries. The words are accented, origins are suggested in many instances, and the entries are very clearly defined, often with lengthy explanations of the circumstances under which they would occur. The appendices contain 96 proverbs and sayings, the words to 18 prison songs, and a list of the words contained in the eighteenth-century Mejer manuscript mentioned above. The editor, I. A. Baudouin de Courtenay, has also added either to the dictionary, or to the foreword, a number of words and expressions of criminal origin from other sources.[24] We might have expected some penetrating observations on argot to be made by Baudouin de Courtenay in his foreword, but it is rather brief and uninformative, perhaps because it was written at a time when real interest in criminal argot (as opposed to the jargons of other groups) was just awakening, and the serious collection of materials was just beginning.

24. Specifically, those terms appearing in Брейтман 1901.

A glossary of some 179 words is contained in P. Fabričnyj's "Язык каторги" ("The Language of the Penal Camp") [Фабричный 1923]. The entries, arranged in what the author calls a "logical," rather than alphabetical order, are in some cases fully defined, and contain the author's ideas as to the origin of the terms. Although words are not accented and the author's topical arrangement is somewhat inconvenient, the work is nevertheless a useful supplement to Traxtenberg; it covers the period of time between the appearance of Traxtenberg in 1908 and Fabričnyj's compilation.

The first serious attempt to write about jargon at any length (to this day it remains perhaps the best general study) is V. V. Straten's "Арго и арготизмы" ("Argot and Argotisms"), published in 1931 [Стратен 1931]. Straten enjoyed the advantage of having at hand a number of dictionaries of argot, including especially Traxtenberg's [Бец 1903, Лебедев 1909, Попов 1912, Виноградов 1927]. These dictionaries are frequently mentioned in the bibliographies and scholarly literature, although I have been unable to obtain them. The two editions of Potapov [Потапов 1923 and 1927], for some reason unavailable to Straten, are also frequently mentioned in the literature. They too have become a bibliographical rarity.

Like many western scholars, Straten finds the beginnings of criminal argot in the numerous medieval artisan and trade jargons, and in the speech of beggars, vagabonds, and thieves. According to him, the demise of these groups, caused by changing social conditions, industrialization, and urbanization, resulted in the passing on of large portions of the jargons as a kind of inheritance to the new groups which arose to take their place. A cursory look at the titles of works appearing in the nineteenth century might lead one to think that this early, or medieval, stage is reflected there, since we find works describing the speech of such diverse groups. Straten shows, however, by carefully comparing the vocabularies of these groups, that the titles are often either misleading or wrong. So it is, for example, with the words in Pallas's dictionary (which were labeled "Suzdal' dialect"), with Mejer's "secret" Belorussian vocabulary, and with the several contributions to the volume published by the Society of Lovers of Russian Literature. All turn out to be examples from the jargon of peddlers. Although scholars began to recognize peddlers' jargon by 1828, numerous works continued to appear throughout the rest of the century which dealt with what were thought to be specific trade jargons, or urban or regional dialects. By studying their vocabularies, Straten shows that nearly all in fact describe peddlers' jargon. In other words, what is attested in the nineteenth century is not the original medieval stage, but a later stage, where the legatee of numerous forms from earlier jargons is the nomadic peddler.

Peddlers' jargon, according to Straten, was itself dying out in the last part of the nineteenth century, and was contributing much of its vocabulary in turn to the newly developing urban jargons. The most important of these, criminal argot, began to be recorded in literature in the 1860s (for example, in Krestovskij's Петербургские трущобы [*The Dens of St. Petersburg*]) and in scholarly work (in the introduction to the first edition of Vladimir Dal''s dictionary). Nowhere does Straten refer to Van'ka Kain's autobiography, thought by most scholars to contain the earliest examples of argot. This блатная музыка (thieves' cant), as it was called by its users at that time, varied somewhat from region to region, and from criminal specialty to criminal specialty, but in general it was the same jargon throughout Russia. Investigations show that its greatest debt was to peddlers' jargon, but the vocabulary was also enriched by foreign borrowings, by borrowings from dialects, and by altering the meanings of standard Russian words.

Straten next turns his attention to the post-revolutionary period. In separate sections he takes up criminal argot, the jargon of the homeless, and the jargon of schoolboys. The post-revolutionary documents are, as he admits, insufficiently numerous, and his findings for the period are necessarily tentative, but he concludes that, by and large, the contemporary jargons still contain numerous "old acquaintances" from earlier periods. It appears, thus, that whenever older jargon-using groups disappear, or become greatly altered by social changes, many forms are "willed" to succeeding groups. The new forms, or the old forms with new meanings which appear, are merely a necessary consequence of the changed conditions. His separate investigations of these three different groups, criminals, the homeless, and schoolboys, also reveal a large common vocabulary, one, indeed, which was used or understood by a large portion of the society.

Not least of the article's virtues is Straten's method of beginning each new topic with a listing of the pertinent major sources. So, for example, we find there a list of the major works dealing with peddlers' speech, another of works dealing with Belorussian "secret" languages, a third of works dealing with Ukrainian jargons, and so on. The article is, for this reason, a useful guide to anyone wishing to find his way in Lixačev's enormous, but unannotated and unclassified, bibliography.

The widespread acceptance and use of jargons disturbed many pedagogues and other defenders of the purity of Russian, and evoked numerous protests during the 1920s and 1930s. During this period we find a rather large number of articles which deal with the penetration of argot into the speech of schoolboys and even into the literature appearing at the time [Копорский 1927, Рыбникова 1927, Луп(п)ова 1927]. Many of these articles I have not been able to examine, but a common theme seems to be the objection to the "perversion" and "coarsening" of Russian speech by the inclusion in it of elements of argot. The same theme is *de rigueur* in the more substantial and scholarly works that appeared at this time. After listing numerous examples of argot that had appeared in belles-lettres and in the popular press, Vjačeslav Tonkov, for example, concludes his work with a criticism of the widespread popularity of argot, and indicts the capitalistic system which, according to him, spawned it. He believed that the socialistic rebuilding of society would eventually destroy the conditions which nourish argot.[25] Lixačev, in his article, labeled argot a disease, and, like Tonkov, believed that the cure lay in the elimination of the social milieus which caused it. Lixačev saw the beginnings of this process in the virtual disappearance by the turn of the century of some trade jargons from the economic scene and believed that the remaining examples (such as criminal argot) were in the process of disappearing at the time he wrote.[26]

Something of an exception to these views, at least in tone, is expressed by E. D. Polivanov in an article entitled "О блатном

25. Тонков 1930, pp. 82–83.
26. Лихачев 1935, pp. 49–50.

языке учащихся и о « славянском языке » революции"
("Concerning the Thieves' Cant of Schoolboys and the 'Slavonic
Language' of the Revolution") [Поливанов 1931]. This well-
known linguist (who was to become a victim of the 1937 purges)
views the popularity of slang with considerably less alarm. While
not denying that the chaotic conditions of life following the
Revolution had caused an increase in the use of jargons and
argot and that excessive acceptance by the literary language of
such elements would be harmful, he nevertheless expresses little
of the concern of the others. He points out that the use of nonstandard speech by young people is no new phenomenon, and
that it has always been employed by them out of a desire to set
themselves apart from the rest of society. He states that jargons
and argot are used almost entirely by young people and that
most of them will die out without leaving a trace on the literary
language.

Vjačeslav Tonkov's study, Опыт исследования воровского
языка (*An Essay in the Study of Criminal Argot*), contains the
dictionary of current jargon which Straten was looking for, and
an essay, "Воровской жаргон" ("Criminal Argot") [Тонков
1930]. Although Straten's article is undoubtedly the better study
of jargons, Tonkov's dictionary of some 502 items goes far
towards compensating for his weaker essay. The dictionary is
based on materials collected by the author in the Kazan' area
in orphanages, houses of correction, reformatories, and the like,
during the years 1923–27. The dictionary, unfortunately arranged in the same "logical" manner favored by Fabričnyj,
contains, in addition to the author's own materials, numerous
items from earlier dictionaries and sources (including, for example, the eighteenth-century work of Van'ka Kain). Although
containing very good definitions, it does not always indicate the
place of accent, and the size of the dictionary makes its non-
alphabetical arrangement a definite inconvenience.

The most important part of Tonkov's article is its long
section devoted to the penetration of argot into literature. He
cites numerous examples taken from the literature of the 1920s
and, in a special section, he lists 102 works going back to the
1860s which contain examples of argot. For each work he gives
references to the pages where the examples are to be found. He
does the same in a much smaller section with the popular press

and newspapers, listing some 17 items. He concludes his article with the usual criticism of the use of argot and with an indictment of capitalism.

Four articles on the sources of Russian criminal argot vocabulary, the work of a group of scholars formed to study the language of the city, with special emphasis on the various urban jargons, appeared in 1931.[27] They are B. A. Larin, "Западноевропейские элементы русского воровского арго" ("Western European Elements of Russian Criminal Argot"), M. M. Fridman, "Еврейские элементы « блатной музыки »" ("Jewish Elements of 'Thieves' Cant'"), A. P. Barannikov, "Цыганские элементы в русском воровском арго" ("Gypsy Elements in Russian Criminal Argot"), and N. K. Dmitriev, "Турецкие элементы в русских арго" ("Turkish Elements in Russian Argots") [all in Язык 1931]. The titles clearly describe the contents of the articles: each consists mainly of lists of words taken from Russian argot, with the corresponding source words in Hebrew and Yiddish, Turkish, Gypsy, and Western European languages. It is possible that each author exaggerates the contribution of his respective source language, but they nevertheless contain useful material, and illustrate the very specialized interest scholars had in argot at this time.

D. S. Lixačev's [Лихачев 1935] appears to have been the last work dealing with criminal argot to be published in the Soviet Union for nearly thirty years. A later article by the same author, written in 1938, was not published until 1964. Both articles are impressive efforts, revealing the author's considerable erudition, his extensive familiarity with both Russian and foreign scholarly literature on the subject, and a profound understanding of the life and outlook of the criminal world. The main thesis of the first article is that the speech of criminals bears many similarities to, and therefore represents a kind of reversion to, the primitive speech of mankind. Despite the extensive evidence marshalled by the author

---

27. According to an introductory note to the articles, two additional contributions on the same theme were to have been published later, but they apparently never appeared. They are I. I. Sokolov, "О греческих элементах русских арго" ("Concerning Greek Elements of Russian Argots") and N. N. Filippov, "Румынизмы в русском арго" ("Rumanianisms in Russian Argot").

in support of his contention, it is unlikely that many will be convinced. Although the article does contain a number of very interesting observations about argot, its chief value lies in its extensive bibliography cited above.

Lixačev's second article, "Арготические слова профессиональной речи" ("Argotic Words in Professional Speech"), is concerned primarily with the use of jargon in legitimate professional and technical speech; nevertheless, many of his observations apply as well to the argot of criminals [Лихачев 1964]. The difference between jargon and the standard word, he tells us, lies in the expressiveness of the former: jargon is humorous, jocular, or derisive, while the standard word is neutral. The function of jargon is to use its uniquely expressive nature to reduce someone or something to an equal or inferior status. It is for this reason, he continues, that to an outsider (against whom it is often directed) jargon seems cynical and vulgar, while to the user it is elevated or even heroic. Jargon is evoked by the disruption of normal, rhythmical processes and activities (here Lixačev uses examples from the manufacturing process), for it is frequently at those points in an activity where something may go wrong that jargon develops. Lixačev feels that in time, with the increase in well-organized activities, such as mass production in industry, disruptions will be fewer and jargons will gradually disappear.

This article also devotes considerable attention to refuting the notion that secrecy is an essential ingredient of criminal argot, a commonly held view among Russian scholars at the time. Tonkov, for example, in the article described above, lays great emphasis on this point, arguing that argot arises because of the illegal nature of the activities of criminals for the express purpose of disguising their intentions from their intended victims. Lixačev attacks this view, in particular as expounded by Tonkov, and shows rather convincingly, in part by demonstrating contradictions in the statements of many proponents of the idea, that secrecy is not essential to argot.[28] While admitting that there might be motivation for a few groups, such as criminals and dishonest traders, to develop a secret vocabulary, he points out that numerous other groups lack such motivation,

28. Лихачев 1964, p. 319.

and yet use jargons. The popularity of the notion he attributes to several factors: the lack of linguistically satisfactory investigations (most often they were made by ethnographers, police officials, or interested amateurs); the investigators' ignorance of the groups being investigated and the suspicion with which they were met, which tended to make the jargons seem exotic and secret; the tendency to sensationalize their findings, with resultant distortion and exaggeration of the material; and, above all, unfamiliarity with or careless reading of the western authorities, many of whom doubted or denied that maintaining secrecy was the primary purpose of argot.[29]

One may argue with some of Lixačev's conclusions and, as he himself states, he has by no means exhausted the subject. Nevertheless, most of his observations are so interesting that we can only regret that he did not find it possible to continue his investigations in this area.

For works on Russian jargon written after 1938, one must, apparently, look to western sources, but the materials are sparse. Few that I have seen are really investigations at all, but are rather word lists or dictionaries. An exception is B. O. Unbegaun's article, "Les argots slaves des camps de concentration" [Unbegaun 1947]. Unbegaun's article deals mostly with the Slavic-German vocabulary that arose in German concentration camps, rather than with Soviet prison camp speech. Another exception is Andrej and Tat'jana Fesenko's Русский язык при Советах (*Russian Language Under the Soviets*) [Фесенко 1955]. The authors, World War II émigrés and graduates in philology of the University of Kiev, have not written a study of argot per se, but their work does contain a chapter of some twenty pages devoted to the penetration of argot into the standard language. The Fesenkos add little to what has been said in earlier works. They discuss the route argot followed into the standard language (i.e., from urban underworld groups to homeless orphans in the streets to the speech of schoolboys, thence into schools, *komsomols*, and factories), the writers who made literary use of argot (Leonov, Kaverin, Babel'), and some

---

29. Among western scholars, Lixačev mentions Sainéan 1920, Dauzat 1923, and Krapp and Bradley 1930, as doubters of the secrecy hypothesis. The only Russian writer to do so was Лебедев 1909.

of the Soviet writers on argot (including, among others, Straten and Polivanov). The work is, however, unusual in that it properly emphasizes the importance of the argot element in Soviet speech. Unhindered by Soviet censorship, the Fesenkos are also able to note the important role of the secret police and the labor camps as sources for the "enrichment" of the vocabulary. The remaining works on Russian jargons have already been mentioned and discussed in the first section of this Introduction.

This Glossary is, then, in a sense, a continuation of a long line of dictionaries of nonstandard Russian going back to the early nineteenth century. It is not, however, like any of its predecessors. The earliest dictionaries, or, more accurately, word lists, recorded the speech of itinerant peddlers, although it was frequently not recognized as such at the time. Next, there appeared a number of dictionaries of the argot of criminals, with one of the earliest, that of Traxtenberg, being one of the best, a model of what such a dictionary should be. The tradition, which comes to a virtual end in the 1930s in the Soviet Union, is picked up in the West following World War II with the publication of a handful of glossaries of labor camp and prison speech. Although in the 150 years of this tradition, at least three substandard varieties of speech may be identified (i.e., peddlers' speech, argot, and now, prison camp speech), a unifying thread may be traced throughout this entire period. It consists of the fact that each succeeding jargon owes a portion of its vocabulary to the preceding jargon. Just as criminal argot contains elements from the earlier speech of peddlers, and the latter contains (presumably) elements from the jargons that preceded it, so prison camp speech contains an important component from criminal argot. To borrow Straten's felicitous metaphor, prison camp speech has inherited many forms from criminal argot, although, in this case, criminals themselves and their distinctive jargon have yet to "pass on" from the Soviet scene. This Glossary of prison camp speech is part of this long tradition.

H. E. M.

LIST OF REFERENCES

Артемьев, А. И., Описание рукописей, хранящихся в библиотеке Императорского Казанского университета. « Летопись занятий Археографической комиссии (1876–1877) », вып. VII, СПб., 1884.

Артемьев, Вячеслав П., Режим и охрана исправительно-трудовых лагерей МВД. « Исследования и материалы Института по изучению СССР », сер. I, вып. 26, Munich, 1956.

Ахманова, О. С., Словарь лингвистических терминов, изд. « Советская энциклопедия », М., 1966.

Баранников, А. П., Цыганские элементы в русском воровском арго. « Язык и литература », т. 7, Л., 1931, стр. 139–158.

Бец, Ванька, Босяцкий словарь: Опыт словотолкователя выражений, употребляемых босяками: Составлен по разным источникам, Одесса, 1903.

Білинський, Андрій, В концтаборах СРСР, 1944–55, Chicago, Munich, 1961.

Бойков, Михаил, Люди советской тюрьмы, чч. 1–3, Buenos Aires, 1957.

Брейтман, Григорий Н., Преступный мир: Очерки из быта профессиональных преступников, Киев, 1901.

Виноградов, Н. Н., Словарь соловецкого условного языка. Соловки, 1927.

Гинзбург, Евгения Семеновна, Крутой маршрут. « Грани », 1967–1968, №№ 64–68.

Даль, Владимир И., Пословицы русского народа, Изд. худож. лит., М., 1862; 1957.

———, Толковый словарь живого великорусского языка, тт. I–IV, ГИИНС, М., 1955, с изд. 1880–1882.

———, Толковый словарь живого великорусского языка, тт. I–IV, изд. 3-е, под ред. И. А. Бодуэна де Куртенэ, СПб., М., 1903–1909.

Дмитриев, Н. К., Турецкие элементы в русских арго. « Язык и литература », т. 7, Л., 1931, стр. 159–179.

Жуков, В. П., Словарь русских пословиц и поговорок, изд. « Советская энциклопедия », М., 1966.

Зайцев, И. М., Соловки, Shanghai, 1931.

Иванов-Разумник, Р. В., Тюрьмы и ссылки, изд. имени Чехова, New York, 1953.

Ишутина, Елена, Нарым: Дневник ссыльной. « Новый журнал », New York, 1964, 1965, №№ 76, 77, 78, стр. 5–54, 5–37, 96–119.

Каин, Ванька, История славного вора, разбойника и бывшего московского сыщика Ваньки Каина, со всеми обстоятельствами, разными любимыми песнями и портретом, писанная им самим при балтийском порте в 1764 году, изд. 4-е, М., 1793.

Копорский, С., Воровской жаргон в среде школьников. « Вестник просвещения », М., 1927, № 1, стр. 7–12.

Краснов, Н. Н., Незабываемое, 1945–1956, New York, 1957.

Крестинский, М. М. и Б. П. Крестинский, Краткий словарь современного русского жаргона, изд. « Посев », Frankfurt, 1965.

Ларин, Б. А., Западноевропейские элементы русского воровского арго. « Язык и литература », т. 7, Л., 1931, стр. 113–130.

Лебедев, В., Словарь воровского языка. « Вестник полиции », 1909, №№ 22, 23, 24.

Лихачев, Д. С., Арготические слова профессиональной речи. « Развитие грамматики и лексики современного русского языка », изд. « Наука », М., 1964.

———, Черты первобытного примитивизма воровской речи. « Язык и мышление », тт. III–IV, Л., 1935.

Луп(п)ова, Е. П., Из наблюдений над речью учащихся в школах II ступени Вятского края. « Труды Вятского Научно-исследовательского Института краеведения », т. III, 1927, стр. 105–125.

Максимов, Сергей, Тайга, изд. имени Чехова, New York, 1952.

Марголин, Юлий, Путешествие в страну зэ-ка, изд. имени Чехова, New York, 1952.

Марченко, Анатолий, Мои показания, изд. « Посев », Frankfurt, 1969.

Мейер, Андрей, Описание кричевского графства или бывшего староства Гр. Ал. Потемкина, в ста верстах от Дубровны, между Смоленскою и Могилевскою губерниею. 1786.

Никонов-Смородин, М. З., Красная каторга (Записки Соловчанина), Sofia, 1938.

Паллас, П. С., *Linguarum totius orbis vocabularia comparativa*

(1786–1789), with added title page, Сравнительные словари всех языков и наречий, собранные десницею Высочайшей Особы [императрицею Екатериною], СПб., 1787–1789.

Петрус, К., Узники коммунизма, изд. имени Чехова, New York, 1953.

Поливанов, Е. Д., О блатном языке учащихся и о « славянском языке » революции. « За марксистское языкознание », изд. « Федерация », М., 1931, стр. 161–172.

Попов, В. М., Словарь воровского и арестантского языка. Киев, 1912.

Потапов, С. М., Словарь жаргона преступников: Блатная музыка, М., 1923; 1927.

Ржевский, Л., Язык и тоталитаризм. « Исследования и материалы Института по изучению истории и культуры СССР », сер. I, вып. 6, Munich, 1951.

———, Творческое слово у Солженицына. « Новый журнал », New York, 1969, № 96, стр. 76–90.

Романенко, Михаил [Розанов, М.], Завоеватели белых пятен, Limburg, 1951.

Рыбникова, М. А., Об искажении и огрубении речи учащихся. « Родной язык в школе », М., 1927, № 1, стр. 243–255.

Селищев, Афанасий М., Язык революционной эпохи, изд. « Работник просвещения », М., 1928.

Семенов, Н., Советский суд и карательная политика. « Исследования и материалы Института по изучению истории и культуры СССР », сер. I, вып. 9, Munich, 1952.

Словарь русского языка, тт. I–IV, ГИИНС, М., 1957–1961.

Словарь современного русского литературного языка, тт. 1–17, изд. АН СССР, М.—Л., 1950–1965.

Словарь сокращений русского языка. Под ред. Б. Ф. Корицкого, ГИИНС, М., 1963, стр. 18–19.

Смирнов, Н., Слова и выражения воровского языка, выбранные из романа Вс. Крестовского - « Петербургские трущобы ». « Известия Отделения русского языка и словесности Императорской Академии Наук », т. IV, кн. 3, СПб., 1899, стр. 1065–1087.

Солженицын, Александр И., В круге первом, изд. « YMCA-Press », Paris, 1969a.

———, Один день Ивана Денисовича. « Новый мир », М., 1962, № 11.

———, Олень и шалашовка. « Грани », 1969b, № 73.

———, Раковый корпус, изд. « YMCA-Press », Paris, 1968.

Солоневич, Иван Л., Россия в концлагере, тт. I–II, Sofia, 1936.

Список русских сокращений, применяемых в СССР. « Исследования и материалы Института по изучению истории и культуры СССР », сер. I, вып. 13, Munich, 1954.

Стратен, В. В., Арго и арготизмы, « Известия Комиссии по русскому языку », т. I, Л., 1931, стр. 111–147. [The cover shows « Труды », rather than « Известия ».]

Толковый словарь русского языка. Под ред. Д. Н. Ушакого, тт. I–IV, изд. « Советская энциклопедия », М., 1935–1940.

Тонков, Вячеслав, Опыт исследования воровского языка, Казань, 1930.

Трахтенберг, В. Ф., Блатная музыка (« Жаргон » тюрьмы), СПб., 1908.

Трегубов, Юрий А., Восемь лет во власти Лубянки; записки члена НТС, Frankfurt, 1957.

« Труды Общества любителей российской словесности при Московском университете », т. XX, М., 1820, стр. 115–243.

Фабричный, П., Язык каторги. « Каторга и ссылка », М., 1923, № 6, стр. 177–188.

Фасмер, Макс, Этимологический словарь русского языка, тт. I, II [А—Муж]. Vasmer 1953–1957, trans. and supp. О. Н. Трубачев, изд. « Прогресс », М., 1964–1967.

Фесенко, Андрей и Татьяна Фесенко, Русский язык при Советах, New York, 1955.

Фразеологический словарь русского языка. Под ред. А. И. Молоткова, изд. « Советская энциклопедия », М., 1967.

Фридман, М. М., Еврейские элементы « блатной музыки ». « Язык и литература », т. 7, Л., 1931, стр. 131–138.

Шиляев, Евгений, « Лагерный язык » по произведениям А. И. Солженицына. « Новый журнал », New York, 1969, № 95, стр. 232–247.

Юкшинский, В. И., Советские концентрационные лагери в 1945–1955 гг. « Исследования и материалы Института по изучению СССР », сер. II, вып. 66, Munich, 1958.

Яковлев, Б., Концентрационные лагери СССР. « Исследования и материалы Института по изучению истории и культуры СССР », сер. I, вып. 23, Munich, 1955.

« Язык и литература », т. 7, Л., 1931, стр. 111–179.

Bessonov, Yuri. *Mes 26 prisons et mon évasion de Solovki*. Paris, 1928.

Dallin, David J. and Nicolaevsky, Boris I. *Forced Labor in Soviet Russia*. New Haven, 1947.

Dauzat, Albert. *La langue française d'aujourd'hui.* Paris, 1923.

———. *Les argots; caractères, évolution, influence.* Paris, 1929.

Ginzburg, Eugenia Semyonovna. *Journey Into the Whirlwind.* Гинз-бург 1967–1968, trans. Paul Stevenson and Max Hayward. New York, 1967.

Gliksman, Jerzy. *Tell the West.* New York, 1948.

Goldin, Hyman E., ed. *Dictionary of American Underworld Lingo.* New York, 1950.

Graf, A. E. *6000 deutsche und russische Sprichwörter.* Halle [Saale], 1960.

Herling, Gustav. *A World Apart.* Melbourne, 1951.

Ivanov-Razumnik, R. V. *The Memoirs of Ivanov-Razumnik.* Иванов-Разумник 1953, trans. P. S. Squire. London, 1965.

Kluge, Friedrich. *Rotwelsch, Quellen und Wortschatz der Gaunersprache und der verwandten Geheimsprachen.* Strassburg, 1901.

Krapp, George Philip and Bradley, Henry. "Slang," *Encyclopedia Britannica.* 14th ed. Chicago, 1930, 20:765–67.

Krasnov, Nikolaj Nikolaevič Jr. *The Hidden Russia: My Ten Years as a Slave Laborer.* Краснов 1957, trans. New York, 1960.

Magner, Thomas F. "The *Stiljaga* and His Language." *The Slavic and East European Journal* 15 (1957): 192–95.

Malsagoff, S. A. *An Island Hell.* London, 1926.

Marchenko, Anatoly. *My Testimony.* Марченко 1969, trans. Michael Scammell. New York, 1969.

Partridge, Eric. *A Dictionary of the Underworld.* 2nd ed. New York, 1961.

Sainéan, L. *Le langage parisien au XIXe siècle.* Paris, 1920.

Schöne, Lucien. *Le jargon et jobelin de F. Villon.* Paris, 1887.

Solonevich, Ivan. *The Soviet Paradise Lost.* Солоневич 1936, Vol. 1, trans. Warren Harrow. New York, London, 1938.

Solženicyn, Aleksandr I. *One Day in the Life of Ivan Denisovich.* Солженицын 1962, trans. Ronald Hingley and Max Hayward. New York, 1963.

———. *The Cancer Ward.* Солженицын 1968, trans. Rebecca Frank. New York, 1968.

———. *The First Circle.* Солженицын 1969a, trans. Michael Guybon. London, 1968.

———. *The Love-Girl and the Innocent.* Солженицын 1969b, trans. Nicholas Bethell and David Burg. New York, 1969.

Unbegaun, B. O. "Les argots slaves des camps de concentration." *Publications de la Faculté des Lettres de l'Université de Strasbourg,* 108—*Mélanges* 1945. Vol. 5, *Études linguistiques,* pp. 177–93. Paris, 1947.

Vasmer, Max. *Russisches etymologisches Wörterbuch*. Heidelberg, 1953–57.

Viles, E. and Furnivall, F. S., eds. *Extra Series of the Early English Text Society* 9 (1869).

Vitu, Auguste. *Le jargon au quinzième siècle*. Paris, 1883.

Wentworth, Harold and Flexner, Stuart Berg. *Dictionary of American Slang*. 2nd ed. New York, 1967.

How to Use the Glossary

THE SCOPE OF THE GLOSSARY

1. A number of words and expressions are listed in this Glossary which can be found in standard dictionaries. This was done primarily in order to make the Glossary more serviceable to those who might wish to use it as an aid in reading prison camp literature. It would obviously be more convenient if all, or nearly all, the camp words and expressions that might be encountered were contained in a single handbook. Therefore, many items which can be found in the standard, four-volume Academy Dictionary with essentially the same meanings as those given in the Glossary are nevertheless included. These items are marked with the abbreviation "AD" in square brackets following the entry. The AD was used, rather than the seventeen-volume Словарь современного русского литературного языка (*Dictionary of the Contemporary Russian Literary Language*) [Словарь 1950–1965] because it was felt to be more generally accessible to most readers and hence a more useful reference point. The general principle followed for the listing in the Glossary of such words and expressions is pertinence to camp or prison life. Accordingly, the words волчок 'a judas hole in a cell door' and баланда 'prison gruel,' both of which may be found in the AD, are included. However, numerous abusive or derisive words, such as обалдуй 'blockhead' and сволочь 'swine,' are not included, since the use of such words is not restricted to camps and prisons.

2. A number of other items found in the AD are included in the Glossary, in violation of the principle stated above. These items

are included because they deal with the day-to-day concerns of the prisoner, with the events that loom large in his life, and thus tend to give a revealing picture of camp and prison conditions. It was thought that by including the many words and expressions which have to do with "stealing," "eating," "drinking," "beating," "escaping," and the like, the Glossary might be of considerable interest to many readers simply as a kind of historical or sociological document dealing with Stalin's concentration camps and prisons.

3. If a derivative of a word which appears in the AD does not itself appear there, both the derivative and the word from which it is derived are included in the Glossary. For example, манкировать 'to shirk' appears, but манкирант 'a shirker,' does not. Both forms are included in the Glossary.

4. It of course goes without saying, that words and expressions which do not occur in the AD are included in the Glossary. This includes a small number of obscene words and expressions which, while surely not restricted to camp and prison usage, have rarely, if ever, been listed in any dictionary.

THE STRUCTURE OF THE GLOSSARY

1. All entries in the Glossary are listed in strict alphabetical order. Abbreviations are treated as words, without regard for what the constituent letters represent. Thus, the entry АД occurs before актировка, although, in its resolved form, алиментарная дистрофия, it would follow. No consistent policy has been followed with respect to the listing of adjective-noun phrases. Where the adjective, rather than the noun, is the unusual form, the phrase is listed under the adjective. Thus, блядское отродье is to be found under блядский. Otherwise, phrases are rather arbitrarily listed under the noun.

2. Variants of words are each listed in their proper place, with a reference to the one of them where the meaning can be found. Where a word has one or more variants, they are listed following the English translation of the illustrative sentence. Thus, following the entry хамса we find "See камса. Following the definition

and illustrative English sentence under камса, we find the notation, "*Also* хамса.

3.   When there is more than a single meaning for a word, or if it appears in a number of expressions, that word is listed once, and its various utilizations are numbered consecutively with Arabic numerals within the entry. So, for example, the word лагерь is followed by ten separate utilizations. Each separate usage is usually illustrated by a Russian sentence and an English translation.

4.   Verbs are listed only by one aspect, the perfective whenever possible, with the other aspect following it. If the verb happens to be standard Russian, the other (imperfective) aspect is not given at all. When the verb is not standard Russian, the other aspect is given only when it could be elicited by discussion with Galler, or when it could be determined from sentences supplied by him. When only a single verb is listed (for whatever reason), it is labeled as to aspect.

5.   Phrases are listed under each main word in the phrase, with the word being given in its usual dictionary form. Each entry is followed by a reference to the one place in the Glossary where the definition is given. So, for example, the phrase От работы лошади дохнут is listed under работа, sense 7, with a reference "*See* лошадь, and under лошадь, where the phrase is defined.

THE STRUCTURE OF ENTRIES

1.   The head word in entries is in the usual dictionary form: infinitive for verbs, nominative case singular for nouns, and masculine nominative singular for adjectives and participles. A double dagger, ‡, appearing in the margin before the head word, indicates an entry culled from the works of Solženicyn and added to Galler's list.

2.   Abbreviations are followed immediately by a phonetic transcription within square brackets, by their resolution in Russian, and then by an English translation. For example, КВЧ [ka-ve-čé], культу́рно-воспита́тельная часть, 'KVČ,' culture and education section.

3.   Accents are indicated by acute accent ´. In some instances, the written sources indicate a different accentuation from that shown in this Glossary. Such disagreement is indicated in square brackets at the end of the entry. For example, the word баланда, stressed on the final stem vowel by this Glossary and by the AD, is ending-stressed in Traxtenberg's dictionary. This fact is indicated by the notation "[Tr, баландá] at the end of the entry.

4.   In the case of phrases, the head word is separated from the phrase by the sign, ⊂, "included in." Following the phrase is either its definition or a reference to the entry where it is defined.

5.   Grammatical information has been kept to a minimum, but where necessary, such notes as verbal aspect, diminutive, indeclinable, gender, and the like follow immediately after the word in question.

6.   Nearly all definitions are followed by one or more illustrative sentences, with an English translation. These translations frequently give much more of the flavor of the word than the explanatory definition, and should always be taken into account by the user of the Glossary.

7.   The notation "*Also*" indicates merely that a synonym is listed elsewhere in the Glossary; there is no reason to refer to such entries, since they will contain no additional information. The reference "*See*" indicates that additional information, or all the information, is to be found at another location. The notation "*Cf.*" indicates either an antonym, or additional information on a related topic.

8.   At the end of many entries, enclosed within square brackets, are to be found references to other sources, and to various kinds of additional information. Generally speaking, an abbreviation alone means simply that the entry has been found in another source, with substantially the same meaning and with the same accent. Where the accent differs, or where the meaning is different (though possibly related), or where the form itself is different (an adjective instead of a noun, for example), this information will follow the abbreviation. For example, папáн 'the old man, father' is followed by [AD, папáня], which means that the AD contains a similar form, папáня, with the same meaning. Парáшник 'rumormonger' is followed by [D, one who cleans the latrine pail],

which means that an identical form appears in Dal''s dictionary, but with a different meaning. The usage labels "popular", "colloquial," and others employed by some sources, are frequently to be found following the abbreviation for the sources. Some forms not listed in the AD can be found in other sources, such as Ушаков 1935–40, Селищев 1928, Молотков 1967, Даль 1862; 1957, Даль 1903–9, and Goldin 1950. These sources are usually cited, in chronological order of publication, only when the entry does not appear in the AD. (Note, however, the exception to this principle in the next paragraph.)

9.   Providing etymological identifications for items in the Glossary is beyond the scope of this work, although origins have been indicated, or suggested, in some instances. In particular, criminal argot origin has been assumed for all items that have previously been listed in dictionaries of argot, or in articles devoted to argot. These sources are Смирнов 1899, Трахтенберг 1908, Фабричный 1923, Тонков 1930, Стратен 1931, Лихачев 1935, and Лихачев 1964. Since many words of argot origin are now listed in the AD (but with no indication of their source), such words will be followed both by the abbreviation "AD" and by the abbreviations of the pertinent argot sources.

GLOSSARY

ABBREVIATIONS

AD	Словарь 1957–1961
aLi plus page number	Лихачев 1935
bLi plus page number	Лихачев 1964
c.	coarse [грубое]
coll.	collective
colloq.	colloquial [разговорное]
conj.	conjunction
D	Даль 1903–1909
DPos plus page number	Даль 1862; 1957
decl.	declinable
derog.	derogatory
dim.	diminutive
F plus page number	Фабричный 1923
Fraz.	Фразеологический 1967
G	Graf 1960
hum.	humorous(ly)
impf.	imperfective aspect
indecl.	indeclinable
K	Словарь 1963
KK	Крестинский 1965
Lingo plus page number	Goldin 1950
M	Magner 1957
obs.	obsolescent [устарелое]
pert.	pertaining
pf.	perfective aspect
pop.	popular [просторечное]
prov.	provincial [областное]
S plus page number	Селищев 1928
Sm	Смирнов 1899
St plus page number	Стратен 1931
tech.	technical term
To plus entry number	Тонков 1930
Tr	Трахтенберг 1908
U	Толковый 1935–1940
Ž	Жуков 1966

A, a

АД [a-dé], алиментáрная дистрофúя, 'AD,' alimentary dystrophy, the abbreviation used in death certificates. Причúна смéрти: АД. Cause of death: AD.

актúрование. *See* актирóвка.

актúровать. *See* сактúровать.

актирóвка, 'a write-off.' In camps and prisons clothing completely worn out by a succession of prisoners is written off the clothing supply records. Prisoners too ill to work are also written off. Unless they are political prisoners, they are sometimes released. Otherwise they are transferred to special barracks, where they receive somewhat better food and care. If their health improves, they are returned to work. Вещкаптёр был постоя́нным чле́ном коми́ссии для актирóвки одéжды в лáгере. The clothing clerk was a permanent member of the commission to write off camp clothing. Начáльник лáгеря назнáчил медици́нскую коми́ссию для актирóвки заключённых. The camp commandant appointed a medical commission to write off prisoners. *Also* актирóвание.

áмба, 'curtains, the jig is up, no chance remains.' Когдá я уви́дел, что легковáя маши́на подъéхала к моемý дóму, я знал, что мне áмба. When I saw the car drive up to my house, I knew the jig was up. [Sm, movement of arm in delivering a death blow; D, a deuce (in gambling); Tr; To 369, death]

амбулатóрия, 'camp dispensary,' to which prisoners can report before morning roll call or after returning from work. Treatment and release from work are given only in case of high temperature or serious illness. Пря́мо из вáхты я напрáвился в амбулатóрию к лекпóму. From the guard shack I went straight to the dispensary to see the medic. [AD]

америкáнка, 'a vodka stand.' Лáгерный экспеди́тор забежáл в америкáнку, раздави́л пол-ли́тра, закуси́в солёным огурцóм, и погнáл обрáтно в зóну. The camp forwarding agent dashed into a vodka stand, polished off a bottle of vodka and a pickle, and ran back to the compound.

арáп ⊂ заправля́ть арáпа, 'to brag.' Пéтька арáпа заправля́ет, что был на вóле больши́м дельцóм, когдá егó друзья́ заверя́ют, что на вóле он был сáвкой. Pet'ka brags that he was a big wheel in free life, but his friends assure us that he was a small-time crook. [Fraz., pop.]

арматýрный ⊂ арматýрная кни́жка, 'clothing record book or cards,' in which all items of clothing and footwear supplied by camp authorities are entered and signed for by the prisoner. Собáки всучи́ли мне телогрéйку в арматýрную кни́жку, котóрую я никогдá не получáл. In the clothing record book, the bastards charged me with a padded jacket which I never got.

АСА [a-sá], антисовéтская агитáция, 'ASA,' anti-Soviet agitation, a reference to article 58.10 of the Soviet Criminal Code of 1926. Наш дневáльный сиди́т по АСА. Our barracks orderly is serving a term for ASA.

ассенизáтор, 'a latrine cleaner.' Дани́ло согласи́лся рабóтать ассенизáтором в жéнской зóне и действи́тельно зáжил, как корóль. Danilo agreed to work as latrine cleaner in the women's compound and he really began to live like a king. [AD]

атáнде   **1.** 'attention! watch it!' an exclamation of alarm or warning, sounded by a lookout to his partners in crime. The word is sometimes stressed on the final syllable. [D, атáнде] *Also* атáндо, шýхер.   **2.** indecl. *See* зекс.

атáндо. *See* атáнде 1, 2.

атáсе ⊂ на атáсе, 'on lookout, on watch.' Вáнька, ты побýдь на атáсе, а я постарáюсь пошуруди́ть э́того фрáйера. Van'ka, you watch out, and I will try to rob this pigeon. *Also* на атáнде, на зекс.

АТПéровец [a-te-péraɣic], администрати́вно-техни́ческий персонáл, 'an ATP,' an administrative-technical staff worker, a prisoner who works as camp cook, barber, work assigner, bathhouse manager, or the like. В нáшем лáгере АТПéровцы жи́ли лýчше, чем вольня́жки. In our camp the ATPs lived better than the free employees.

АТПéровский [a-te-pérafsķij], 'ATP,' pertaining to the administrative-technical staff. *See* АТПéровец.

аттеста́т, 'certificate.' Аттеста́т — э́то спра́вка, в кото́рой ука́зано до како́го числа́ з/к получи́л проду́кты при перево́де в друго́е ме́сто заключе́ния. A certificate is a document which indicates how many days' rations the prisoner was given when being transferred to another camp.

Б, б

‡ **балала́ечник,** 'a balalaika player,' a term used for a prisoner arrested under article 58.10 of the Soviet Criminal Code of 1926. « Ты — с фро́нта пря́мо? » — « Да ». — « Балала́ечник? » — « Называ́ют ». — « Трень-бре́нь, антисове́тская агита́ция? » "Are you straight from the front?" "Yes." "A balalaika player?" "That's what they call it." "Plunka-plunk, anti-Soviet agitation?" (Олень и шалашовка) [AD].

бала́н, 'a log,' a technical logging term. В арха́нгельских лагеря́х мой шу́рин рабо́тал на погру́зке бала́нов. My brother-in-law loaded logs in the Archangel camps.

бала́нда **1.** 'gruel,' a deprecatory term for the thin, watery soup served in camps. The use of the term is often a punishable offense. Поду́май то́лько — в тече́ние пяти́ лет жрать одну́ и ту же бала́нду. Just imagine—eating nothing but watery gruel for five years! [AD, pop.; Tr, баланда́; F 183; To 250] *Cf.* лю́ра, ю́шка. **2.** 'cooked food,' the cooked portion of the food ration, so-called because it generally consisted of бала́нда. *See* прива́рок.

бала́ндёр, 'the gruel ladler,' a prisoner responsible for distributing portions of бала́нда (q.v.).

балдо́ха, 'the sun.' Как то́лько балдо́ха появи́лась, Ва́ня скры́лся. As soon as the sun appeared, Vanja disappeared.

бан, 'railway station.' Эта́п повели́ че́рез бан пря́мо в пересы́льную тюрьму́. The transport was led through the railway station straight to the transit prison. [Tr; To 90; St 135]

банде́ровец, 'Banderite,' a member of the Ukrainian nationalist movement of Stepan Bandera (1909–1959), or, loosely, any Ukrainian nationalist who fought the Soviets. Although the name is borne proudly by its members, it is applied in contempt by Russian prisoners, even to other Russian prisoners. Не рассчи́тывай на него́; ведь он банде́ровец. Don't count on him; after all he's just a Banderite.

барахли́шко ⊂ ла́герное барахли́шко, 'camp clothing,' issued by the authorities. Во вре́мя эта́па Ми́шку обобра́ли. Когда́ он на́чал рабо́тать, нача́льник вы́дал ему́ ла́герное барахли́шко. Miška was robbed during his transport. When he began to work, the commandant issued him camp clothing.

барахо́лка, 'second-hand market, flea market' of necessity clandestine in camps, where one can buy or barter for meal tickets, used foot cloths, scraps of newspapers for cigarettes, and the like. Сего́дня я пошёл на барахо́лку, про́дал па́йку хле́ба и купи́л за э́ти де́ньги две ка́ши и бала́нду. Today I went to the second-hand market, sold a bread ration, and bought two bowls of cereal and a bowl of gruel with the money. [AD, pop.]

‡ **барда́к,** 'all fucked up,' said of a plan, a task, or a place; confused, unnecessarily complex. Всю доро́гу барда́к! Things are always fucked up here! (Оле́нь и шалашо́вка) [D, a whorehouse].

баро́ха, 'a broad,' a mildly derogatory term for a woman. Смотри́ на э́ти баро́хи! Look at those broads! *Also* боро́ха. [To 55, боро́ха]

бары́га, 'a fence, a dealer in stolen goods.' Ах, э́тот бары́га всё спла́вит. Ah, that fence can sell anything. [Tr; To 48]

бары́жничать, impf., 'to be a fence (бары́га, q.v.), to deal in stolen goods.' Воло́дя притворя́лся блатны́м, а на са́мом де́ле он всю жизнь бары́жничал. Volodja pretended to be a criminal, but as a matter of fact he was a fence all his life.

басма́ч, 'Basmač,' a member of an anti-Communist resistance movement in Central Asia, active intermittently since 1917 and as late as World War II. It is applied as a term of abuse to all Asiatic national minorities. Боже́ева посади́ли за басма́чество; он уверя́л нас, что до тюрьмы́ не знал сло́ва « басма́ч ». Božeev was imprisoned for belonging to the Basmač movement; he assured us that before his imprisonment he didn't know the word "Basmač." [AD]

ба́тя, 'dad, uncle,' a common term of address for an older criminal. Гей, ба́тя, дава́й махнёмся боти́нками. Hey, uncle, let's trade boots. [AD, prov. 'father']

ба́хнуть, ба́хать 1. 'to unload, to get rid of, to sell illegally.' Я ба́хнул [спла́вил] мою́ спецоде́жду че́рез бесконво́йного. I got rid of my work clothes with the help of a trusty. *Also* спла́вить. **2.** ——— получку, 'to blow one's pay, to squander one's pay,' usually on alcohol, or prostitutes. Васёк ба́хнул всю получку за одну́ ночь. Vasek blew all his pay in one night. [AD, colloq. 'to make a loud, deep noise; to strike, throw noisily']

баци́лловый ⊂ баци́лловые проду́кты. [AD] *See* баци́льный.

баци́ллы, pl., ' "gourmet" food,' (lit., bacilli). [AD] *See* баци́льный.

баци́льный ⊂ баци́льные проду́кты, pl., ' "gourmet" food,' a name given by ordinary prisoners to the fats, sugar, and other foods denied them. Смотри́, как каптёр отрасти́л себе́ ря́шку на баци́льных [баци́лловых] проду́ктах [на баци́ллах]. Look how the supply clerk has fattened his ugly mug on "gourmet" food. *Also* баци́ллы, баци́лловые проду́кты.

бегле́ц, 'an escapee.' Обыкнове́нно беглеца́, изби́того и в незави́дном состоя́нии, привози́ли обра́тно в зо́ну, чтобы напуга́ть остальны́х заключённых. Usually the escapee, beaten and in very bad condition, was brought back to the compound in order to frighten the other prisoners. [AD]

бе́ленький. *See* цветно́й, блатно́й 1.

бесконво́йный, 'a trusty.' Я спла́вил мою́ спецоде́жду че́рез бесконво́йного [расконвои́рованного]. I sold my work clothes with the help of a trusty. *Also* расконвои́рованный.

бзди́тельность ⊂ социалисти́ческая бзди́тельность, 'socialistic farting,' a play on the phrase, социалисти́ческая бди́тельность 'socialistic vigilance.' Благодаря́ социалисти́ческой бзди́тельности мы постро́или коммуни́зм в стране́. Thanks to socialistic farting, we have built communism in the land. [D, бздеть 'to fart quietly']

би́кса, 'a whore.' Ма́ша — э́то така́я би́кса; ка́ждую ночь в мужско́й бара́к ле́зет. Maša is such a whore; she goes to the men's barracks every night. [То 41]

би́тый, 'experienced,' a term applied to noncriminals who are nevertheless experienced in camp life. Воло́дя не́ был блатны́м, то́лько би́тый па́рень, челове́к, и поэ́тому нача́льник уча́стка назна́чил его́ бригади́ром строи́тельной брига́ды. Although not a criminal, Volodja was an experienced fellow, and therefore the section commandant made him boss of the construction gang. [D, intelligent; prompt, efficient]

битьё ⊂ Битьё определя́ет созна́ние. 'Beating determines (one's) consciousness,' a play on the Communist dictum, Бытие́ определя́ет созна́ние 'Being determines (one's) consciousness.'

блат   1. 'pull, influence.' Блат вы́ше [сильнéе] совнаркóма. Pull is more important than the Council of People's Commissars. [Tr]   **2.** блáтом обзавести́сь, 'to acquire pull, influence.' Ивáнов обзавёлся блáтом. Ivanov has acquired pull. **3.** Совéтские лагеря́ дéржатся на трёх китáх: блат, мат и тухтá. 'Soviet camps are supported by three principles (lit., whales): pull, obscene oaths, and chiseling,' a paraphrase of the saying, Мир дéржится на трёх китáх 'The world is supported by three whales.'

блатáрь. *See* блатнóй 1.

блатнóй   1. 'a hardened, professional criminal,' one covered by the criminal code (*see* закóн 1). Criminals are composed of two antagonistic groups, крáсненькие 'the reds' and бéленькие 'the whites,' who frequently engage in bloody fights. These criminals (also called цветны́е 'colored') should be distinguished from the criminals who are not covered by the code (such as the Maxnoites and the small-time petty crooks) and from the political prisoners. Как тóлько блатны́е [блатя́ги, блатняки́, блатари́] вошли́ в пересы́льный барáк, чтобы обрабóтать вновь прибы́вших кóнтриков, послéдние скучи́лись в оди́н уголóк, готóвые защищáться. As soon as the criminals entered the transit barracks to rob the newly arrived politicals, the latter huddled together in a corner, ready to defend themselves. [Tr; F 180; To 59] *Also* блатáрь, блатня́к, блатя́га. *Cf.* махнóвец.   **2.** 'cushy, easy, soft,' something associated with the criminals' privileged position in camps (*Cf.* закóн 1). Сегóдня мне попáлась блатнáя работёнка: пошёл руби́ть дровá начáльнику учáстка, и егó женá далá мне кусóк сáла и стакáн вóдки. Today I fell into a cushy job: I went to the commandant's to chop wood and his wife treated me to a lump of lard and a glass of vodka.

блатня́к. *See* блатнóй 1.

блатня́чка, fem. form of блатня́к (q.v.).

блатя́га. *See* блатнóй 1.

блокпóст, 'block station,' where a watchdog is stationed outside the camp. The dog has a kennel for protection from bad weather, and can move back and forth along a wire. Вожáтый вы́ставил собáк по блокпóстам. The dog handler stationed dogs at the block stations.

блядовáть, impf., 'to fuck.' Наш бригади́р блядовáл всю

ночь; с утра́ его́ помо́щник до́лжен был вы́вести брига́ду на рабо́ту. Our gang boss fucked all night long; in the morning his deputy had to lead the brigade to work. [D]

бля́дский ⊂ бля́дское отро́дье, 'spawn of a prostitute.' Ах, ты су́кин сын, ты бля́дское отро́дье! You son of a bitch, you spawn of a prostitute! [D]

блядь, 'prostitute.' [D]

бля́хи, pl. *See* полти́нники.

бобёр, 'a rich pigeon,' a prisoner who arrives in camp well-dressed and with many belongings. С после́дним эта́пом приве́ли одного́ бобра́, бы́вшего румы́нского мини́стра; носи́л шевио́товый костю́м, хро́мовые прохоря́, а в рука́х два угла́. A rich pigeon, an ex-Rumanian minister, arrived with the last transport. He was wearing a wool suit, chrome-leather boots, and was carrying two suitcases. [AD, beaver fur; pop. 'a beaver']

Бог ⊂ Дай, Бо́же, за́втра то́же. 'May God give us a tomorrow,' a toast used when drinking vodka.

бока́, pl., 'a pocket watch.' Во вре́мя пове́рки Ва́ська спи́здил бока́ у нача́льника режи́ма. During a checkup Vas'ka swiped the disciplinary officer's pocket watch. [Tr; F 183; To 183]

болту́н, 'a chatterbox.' This normal, colloquial term, used for a prisoner arrested under article 58.10 of the Soviet Criminal Code of 1926, enjoyed nearly official standing in camps, at least before the Legal Reforms of 1958. « Кака́я статья́? » — « Болту́н [Болту́ха, Болту́шка] », — отве́тил заключённый. "Which provision?" "Chatterbox," answered the prisoner. [AD, colloq.] *Also* болту́ха, болту́шка, язы́чник.

болту́ха. *See* болту́н.

болту́шка 1. 'flour soup,' made by stirring flour into boiling water, but without fats. К весне́ в лагеря́х уже́ овоще́й не́ было, и поэ́тому корми́ли з/к одно́й болту́шкой до но́вого урожа́я. By spring the vegetables were used up in the camps so the prisoners were fed flour soup until the new crop. [AD, pop. prov.] 2. *See* болту́н.

боро́ха. *See* баро́ха.

бо́тать ⊂ бо́тать по-фе́не [на фо́не], impf., 'to speak in criminals' argot.' По-фе́не [На фо́не] бо́таешь [хрю́каешь]? Do you speak criminals' argot? [To 393; M, to speak *stiljaga* slang] *Also* хрю́кать по-фе́не [на фо́не].

бочáта, pl., 'a watch,' dim. of бокá (q.v.). Я долбанýл нóвые бочáта из ювелúрного магазúна. I stole a new watch from a jewelry store. [КК, бачáта (*sic*)]

браслéты, pl., 'handcuffs.' Когдá я попáлся, уполномóченный мне срáзу надéл браслéты и повёл в изолятор. When I was caught the officer immediately handcuffed me and took me to the isolator. [Sm, браслетики; F 183; To 452]

братýха, 'chum, close friend.' Гей, братýха, давáй махнёмся ботúнками. Hey, chum. Let's trade boots.

брáшка. [КК] *See* хéвра.

брехáло, 'mouth.' Заткнú брехáло! Shut up! [AD, брехáть pop. prov. 'to bark, bay']

бригáда 1. 'brigade, gang.' Сегóдня нáша бригáда вышла на плотúну. Today our gang went out to the dam site. **2.** ——— ширпотрéба, 'consumer goods gang,' made up of goners and the weak, who repair clothing, make baskets, mats, wooden spoons, and the like. Сúдоров дошёл, и начáльник колóнны перевёл егó в бригáду ширпотрéба. Sidorov was on his last legs and the column chief transferred him to the consumer goods gang. **3.** ——— штрафнáя, 'penalty brigade,' composed of prisoners who have violated some camp rule. They live in special barracks and do hard labor under strict discipline. Иванóв промотáл свою нóвую одéжду и спецóвку; начáльник лáгеря велéл перевестú егó в штрафнýю бригáду. Ivanov sold his new clothing and coveralls; the commandant ordered him transferred to the penalty brigade. [AD]

бригадúр, 'gang boss, brigadier,' a prisoner, usually a criminal, in charge of a brigade or gang. Наш бригадúр бушевáл весь день, потомý что егó зазнóбу отпрáвили нóчью в этáп. Our brigadier raged the whole day because his sweetheart was transported during the night. [AD]

бригадúрша, fem. form of бригадúр (q.v.).

бригáдник, 'a member of a brigade.' [AD, colloq.]

брюхо ⊂ Не пáдай дýхом, а брюхом. *See* дух.

бýбен ⊂ **1.** бýбну выбить, 'to beat.' Доходяга заикнýлся, что пáйка мáленькая; бригадúр доходяге выбил бýбну. The goner started to mention that his bread share was small; the brigadier gave the goner a beating. [St 143] **2.** бубнéй дать [навéсить], 'to beat.' Кóлька заикнýлся бригадúру, что пáйка слúшком мáлая, и бригадúр емý такúх бубнéй дал [навéсил], что Ко́лька не забу́дет э́то надо́лго. Kol'ka started to mention to the brigadier that his bread ration was too small, and the brigadier gave him such a beating that he won't soon forget it.

бу́дка ⊂ проходна́я бу́дка, 'control post,' a part of the guard shack where special permits are shown to enter or leave the area. Вольнонаёмные и бесконво́йные проходи́ли че́рез проходну́ю бу́дку, чтобы предъяви́ть про́пуск вахтёру. The free workers and trusties passed through the control post in order to show their permits to the guard. [AD]

бузотёр, 'a troublemaker.' Си́доров — э́то настоя́щий бузотёр; держи́сь пода́льше от него́. Sidorov is a real troublemaker; stay away from him. [AD, c. pop.; F 186; St 138]

БУР [búr], бара́к уси́ленного режи́ма, 'BUR,' strict discipline barracks, where political prisoners with heavy sentences and especially recalcitrant criminals are assigned. It is also used as a camp prison for prisoners being interrogated. Я проваля́лся в БУ́Ре пять дней за чепуху́. I lolled around in the BUR five days for a trifle. [K]

бурда́, 'slop.' Сего́дня таку́ю бурду́ навари́ли на ку́хне, что да́же работя́ги не могли́ её в рот взять. They prepared such slop in the kitchen today, that not even the hard workers could swallow it. [AD, colloq.]

бу́сать, impf., 'to drink, swallow.' Ко́стя комменда́нт бу́сает сиву́ху, как води́чку. The barracks chief, Kostja, swallows vodka like water. [Tr, бусну́ть; To 403, бу́сать; St 133, буси́ть, бусну́ть]

Буты́рка, sometimes construed as pl. *Cf.* following sources. 'Butyrka,' a popular designation for Буты́рская тюрьма́, a notorious prison in Moscow. Я год просиде́л в Буты́рке. I spent a year in Butyrka. [Tr, Буты́рки (see his entry кича́) and из Буты́рки (see his entry милосе́рдная); F 178, в Буты́рках]

буфера́, pl., 'knockers, breasts.' Когда́ Ма́ша со свои́ми буфера́ми появи́лась на сце́не, все на́чали аплоди́ровать. When the audience saw Maša's knockers, it burst into applause. [Tr; To 318]

буферя́стый, 'having large breasts,' pertaining to буфера́ (q.v.).

бушла́т 1. 'jacket,' long-sleeved, quilted, and lined with corded cotton wadding. Хотя́ я рабо́тал хорошо́, соба́ки всучи́ли мне бушла́т второ́го сро́ка. Although I worked hard, the bastards only issued me a secondhand jacket. [AD, a sailor's cloth jacket; Tr; F 183] **2.** деревя́нный ———, 'a wooden jacket' [i.e., a coffin]. Не горю́й, ско́ро полу́чишь от нача́льника деревя́нный бушла́т. Don't worry, you'll soon get a wooden jacket from the commandant.

бытови́к, 'nonpolitical prisoner.' В Ста́линские года́ бытовики́ бы́ли привилегиро́ванные во всéх лагеря́х. In the years of Stalin nonpolitical prisoners had special privileges in all the camps.

бытови́чка, fem. form of бытови́к (q.v.).

бычо́к, 'cigarette butt.' Си́доров дошёл до тако́й сте́пени, что он бессты́дно пыта́лся стреля́ть бычки́ у ка́ждого встре́чного и попере́чного. Sidorov was reduced to such a state that he would shamelessly try to finagle cigarette butts from anybody and everybody. [St 138]

В, в

вагонзак, вагон заключённых. *See* столыпинский.

вагонка, 'wooden plank bunk,' used in вагонная система. (*See* система.) *Also* нара.

вахлак, 'a goner, a wreck, a prisoner on his last legs.' Не трогай этого вахлака, убьёшь его. Don't touch that wreck, you'll kill him. [AD, pop. obs., usually abusive, 'a clumsy, rather stupid person']

вахта, 'guard shack.' Когда колонна заключённых приблизилась к вахте, все охранники и внутренники высыпались, чтобы обыскивать их. When the column of prisoners approached the guard shack, all the camp guards and prisoner guards spilled out to search them. [AD, a watch; the watch crew (at sea)]

вахтёр, 'guard,' on duty in the guard shack. Когда бригада увидела, что Шмаков сегодня вахтёром, они знали, что шмонать будет крепко. When the gang saw that Šmakov was on duty in the shack, they knew there would be a thorough frisk. [AD, pop. 'watchman in an institution']

век ⊂ **1.** Век живи, дураком помрёшь. 'Though you live to be a hundred, you will die a fool.' In camps, this old proverb is very frequently used. It implies that even the wiliest and most experienced camp veteran will eventually be tripped up. [Ž] **2.** Век свободы не видать, если подведу. 'May I never see liberty if I fail,' a strong criminals' oath.

вертухай. [КК] *See* попка.

верхотура 1. 'the upper bed boards.' Летом камера была настоящей парилкой; блатари загнали всех фраеров на верхотуру, а сами легли на нижние нары. The cell was a real steam bath in the summer; the criminals drove the pigeons to the upper bed boards and occupied the lower ones themselves. **2.** 'the upper hand.' Фраера сорганизовались и загнали блатных под нары. С того момента фраера заняли верхотуру. The pigeons organized themselves and forced the criminals under the bed boards. From that moment on the pigeons had the upper hand (in the barracks). [AD, pop. hum. 'upper part of a lodging; the upper storey']

вещь ⊂ с вещáми на вáхту, 'to the guard shack with your gear,' the usual order to prepare for transport. Иванóв, Петрóв — с вещáми на вáхту! Ivanov, Petrov! To the guard shack with your gear!

вещкаптёр, from завéдующий вещкаптёркой, 'clothing clerk,' prisoner-manager of the clothing supply, responsible for assigning clothing to prisoners and maintaining clothing records. Вещкаптёр получи́л спи́сок на раздáчу одéжды в контóре и напрáвился в вещкаптёрку. The clothing clerk received the distribution list at the office and set out for the supply room.

вещкаптёрка, вещевáя каптёрка, 'clothing supply.' *See* вещкаптёр.

вещстóл 1. вещевóй стол, 'the clothing desk,' an office where clothing is ordered for a camp district or camp section. Пóсле рабóты я реши́л пойти́ в вещстóл, чтóбы провéрить, чтó за мнóй чи́слится. After work I decided to go to the clothing desk to verify what I was charged with. 2. from начáльник вещстолá, 'head of the clothing desk,' a prisoner accountant in charge of the clothing desk, the immediate superior of the вещкаптёр (q.v.). Вещстóл нáшего отделéния был óчень дурнóй человéк и за наимéньший промóт писáл жáлобу начáльству лáгеря. The head of the clothing desk in our district was a very harsh man and for the least misappropriation would complain to the camp authorities.

взять ⊂ 1. ——— в рабóту, 'to work someone over,' to beat unsparingly to obtain a desired result. Слéдователь взял в рабóту Николáя и пóсле э́того Николáй расколóлся, как цéлочка. The interrogator worked Nikolaj over and then he broke like a hymen. 2. ——— на понт, 'to cheat, dupe.' Блатны́е в лагеря́х пытáлись взять на понт вновь при́бывших фрáйеров, чтóбы отня́ть у них вся́кую цéнную вещь, привезённую с вóли. In the camps criminals tried to cheat newly arrived pigeons out of every valuable which they had brought in from the outside world. [Tr; F 180; St 142]

винт, винтóвка, 'a rifle.' Пóпка шлёпнул доходя́гу из винтá. The screw shot a goner with a rifle. [St 140]

вка́лывать, impf., 'to work very hard.' Вчера́ я це́лый день вка́лывал. Yesterday I worked very hard all day. [KK]

вла́совец, 'Vlasovite,' a follower of General Andrej Andreevič Vlasov (1900–1946), who, after his capture by the Germans in 1942, was induced to play a leading part in the Russian anti-Communist movement. Нача́льник УРБ сказа́л мне, что у Ивано́ва в ли́чном де́ле запи́сано « вла́совец ». The head of the URB (registration-distribution office) told me the designation "Vlasovite" was entered in Ivanov's personal dossier.

власть ⊂ Сюда́ Сове́тская власть не дохо́дит. 'Soviet power does not reach here,' an expression emphasizing the futility of complaining to Moscow. Выполня́й приказа́ния, и ни на что не наде́йся; сюда́ Сове́тская власть не дохо́дит. Carry out orders and hope for nothing; Soviet power does not reach here.

в/н [ve-én], вольнонаёмный, 'free employee,' often a discharged prisoner. The abbreviation is also used in official documents and announcements. За связь с заключённым в/н Петро́ву, Си́дору Ива́новичу, объяви́ли вы́говор. The free employee Petrov, Sidor Ivanovič, was reprimanded for fraternizing with a prisoner.

внеза́пка, внеза́пная прове́рка, 'a sudden prisoner check,' sometimes followed by a search of the prisoners and barracks. Весь бара́к уже́ собира́лся спать, как дежурня́к с комен-да́нтом вошли́ в бара́к, что́бы сде́лать внеза́пку. The whole barracks was settling down to sleep when the duty noncom and the barracks chief entered to conduct a sudden prisoner check.

вну́тренник, 'a prisoner guard,' most frequently a criminal. Since he is usually an informer, he is hated more than camp guards. Вновь назна́ченный вну́тренник Ивано́в повёл брига́ду бесконво́йных к трактора́м. The newly appointed prisoner guard Ivanov led a brigade of trusties to the tractors.

вну́трянка, вну́тренняя тюрьма́. *See* тюрьма́ 1.

вода́ ⊂ **1.** Вода́ ме́льницы лома́ет. 'Water wears down mills,' a warning given to those who drink too much water (and too much of the watery camp soup, бала́нда) in an attempt to combat hunger. Ва́ня, не продолжа́й во́ду пить; ведь вода́ ме́льницы лома́ет. Vanja, don't keep drinking water; you know, water wears down mills. [Ž, Вода камень точит] **2.** Пей вода́, ешь вода́, еба́ть не захо́чешь никогда́! 'Drink water, eat water, and you'll never feel like fucking!' a proverb referring to the low caloric value of the food ration. The ungrammaticalness of this proverb (пей, ешь вода́, instead of во́ду) is determined by the rime.

вожа́тый, 'dog handler,' a guard in charge of the watch dogs. Как то́лько охра́на обнару́жила следы́ ног в запре́тной зо́не, вожа́тый привёл лу́чшую соба́ку, чтобы она́ шла по следа́м. As soon as the guards discovered tracks in the forbidden zone, the dog handler led up the best dog to follow the tracks.

волчо́к, 'a judas hole,' an opening located in the door of a cell and covered with a small hatch. По́пка всё вре́мя открыва́л волчо́к [глазо́к] и осма́тривал всех в ка́мере. The screw kept opening the judas hole and looking at everyone in the cell. [AD, pop. obs.; F 183] *Also* глазо́к.

волы́нщик. *See* рези́нщик.

вольня́га. *See* вольня́жка.

вольня́жка, dim. of вольня́га, 'free employee,' often an ex-prisoner who stays on to work in the camp. Как то́лько я получи́л но́вое одея́ло из вещкаптёрки, я сра́зу спла́вил его́ вольня́жке. As soon as I received a new blanket from the clothing storage, I sold it to a free employee.

во́ля, 'outside (camp or prison).' Зу́бов получи́л посы́лку с во́ли [жилу́хи]. Zubov received a parcel from the outside. [AD, pop. 'out of doors'] *Also* жилу́ха.

во́рон ⊂ чёрный во́рон, 'a paddy wagon, a Black Maria,' a closed truck used to transport prisoners. Ивано́ва вы́вели из ка́меры и чёрным во́роном повезли́ к областно́му прокуро́ру. Ivanov was taken from his cell and driven to the district prosecutor in a paddy wagon. [KK]

вороно́к, dim. of чёрный ворон, 'a paddy wagon, a Black Maria.' Вороно́к подкати́л к кварти́ре Ивано́ва и по́сле о́быска повёз его́ в МГБ. The paddy wagon rolled up to Ivanov's apartment and after a search it carried him to the Ministry of State Security.

ворю́га, 'thief.' Бригади́р Воло́дя — э́то бы́вший ворю́га. The brigadier Volodja is an ex-thief. [D, воря́га]

воспита́тель, 'education officer,' whose duty is to transform prisoners into loyal, hard-working supporters of the regime. Раз в неде́лю воспита́тель на́шего отделе́ния стара́лся организова́ть чи́тку газе́ты в бара́ках. Once a week the education officer of our camp district tried to organize a newspaper reading session in the barracks. [AD, tutor]

вóхра, военизи́рованная охра́на, 'camp garrison.' Команди́р вóхры приказа́л надзира́телям на ва́хте и охра́нникам на вы́шках стреля́ть в заключённых, пыта́вшихся нару́шить запрéтную зóну. The commander of the camp garrison ordered the overseers at the guard shack and the guards in the towers to shoot at prisoners who tried to enter the restricted area. [К, вохр]

вóхровец, 'soldier,' a member of the camp garrison. Вóхровцы чередова́лись, рабóтая по нéсколько дней в внéшней вóхре и нéсколько дней, как карау́льные. Soldiers in the camp garrison alternated, working several days outside camp as escorts, several days as tower guards.

вошь ⊂ вошь на арка́не, 'a louse on a leash,' a frequent, jocular response of a prisoner to a guard who is searching him. The phrase is from an old proverb, В однóм карма́не вошь на арка́не, в другóм блоха́ на цéпи 'In one pocket a louse on a leash, in the other a flea on a chain.' « Что у тебя́ в карма́не? » — « Вошь на арка́не ». "What do you have in your pocket?" "A louse on a leash." [DPos 91]

впра́вить мозги́. *See* мозг.

враг ⊂ враг нарóда, 'enemy of the people,' since 1937, a term applied to political prisoners both by the authorities and by nonpolitical prisoners. Before this date, the epithet кла́ссовый враг 'class enemy' was more common. Чегó ожида́ть от тебя́? Ведь ты же настоя́щий враг нарóда. What can one expect of you? After all, you're a real enemy of the people.

врéзать, pf., 'to hit.' Фéдя жа́ловался бригади́ру, что па́йка ма́ленькая, а тот врéзал ему́ по башкé. Fedja complained to the brigadier that his bread ration was small, and the latter hit him on the head.

врéменный ⊂ врéменно изоли́рованный, 'temporarily isolated.' *Cf.* изоля́ция.

времянка, 'a temporary barracks.' Большинствó пострóек в зóне — это бы́ли время́нки-лепя́нки, котóрые под дéйствием дождéй начина́ли раскиса́ть и распада́ться. The majority of the camp buildings were temporary ones made of clay, which began to sag and fall apart in the rainy season. [КК, anything temporary]

врйдло, вре́менно исполня́ющий до́лжность ло́шади, 'human labor,' used as tractive power (lit., one temporarily doing the work of a horse). Во вре́мя войны́ и в послевое́нные го́ды из-за отсу́тствия тракторо́в и живо́го тя́гла большинство́ трудоёмких рабо́т в лагеря́х выполня́лось врйдлом. During the war and postwar years, owing to the absence of tractors and draft animals, most of the heaviest work in the camps was done by human labor. [КК; AD, K, both list врид]

всу́нуть, pf., 'to stick (with a sentence), to impose.' Петро́ву всу́нули де́сять лет ИТЛ. Petrov was stuck with ten years of ITL (corrective labor camps).

всучи́ть, pf., 'to charge with (illegally),' to insert into a written record, as, for example, a new item for a used one actually given to a prisoner. Соба́ки всучи́ли [втри́нили] мне телогре́йку в армату́рную кни́жку, кото́рую я никогда́ не получа́л. In the clothing record book the bastards charged me with a jacket which I never got. [D] *Also* втри́нить 1.

ВТеК [fték], внеочередна́я [враче́бная] трудова́я коми́ссия, 'VTeK,' a special [medical] commission to determine the working ability of prisoners. После́дний ВТеК призна́л меня́ дистро́фиком. The last VTeK diagnosed my illness as dystrophy (lit., recognized me as a dystrophic).

втере́ть очки́. *See* очки́.

втри́нить, pf. **1.** *See* всучи́ть. **2.** 'to palm off, to dispose of by deceit.' Я втри́нил [толкану́л] ему́ подде́ланный тало́н на обе́д. I palmed a counterfeit dinner ticket off on him. [AD, pop. 'to push, incite'] *Also* толкану́ть. **3.** 'to sentence.' Никола́й ворова́л года́ми зерно́ из колхо́зного зернохрани́лища; после́дний раз засы́пался и ему́ втри́нили 15 лет. For years Nikolaj stole grain from the collective farm's granary; the last time he was caught red-handed and sentenced to 15 years.

втыка́ть, impf., 'to work like a dog.' Ивано́в втыка́л весь день, а ве́чером получи́л то́лько 400 грамм. Ivanov worked like a dog all day, but in the evening he received only 400 grams (of bread).

входи́ть ⊂ Входя́щий, не грусти́; выходя́щий, не ра́дуйся. 'You who are entering, don't be sad; you who are leaving, don't rejoice,' an expression which indicates both to newcomers and those being released that living conditions inside camps are little different from those on the outside. It also implies, to the latter, that they may soon be back.

выблядок, 'son of a bitch' (lit., son of a whore). Этот выблядок, эта продажная шкура; он готов продать родную мать. That son of a bitch, that mercenary bastard; he's ready to sell his own mother. [D]

вывод ⊂ с выводом на работу. *See* работа 3.

‡ **выгрябываться,** impf., 'to put on airs.' С кублом разошёлся. Рубен, гадища, сети плетёт. Хомич выгрябывается. I've had a falling out with the "family" [of *priduroks*]. That bastard Ruben keeps setting traps, and Xomič keeps putting on airs. (Олень и шалашовка) [D, грёбоваться 'to scorn, to disdain']

выебать, pf. **1.** 'to fuck.' Ванька поставил Машу раком возле скирды и выебал. Van'ka took Maša near the hay stack and fucked her standing up. **2.** Выеби, а скажи « нашёл ». 'Get the fuck out, and say you've found it!' This might be said by a criminal to a subordinate whom he has ordered to steal something, meaning roughly "I don't care how you do it; just do it." Or it might be said by an official to an apprehended thief, meaning "Find and return the stolen goods at once." [D, выеть, see his entry ети]

выколоть ⊂ Глаза выколю! 'I'll pluck out your eyes!' a threat used by criminals to intimidate new arrivals to the camps in order to extort food and clothing from them. While speaking, the criminal approaches his victim with two extended fingers.

вылупить, лупить ⊂ глаза вылупить, лупить, 'to stare.' Чего глаза лупишь? What are you staring at? [AD, pop. лупить глаза; с. pop. вылупить]

выскочить ⊂ выскочить на волю, 'to be released from prison or camp' (lit., to jump to freedom). Благодаря зачётам мне удалось выскочить на волю на два года раньше срока. Because of bonuses I managed to be released two years early. [AD]

вытянуть ⊂ вытянуть копыта, 'to die.' Сидоров вытянул копыта на известковом. Sidorov died at a lime camp. [AD, pop. вытянуть ноги]

выходить ⊂ Входящий, не грусти; выходящий, не радуйся. *See* входить.

вышак. *See* вышка 1.

вы́шка **1.** вы́сшая ме́ра наказа́ния, 'death sentence' (lit., the highest measure of punishment). Его́рову да́ли вы́шку [вышака́] и по́сле ста дней в сме́ртной его́ пригово́р был заменён 25 года́ми. Egorov received a death sentence and after 100 days in death row his sentence was commuted to 25 years. *Also* выша́к. **2.** 'watchtower.' По́пка стоя́л на вы́шке, как истука́н. A screw stood on the watchtower like a statue. [AD]

Г, г

гаврик, 'a guy, a chap,' a somewhat pejorative term for an individual. Начáльник учáстка отобрáл 20 гáвриков и напрáвил на сенокóс. The commandant selected 20 guys and sent them out to cut hay. [D, a ninny, simpleton; aLi 81]

гад, 'snake, stoolie,' a popular term of abuse among criminals, most frequently applied to informers and spies. Мáша, э́та былá настоя́щей пиздóй-разбóйницей. Гад бýду, не забýду. Maša was a real cunt. Even if I turn stoolie, I won't forget her! [AD, pop. abusive 'a disgusting, vile person']

гáдский ⊂ гáдская кровь, 'snake' (lit., reptile's blood), a very derogatory expression common among criminals. Иванóв — э́то такáя гáдская кровь, я бы уби́л егó на мéсте. Ivanov is such a snake I could kill him on the spot. [D]

гаранти́йка, гаранти́йная пáйка, 'a guaranteed ration,' of 450–550 grams of bread, not dependent on work quotas, given to invalids and certain employees (for example, office workers, orderlies). Дневáльный просидéл на гаранти́йке почти́ три гóда и в ус не дул. The orderly received the guaranteed ration for nearly three years so he didn't give a damn. *See* пáйка.

гастроли́ровать, impf., 'to steal,' while traveling about from city to city. Карзýбый гастроли́ровал по всем городáм Совéтского Сою́за. Karzubyj stole in all the cities of the Soviet Union. [AD, гастролёр 'a guest actor'; Tr, гастролёр 'a touring pickpocket']

гвáрдия ⊂ стáрая гвáрдия, 'the old guard,' a designation for communists who participated in the 1917 Revolution, most of whom were arrested during the various purges. Си́доров ужé отбýхал 15 лет в лагеря́х; он ещё из стáрой гвáрдии. Sidorov has already spent 15 years in camps; he is from the old guard.

гéмбил, 'a raucous quarrel.' В жéнском барáке подня́лся такóй гéмбил, что начáльство вы́нуждено бы́ло уйти́. Such a raucous quarrel started up in the woman's barracks that the officials had to leave.

генера́л, 'a "general," ' one who has an advanced case of syphilis. Остерега́йся Ва́ню, он уже́ « генера́л ». Watch out for Vanja. He's already a "general." *Cf.* полко́вник, лейтена́нт.

гепеу́шник. [КК] *See* ГПУшник.

глазо́к 1. [AD, colloq.] *See* волчо́к. **2.** ка́рие гла́зки, 'dark brown eyes,' a fish soup, so-called because of the floating fish eyes found in it. In some camps the name is given to a barley soup, which is bluish in color and in which the floating barley resembles brownish eyes. « Что сего́дня на обе́д? » — « Опя́ть ка́рие гла́зки ». "What's for dinner today?" "Brown eyes again."

глист. [AD, an intestinal worm] *See* глиста́.

глиста́, 'an extremely thin person, a goner,' a term for both males and females, although more frequently applied to the latter. Глист, by contrast, would be used only of a male. Смотри́, Ма́ша така́я глиста́ ста́ла и всё к мужика́м ле́зет. Look how thin Maša has become, but she still chases after the men. [AD, c. pop.]

глода́ть ⊂ Кто кого́ сможет, тот того́ и гло́жет. 'He who can will swallow you,' a proverb by which camp prisoners described the harsh realities of camp life. [DPos 155, 835]

гло́тка ⊂ 1. ——— лужёная, 'tin-plated throat,' applied to someone who raises his voice to intimidate others. Гло́тка лужёная тебе́ не помо́жет. A tin-plated throat won't help you. [AD, pop.] **2.** гло́ткой (не) взять. [DPos 408, горлом не взять] *See* го́рло.

гло́тничать, impf., 'to scream,' to yell at the top of one's voice. Днева́льный на́шего бара́ка гло́тничал це́лый день, и весь бара́к боя́лся его́, как огня́. Our barracks orderly used to scream the entire day and the whole barracks feared him like fire.

говно́ ⊂ конфе́тку сде́лать из говна́, 'to make candy out of shit,' an expression used in complaints about the poor quality of raw material given the prisoners to process. Посмотри́ на э́тот материа́л; нача́льство хо́чет из э́того говна́ конфе́тку сде́лать. Look at this material; the command wants us to make candy out of this shit! [D]

горбу́ша. [D] *See* горбу́шка 1, 2.

горбу́шка, dim. of горбу́ша. **1.** 'the crust of the bread,' highly prized because it has less moisture and is of higher caloric value. Посмотри́, как Алексе́й охо́тится на горбу́шку [горбу́шу], а бригади́р ему́ хер даёт. Look how Aleksej hunts for the crust of the bread, but the brigadier gives him the shaft (lit., prick, penis). [AD; D] **2.** 'the bread ration.' « Горбу́шку [Горбу́шу, Горбы́ль] уже́ получи́л сего́дня? » — « Нет, ещё не получа́л ». "Have you received the bread ration today?" "No, not yet." *Also* горбу́ша, горбы́ль. *See* па́йка.

горбы́ль. *See* горбу́шка 2.

‡ **горе́ть,** impf., 'to be sunk, to end up in a hopeless situation.' ... и он горе́л в ка́рцер на три́ста грамм в день, и горя́чая пи́ща то́лько на тре́тий день. And he'd wind up starving in the cooler on 300 grams a day, with hot food only every third day. (Оди́н день Ива́на Дени́совича)

го́рло ⊂ на го́рло (не) взять, 'to (not) get by shouting, by intimidation.' Напра́сно, Ва́ня, на го́рло [гло́ткой] у меня́ не возьмёшь. You're wasting your time, Vanja, you won't get it from me by shouting. *Also* гло́ткой (не) взять.

горлохва́т, 'a clamorer,' someone who tries to get things by shouting. Бригади́р Ивано́в был тако́й горлохва́т, что все круго́м его́ боя́лись, и да́же нача́льство избега́ло. The brigadier Ivanov was such a clamorer that everyone around feared him, and even the leadership avoided him. [D]

горшо́к ⊂ Хоть горшко́м назови́, то́лько корми́. 'Call me a chamber pot if you wish, but feed me,' an expression of the basic philosophy of the camp prisoner. [G, ... то́лько в печь не станови]

ГПУ [ge-pe-ú], Госуда́рственное полити́ческое управле́ние, 'GPU,' State Political Administration (1922), replaced in the same year by ОГПУ (OGPU). The initials ГПУ continued to be used (not quite accurately) for ОГПУ. Сухачёв был осуждён к двадцати́ года́м тюре́много заключе́ния во вре́мя ГПУ. Suxačev was sentenced to 20 years imprisonment in the time of the GPU. [K] *See* ОГПУ, Чека́.

ГПУшник [ge-pe-úšṇik], 'an employee of ГПУ' (q.v.). *Also* гепеу́шник.

граждани́н, 'citizen,' form of address of prisoners for the camp officials. Prisoners were not allowed to use the term това́рищ 'comrade.' Граждани́н нача́льник! Дава́й докури́ть. Citizen commandant! Let me have the last drag. [AD]

грамм ⊂ получи́ть де́вять гра́ммов, 'to receive nine grams (the weight of a rifle bullet), to be shot.' Говоря́т, что ма́ршал Тухаче́вский получи́л де́вять гра́ммов. It is said that Marshal Tuxačevskij got the nine grams.

губчека́, indecl., according to K., but frequently decl. in colloq. speech, губе́рнская чрезвыча́йная коми́ссия по борьбе́ с контрреволю́цией и сабота́жем, 'provincial Cheka.' [K] *See* Чека́.

гужо́вка. *See* шамо́вка.

гужрабси́ла, гужева́я рабо́чая си́ла, 'tractive force,' a technical term for all kinds of available tractive power—human labor, tractors, and draft animals. По́сле тяжёлой зимы́ состоя́ние гужрабси́лы упа́ло до о́чень ни́зкого у́ровня. Усло́вия для проведе́ния посевно́й бы́ли о́чень тяжёлые. After the severe winter the condition of the tractive force fell to a very low level. The conditions for carrying out the sowing were very hard.

ГУЛАГ [gu-lák], Гла́вное управле́ние исправи́тельно-трудо-вы́х лагере́й, 'GULAG,' main administration of corrective-labor camps. Реше́нием ГУЛА́Га меня́ перебро́сили из Комсомо́льска в Карла́г. I was transferred from Komsomol'sk to Karlag (the Karaganda camp) by a decision of GULAG. [K]

гуля́ш ⊂ гуля́ш по коридо́ру, 'a severe beating.' По́пки при-волокли́ беглеца́ в кабине́т нача́льника режи́ма и там ему́ да́ли тако́й гуля́ш по коридо́ру, что родна́я мать бы его́ не узна́ла. The screws dragged the fugitive into the disciplinary officer's office and beat him so badly that his own mother wouldn't recognize him.

‡ **гумо́вница,** 'woman, mistress.' Вон как бригади́р себе́ и свое́й гумо́внице по килу́ взял! The gang boss took a whole kilo for himself and his woman. (Оле́нь и шалашо́вка)

Д, д

давáлка, 'an easy lay,' a willing sexual partner. [D]

давáха, 'an easy lay,' a willing sexual partner.

‡ **двадцатилéтник,** 'a prisoner with a twenty-year sentence.' А прóтив негó сидúт Х-123, двадцатилéтник ... Х-123, serving a twenty-year sentence, was sitting opposite him. (Один день Ивана Денисовича) *Cf.* десятилéтник.

двуствóлка, 'a broad,' a mildly derogatory term for a woman. Эта двуствóлка опя́ть пришлá на ночь к бригадúру Волóдьке. That broad spent the night with the gang boss Volod'ka again. [AD, a double-barreled gun]

дежурня́к, 'duty noncom,' charged with keeping order, with roll calls, bathhouse and kitchen schedules, and the like. Я хотéл подшухéрить одея́ло в ИТРовском барáке, тóлько дежурня́к накры́л меня́. I tried to steal a blanket from the ITR (engineering-technical workers') barracks, but the duty noncom caught me.

дезкáмера, дезинфекциóнная кáмера. *See* санпропускнúк.

дéло 1. 'a dossier,' containing personal data about the prisoner, a copy of the sentence, and any special instructions. A prisoner could not be admitted to a camp without a dossier. Начáльник конвóя вы́нужден был взять з/к Сúдорова обрáтно в тюрьмý, потомý что егó дéла не оказáлось при сдáче з/к. The convoy chief had to return the prisoner Sidorov to prison because his dossier was missing during the transfer of the prisoners. [AD] **2.** Был бы человéк, а дéло найдётся. *See* человéк 1. **3.** мóкрое дéло, 'robbery with murder.' Я избегáл мóкрого дéла, тóлько в послéдний раз пришлóсь, и э́то мне стóит 10 лет. I tried to avoid bloodshed, but on the last occasion I couldn't, and it's costing me 10 years. [Sm; Tr, мокротá 'murder with bloodletting'; F 180, с мокрой 'robbery with murdeг'; St 137]

‡ **дербанýть,** pf., 'to guzzle.' Ай, ты сегóдня нóрму перехватúл, вторы́е пол-лúтра дербанýл. I see you've over-fulfilled your quota today; you've guzzled your second bottle (lit., second half-liter). (Олень и шалашовка)

‡ **дерьмо́,** 'shit.' Хлеба того́ не стоя́т, что им даю́т. Дерьмо́м бы их корми́ть. They're not worth the bread we give them. We should feed 'em shit. (Один день Ивана Денисовича) [D]

‡ **дерьмо́вый,** 'shitty.' Ну что же вы! Спаса́йте бригади́ра! Вы, пятьдеся́т восьма́я дерьмо́вая, чёрт бы вас драл! What are you doing! Save your gang boss! You shitty article fifty-eighters, may you rot in hell! (Олень и шалашовка)

‡ **десятиле́тник,** 'a prisoner with a ten-year sentence.' Десяти-ле́тников я не могу́ брать. I can't take any ten-year men. (Олень и шалашовка) *Cf.* двадцатиле́тник

деся́тник, 'foreman,' a prisoner or ex-prisoner responsible to the work superintendent of the camp. Жизнь брига́ды зави́села от деся́тника: захо́чет, прокорми́т её, а не захо́чет, так го́ло-дом примори́т. The life of the gang depended on the foreman: if he wished, he could feed it; if not, he could starve it. [AD]

‡ **деся́точка,** 'a ten-year stretch.' А попро́буй в ка́торжном ла́гере оттяну́ть деся́точку на о́бщих! Just try to last out a ten-year stretch in a hard labor camp on general duties! (Один день Ивана Денисовича)

де́тский ⊂ **1.** де́тское наказа́ние, 'a child's punishment.' « Гей, Копыло́в, ско́лько нафуя́рили? » — « Пять лет ». — « Э́то чепуха́, э́то де́тское наказа́ние [де́тский срок] ». "Hey, Kopylov, how much did they give you?" "Five years." "That's a trifle, a child's punishment." *Also* де́тский срок. **2.** де́тский срок. *See* meaning 1.

дешёвка, 'a whore,' an abusive term often applied to men. Ах, ты дешёвка, я предупрежда́л тебя́, чтобы горбу́шку э́ту не тро́гать. You whore! I warned you not to touch this bread. [D, a brothel]

Джёзказга́н, 'Džezkazgan,' an infamous camp in the Karaganda group. Все заключённые без исключе́ния боя́лись эта́па в Джёзказга́н; плоха́я вода́ убива́ла заключённых в о́чень коро́ткий срок. All the prisoners without exception feared transport to Džezkazgan, where bad water killed one in a very short time.

дитя́ ⊂ Чему́ бы дитя́ ни ра́довалось, лишь бы рабо́тало. 'Anything to keep the child happy, so long as it [i.e., the child] works,' a play on the proverb Чем бы дитя́ ни те́шилось, лишь бы не пла́кало 'Anything to keep the child amused, so long as it doesn't cry.' The revised proverb refers to a camp policy at the beginning of the 1950s, which permitted more freedom to obtain better efficiency. Лáгерные влáсти нáчали смотрéть чéрез пáльцы на нéкоторые нарушéния режúма. Онú считáли, что « чемý бы дитя́ ни рáдовалось, глáвное лишь бы рабóтало ». The camp authorities began to wink at certain violations of discipline. They thought "anything to keep the child happy, so long as it works." [Ž]

дневáльный, 'barracks orderly,' usually an invalid or an old criminal. Дневáльный нáшего барáка был уважáем всем начáльством, потомý что наш барáк служúл образцóм для всей зóны. Our barracks orderly was respected by all the higher-ups because our barracks was an example for the whole compound. [AD]

добáвка ⊂ 1. 'an additional sentence.' Акúмов написáл помúлование на úмя Стáлина, а пóсле полугóда получúл добáвку [довéсок] в три гóда. Akimov wrote an appeal for a pardon addressed to Stalin, and after half a year got an additional sentence of three years. [AD, colloq. 'an addition of anything'] *Also* довéсок. 2. Добáвку? Прокурóр добáвит. 'More? You'll get more from the prosecutor,' a frequent response of the cook to a prisoner who asks for more food.

добрó ⊂ Чем добрý пропадáть, лýчше пусть пýзо лóпнет. 'Rather than waste the good, better let the belly burst,' a saying created under camp conditions where everything has to be utilized, even if the results might be harmful. В послéднем трáнспорте ры́ба былá совсéм разложúвшаяся. З/к всё пожрáли. Знáешь, чем добрý пропадáть, лýчше пусть пýзо лóпнет. The last consignment of fish was completely rotten. The prisoners devoured it all. You know, rather than waste the good, it's better to let the belly burst.

довéсок 1. 'an addition' (of bread). In order to distribute the exact amount of bread needed in a ration, one or two smaller portions are frequently attached to a larger loaf by means of a wooden pin. Ужé вторóй день получáю паёк без довéска; навéрно дневáльный утащúл. For the second day I got a ration without the addition; probably the barracks orderly stole it. [AD] 2. *See* добáвка 1.

догнáть ⊂ Догнáть и перегнáть капиталистúческие стрáны. 'Overtake and surpass the capitalistic countries,' one of many slogans emblazoned on barracks walls and other buildings.

дойти, доходить, 'to fail, to be on one's last legs, to become a goner.' Иванóв внезáпно заболéл; пóсле э́того нáчал доходи́ть и чéрез три мéсяца пиздéц. Ivanov suddenly became ill; afterwards he began to fail and in three months he was dead. *Cf.* доходи́ловка, доходя́га.

долбану́ть, pf. 1. 'to drink up, to kill.' Как тóлько полу́чку получи́л, я долбану́л поллитрóвку. As soon as I received my pay, I killed a pint (lit., half a liter) of vodka. [KK] **2.** 'to swipe, to steal.' Сáша-У́рка долбану́л лепёху от одногó из фрайерóв. Saša-Urka swiped a suit of clothes from one of the pigeons. [AD, pop. 'to thrash, beat']

дом ⊂ **1.** ——— свидáний, 'meeting house,' located near the guard shack, where certain prisoners are allowed to see their spouses. Из-за отсу́тствия кóмнат в домáх свидáний, чáсто нéсколько пар встречáлось в однóй кóмнате. Because of the lack of rooms in the meeting house, several couples often met in one room. **2.** казённый ———, 'government house,' sardonic term for a prison. Два дня пéред мои́м арéстом мне присни́лся казённый дом. Two days before my arrest I dreamed about the government house.

домáновец, 'Domanovite,' a follower of T. I. Domanov, an émigré White Guard general who fought the Soviet Union with the German-organized army of General Vlasov. Когдá привезли́ домáновцев в наш лáгерь, начáльник режи́ма велéл уси́лить вáхту вокру́г зóны. When the Domanovites were brought to our camp, the disciplinary officer ordered the watch around the compound strengthened.

домáшник. *See* домашня́к.

домашня́к, 'a burglar.' Никтó из монтáжников не подозревáл, что Сергéй домашня́к [домáшник, скакáрь]; в день рабóтал тóкарем, а нóчью грáбил квартúры. Nobody in the assembly shop suspected that Sergej was a burglar. During the day he worked as a lathe operator and during the night he burglarized apartments. *Also* домáшник, скакáрь, дому́шник.

дому́шник, 'a housebreaker, burglar.' Карзу́бый рабóтал дому́шником [скакарём] ещё в цáрское врéмя; он считáл, что в совéтское врéмя э́та специáльность потеря́ла пóчву из-за óбщей нищеты́. Karzubyj worked as a burglar in tsarist times; he believed that this specialty had lost ground during the

Soviet period because of the general poverty. [D, до́мушник; Tr, КК, дому́шник] *Also* скака́рь, домашня́к.

дополни́тельное, 'an extra portion of food.' Врачéбная ком́ис-сия приняла́ во внима́ние плохо́е здоро́вье Ивано́ва и назна́чила ему́ дополни́тельное. The medical commission took Ivanov's poor health into account and prescribed an extra portion for him. [AD, supplementary]

допр, дом принуди́тельных рабо́т, '*dopr*,' house of forced labor, a term for prisons during the first years after the Revolution, when the word "prison" was out of favor. Усло́вия в до́прах бы́ли насто́лько лу́чше усло́вий в ста́линских тю́рьмах, что заключённые ча́сто мечта́ли о них. Conditions in the *dopr*s were so much better than in Stalinist prisons that the prisoners often dreamed of them. [K]

доска́ ⊂ **1.** ——— почёта, 'board of honor,' where the names of the best workers are posted each day. Such workers are given an additional coupon for meat or soup, and, in large camps, are met at the gates by an orchestra. Бригади́р наш постара́лся, чтобы на́ша брига́да появи́лась на доскé почёта. Our brigadier did his best to get our brigade on the board of honor. [AD] **2.** в до́ску пьян, 'stoned, dead drunk.' Нача́льник отделéния пришёл на ва́хту пьян в до́ску. The commandant returned to the guard shack stoned.

‡ **дострéливать,** impf., 'to scrounge.' Фетюко́в, шака́л, у кавтора́нга оку́рок дострéливал, зазева́лся, в свою́ пятёрку не переступи́л во́время ... That scavenger Fetjukov got distracted scrounging the Captain's cigarette butt, and didn't get back to his own line of five in time. (Оди́н день Ива́на Денисо́вича)

до́хнуть. *See* подо́хнуть.

доходи́ловка, 'a killer camp.' Китла́г — это настоя́щая доходи́-ловка. Там наш брат па́дал, как му́ха. Kitlag (the Kitoj camp) is a real killer. The likes of us died there like flies.

доходи́ть. *See* дойти́.

доходно́й. *See* доходя́га.

доходя́га, 'a goner,' a prisoner on his last legs. Это же доходя́га [доходно́й]. Не тро́гай его́, а то беды́ наживёшься. He's a goner. Don't disturb him, or you're asking for trouble. [KK] *Also* доходно́й.

дрéфить. *See* сдрéфить.

друг ⊂ друг наро́да, 'friend of the people,' a term used for a nonpolitical prisoner or a criminal, in contrast to 'enemy of the people' (враг наро́да, q.v.). У́рки счита́ли себя́ друзья́ми наро́да в отли́чие от 58-ой статьи́, кото́рая счита́лась враго́м наро́да. The criminals considered themselves friends of the people as distinct from the political prisoners, who were regarded as enemies of the people.

дрын, 'a measuring stick,' a meter in length, used in logging. Продолжа́й рабо́ту, а то отлуплю́ дры́ном, что и родна́я мать не узна́ет тебя́. Keep working or I'll flog you with a measuring stick until even your own mother won't recognize you. [KK]

дры́хнуть, impf., 'to sleep.' Брига́да вчера́ дры́хла весь день на на́рах, а сего́дня — дава́й рабо́тать. The brigade slept on its bed boards all day yesterday, but today they're up and at it. [AD, pop.]

дрю́кнуть, pf., 'to give.' Сего́дня Воро́нину посчастли́вилось. По́вар дрю́кнул ему́ доба́вку. Voronin lucked out today. The cook gave him seconds. [To 411, дре́кнуть 'to transfer']

дуб ⊂ дать ду́ба, 'to die.' Бе́дный Васи́льев мечта́л всё вре́мя, чтобы отсиде́ть срок и верну́ться к свое́й семье́, а проше́дшей но́чью дал ду́ба [дубака́, дубаря́]. Poor Vasil'ev dreamed all the time of serving out his time and returning to his family, but last night he died. [bLi 345; Fraz, pop.] *Also* дать дубака́, дать ду́баря.

дуба́к ⊂ дать дубака́. *See* дуб.

ду́барь ⊂ дать ду́баря. *See* дуб.

ду́нуть, pf. *See* настуча́ть.

дура́к ⊂ **1.** Дура́к рабо́ту лю́бит, и рабо́та дурака́ лю́бит. 'A fool likes work and work likes a fool,' a common Russian expression, but in camps it has the additional implication that one must avoid work in order to survive. [Ž, Рабо́та дурако́в лю́бит] **2.** Дурака́м зако́н не пи́сан. *See* зако́н 2. **3.** Век живи́, дурако́м помрёшь. *See* век 1. **4.** Все дураки́ подо́хли, одни́ у́мные оста́лись. 'All the fools perished; only the smart ones made it.' This expression might be used by a camp veteran with the implication: don't try to put anything over on me! **5.** Так и дура́к проживёт. 'In such a job even a fool will get along.' The expression implies that anyone can survive such easy conditions. Ко́лька устро́ился парикма́хером на центра́льном уча́стке. Так и дура́к прожи́вёт. Kol'ka was appointed barber at the central compound. In such a job even a fool will get along.

дуть, impf. **1.** 'to swill, to guzzle.' Год тому́ наза́д Тара́с был тако́й доходно́й, что дул одну́ бала́нду за друго́й. A year ago Taras was such a goner that he swilled down one bowl of gruel after another (which was even more harmful to his health). *Cf.* вода 1, 2. [AD, pop.] **2.** ——— в ка́рты, 'to play cards heatedly.' Блатны́е на́шего бара́ка ду́ли всю ночь в ка́рты. The criminals in our barracks played cards excitedly all night long. [AD, pop.]

дух ⊂ Не па́дай ду́хом, а брю́хом. 'Don't lose your spirit, but your belly,' used by camp veterans to advise newcomers to keep their courage up and be prepared to tighten their belts. [DPos 42, Пости́сь ду́хом, а не брю́хом!]

духа́рик, 'a blowhard, a bluffer,' a man who simulates bravery. Карзу́бый заяви́л бригади́ру, что за́втра не вы́йдет на рабо́ту. Бригади́р отве́тил: « Мы ви́дели таки́х духа́риков и зна́ем, как приспи́чить га́йку ». Karzubyj announced to the gang boss that he wouldn't go to work the next day. He replied "We've seen such blowhards, and we know how to put on the screws." [AD, дух obs. prov. 'air']

душа́ ⊂ Душа́ боли́т за произво́дство, а но́ги тя́нут в санча́сть. *See* санча́сть 2.

душа́-паренёк, 'a stout fellow, a good guy,' used especially by criminals of their own kind. Ко́лька — э́то душа́-паренёк. Хотя́ никогда́ не рабо́тает, никто́ в брига́де не обижа́ется на него́. Kol'ka is a good fellow. Although he never works, no one in the brigade resents him.

ды́шло ⊂ Сове́тский зако́н, что ды́шло: куда́ поверну́л, туда́ и вы́шло. *See* зако́н **4.**

E, e

ебáка, 'a lover' (lit., a fucker). Вáля учётчица рассказáла мне, что онá прогналá нáшего бригадúра, потомý что он плохóй ебáка. The bookkeeper Valja told me that she jilted our brigadier because he was a lousy lover.

ёбарь, 'a lover' (lit., a fucker). Мáша дневáльная э́то настоя́щая пиздá-разбóйница; онá меня́ет ебарéй [хáхалей], как перчáтки. The orderly Maša is a real cunt; she changes lovers like gloves. *Also* хáхаль.

ебáть. *See* поебáть.

ёбнуть, pf., 'to steal.' Пéтя, давáй ёбнем сúдор у э́того фрáйера. Petja, let's steal the parcel from that pigeon.

ежóвщина, 'Ežov purge,' the purge of 1936–1938, after the then head of the NKVD, Nikolaj Ivanovič Ežov (1895–?1939). Ивáн Васúльевич Егóров — э́то ещё жéртва ежóвщины. Ivan Vasil'evič Egorov was a victim of the Ežov purge.

ёлка ⊂ ёлки-пáлки зелёные, a euphemism for ёб твою́ мать. *Cf.* U., where ёлки-пáлки or ёлки зелёные are labeled "pop. and vulgar," and defined чёрт возьмú 'Devil take it'. *See* мать 1.

Ж, ж

жа́хнуть, pf., 'to drink, to swallow.' Вчера́ на рабо́те наш бригади́р жа́хнул 200 грамм, кото́рые получи́л от по́пки. At work yesterday our brigadier swallowed 200 grams (of vodka) he got from a screw. [AD, c. pop. 'to strike hard']

ЖВН [že-ve-én], жена́ врага́ наро́да, 'ŽVN,' wife of an enemy of the people. Ка́тя сиде́ла по ЖВН. Она́ была́ жено́й бы́вшего секретаря́ Моско́вского горко́ма. Katja was in prison as a ŽVN. She was the wife of a former secretary of the Moscow city committee.

жега́н. *See* жига́н.

жена́ ⊂ ла́герная жена́, 'camp wife, mistress.' Кругло́в ушёл к ла́герной жене́ на друго́м уча́стке. Kruglov went to visit his camp wife at another camp section.

женбара́к, же́нский бара́к, 'barracks for female prisoners.'

жено́лп, же́нский ОЛП, 'camp sub-section for female prisoners.' *See* ОЛП, пункт 1.

живу́чий ⊂ живу́чая, как ко́шка. *See* ко́шка.

жига́н, 'a ringleader,' who attains his position because of superior skill and ability. Хотя́ Карзу́бый был о́чень молодо́й, но его́ спосо́бности и прово́рность сде́лали его́ жига́ном блатны́х в на́шем бара́ке. Although Karzubyj was very young, his abilities and hustle made him the ringleader of the criminals in our barracks. *Also* жега́н. [D, an old, experienced penal camp inmate; Tr, prisoner held in contempt by stronger prisoners; To 64, one who loses at cards and flees; aLi 63, a bold thief] *Cf.* паха́н.

жизнь ⊂ жи́зни дать, 'to beat.' Ко́лька ворва́лся в бара́к ко́нтриков и дры́ном на́чал жи́зни дава́ть фрайера́м. Kol'ka burst into the counter-revolutionaries' barracks and began to beat the pigeons with a stick. [Fraz, pop.]

жи́ла, 'a tightwad.' Наш дснева́льный — э́то настоя́щий жи́ла; у него́ и сне́га зимо́й не вы́просишь. Our barracks orderly is a real tightwad; he won't even give away snow in the winter-time. [AD, pop.]

жилгородо́к, жили́щный городо́к, 'housing zone,' for free employees, usually constructed by prisoners. Наря́дчик веле́л на́шу брига́ду вы́вести в жилгородо́к на рабо́ту. The work assigner ordered the brigade to work at the housing zone.

жилзо́на, жили́щная зо́на, 'living zone.' В двадцати́ бара́ках жилзо́ны находи́лось не ме́нее пятисо́т з/к. In the twenty barracks of the living zone, there were at least 500 prisoners.

жилу́ха. *See* во́ля.

житу́ха, 'a good life,' with the implication that a person is well off, or has it made. Кака́я житу́ха бы была́, е́сли бы сво́лочи разреши́ли хоть одну́ забега́ловку в ла́гере. What a good life it would be if the swine would permit just one vodka stand in camp! [D]

жму́ра, 'a whore.' Нача́льник режи́ма посове́товал на́шему бригади́ру бро́сить э́ту жму́ру, е́сли хо́чет избежа́ть неприя́тностей. The disciplinary officer advised our brigadier to drop that whore of his if he wanted to avoid trouble. [D, one who winks]

жму́рик, 'a corpse, a stiff.' Вчера́ привезли́ це́лый ку́зов жму́риков из сангородка́. Yesterday a whole wagon load of corpses was brought in from the hospital-medical block. [D]

жо́па ⊂ На хи́трую жо́пу, хер винто́м. 'For a shrewd ass, a prick will serve as a screw' (to pin you down), a vulgar expression, commonly used by investigators in pressing for confessions. It means that some way will be found to pin a charge on the prisoner. *Also* На хи́трую жо́пу, хер с винто́м найдётся. [D, жо́па]

жо́почник, 'a brown-nose, an ass-kisser, a toady.' Ивано́в — э́то настоя́щий жо́почник [подхали́м]. Он бригади́ру без мы́ла в жо́пу ле́зет. Ivanov is a real brown-nose. He kisses (lit., crawls into) the brigadier's ass without soap. *Also* подхали́м.

жу́жа, 'a young criminal.' *See* жучо́к.

жучо́к, 'a young criminal.' Вчера́ жучки́ разошли́сь, и дава́й шмона́ть работя́г и отнима́ть после́днее. Yesterday the young criminals went on a rampage; they set about frisking the workmen and taking everything they had. [AD, жук с. pop. 'a smart fellow'; D, жучо́к 'a rather miserly person'] *Also* жу́жа.

З, з

забега́ловка, 'a vodka stand.' Хоть бы одну́ забега́ловку разреши́ли сво́лочи. Oh, if the swine would only permit one vodka stand! [KK]

‡ **завали́ть,** pf., 'to denounce.' Она́ держа́лась с зэ́ками пре-зри́тельно ... и сама́ завали́ла двои́х — одного́ на свя́зи с де́вушкой, друго́го — на изготовле́нии чемода́на из казённых материа́лов. She was contemptuous of the zeks... and denounced two of them herself, one for an affair with a girl, the other for making a suitcase out of government materials. (В круге пе́рвом)

завгу́ж, заве́дующий гужевы́м тра́нспортом, 'transportation manager.' Согла́сно разнаря́дке я до́лжен был получи́ть бри́чку с ло́шадью на оди́н день в неде́лю от завгу́жа. According to the work assignment, the manager of transport was supposed to get me a horse and buggy for one day a week.

завербова́ть, pf., 'to implicate.' Мой шу́рин под нажи́мом сле́дствия завербова́л и меня́. Under the strain of the investigation, my brother-in-law implicated me too. [AD, to engage, hire, attract]

загиба́ловка, 'a killer camp.' Известко́вый ла́герь — э́то настоя́щая загиба́ловка; бо́льше полго́да не протя́нешь. A lime camp is a real killer camp; you won't last more than half a year there.

загна́ть под на́ры. *See* на́ра 3.

загну́ться, pf. 1. 'to stagger about, to be on one's last legs.' В не сполна́ полго́да Ва́нька загну́лся в се́верных лагеря́х. After less than half a year in the northern camps, Van'ka was on his last legs. 2. 'to die.' Ивано́в загну́лся, и на со́пку. Ivanov died and was buried. [AD, с. pop.; aLi 63]

‡ **за́дница,** 'ass.' Слу́шай, нача́льник произво́дства!! Что за поря́дки?! Надое́ло э́то га́дство! Па́длы сидя́т, за́дницы гре́ют! Listen, production manager, what's going on around here? I'm sick of this crap! The carrion just sit around here warming their asses! (Оле́нь и шалашо́вка) [D, buttocks]

заём ⊂ госуда́рственный заём, 'state loan.' After World War

II, Soviet employees and prisoners were compelled to buy bonds which were later abolished and the money "donated" to the state. Заключённые во всех лагеря́х Сове́тского Сою́за принужда́лись подпи́сывать госуда́рственные за́ймы. The prisoners in all the camps of the Soviet Union were forced to subscribe to the state loans. [AD]

зажи́лить, зажи́ливать, 'to keep for one's own use.' Наш бригади́р суме́л закоси́ть сто у́тренних па́ек хлеба. Большинство́ хлеба он зажи́лил. Our brigadier managed to finagle a hundred morning shares of bread. Most of the bread he kept for his own use. [AD, pop.]

зазу́ля. *See* зозу́ля.

за́игранный, 'a marked man,' a criminal marked for punishment or death for violating the code. Васёк за́игранный. Vasek is a marked man. [AD, unfit, worthless from frequent use]

‡ **заклада́ть,** impf., 'to put, or stow, away,' to imbibe to excess. Ми́лый, кто тепе́рь не пьёт? Пе́рвая жена́ крепи́лась, а э́та заклада́ет. My dear fellow, who doesn't drink nowadays? My first wife kept herself in hand, but this one really puts it away. (Оле́нь и шалашо́вка)

закла́дывать. *See* заложи́ть.

зако́н ⊂ **1.** быть в зако́не, 'to be covered by the criminals' code, to have the rights of a criminal.' Воло́дька в зако́не; бригади́р никогда́ его́ не заставля́ет рабо́тать. Volod'ka has criminal rights; the brigadier never makes him work. **2.** Дурака́м зако́н не пи́сан. 'The law is not written for fools.' The implication of this expression is that if one is clever, one can evade the law and avoid the punishment. Не зна́ешь, почему́ Макси́ма бро́сили в изоля́тор? Не зна́ешь, дурака́м зако́н не пи́сан? Don't you know why Maksim was put in the isolator? Don't you know the law is not written for fools [i.e., Maksim is a fool]? [Ž] **3.** Зако́н — тайга́. 'The taiga is the law.' В се́верные лагеря́ Сове́тская власть не дохо́дит; там зако́н — тайга́. Soviet power doesn't reach the northern camps. There the taiga is the law. **4.** Сове́тский зако́н, что ды́шло: куда́ поверну́л, туда́ и вы́шло. 'Soviet law is like a wagon tongue: it goes wherever you direct it,' a proverb meaning that the law is always right, that some article will be found under which one can be charged. [Ž, obs. Зако́н, что ды́шло ...]

зако́нник 1. 'a criminal covered by the code.' *Cf.* зако́н 1. ‡ **2.**

'a jail-house lawyer.' Вообще слушайте ... Учтите — такие законники, как вы, — долго в лагере не живут!... Now you just listen and think about this—jail-house lawyers like you don't live long in camp! (Олень и шалашовка)

законвойрованный, 'a prisoner who must be guarded.' Акимов весь свой срок был законвойрованным. Akimov was kept under guard during his entire term.

закорышевать, pf., 'to become friends.' Мишка ещё в этапе закорышевал с урками и стал одним из них. During his transport Miška made friends with the criminals and became one of them. [AD, pop. корешок 'close friend']

закосить, косить, 'to finagle, to get by guile.' Наш бригадир закосил сто утренних паек хлеба. Our gang boss finagled a hundred morning shares of bread. [AD, colloq. 'to mow someone else's field'] *Cf.* косануть.

закрутить, pf., 'to take up with, to begin a love affair.' Пётька закрутил с Машей год тому назад, и до сих пор возится с ней. Pet'ka took up with Maša a year ago and is still going with her. [AD, to twist, wind]

закрутка, 'a hand-rolled cigarette,' usually made of newspaper. За два года тюремного заключения Василий выучился делать закрутки с большой ловкостью. In two years of imprisonment, Vasilij learned how to roll cigarettes with great skill. [AD, pop.]

закрыться. [S 75, 79] *See* заткнуться.

заливайло, 'a liar.' [S 79, заливало (*sic*)]

заливать, impf., 'to lie.' Ты, Васька, лучше не заливай, а то получишь отбивные по рёбрам. Vas'ka, you better stop lying, or I'll break your ribs. [AD, pop.; F 181; St 137]

заложить, закладывать, 'to squeal, to inform.' Следователь измотал Карзубого до такой степени, что последний заложил своего закадычного друга за колбасу и пайку хлеба. The interrogator exhausted Karzubyj to such a degree that he squealed on his bosom friend for a sausage and a bread ration.

‡ **замостырить,** pf., 'to fake an infection.' Ну, я замостырила, чтоб на этап не ехать. I faked an infection to keep from going on that transport. (Олень и шалашовка) *Cf.* мастырка, мастырщик.

заначить, заначивать, 'to stash away, to hide away for future use.' Николай утащил одеяло из соседнего барака и заначил его в известное ему место. Nikolaj stole a blanket from the next barracks and stashed it away in a place known only to him. [Tr; To 380; St 133, 142]

заначка, 'a hiding place.' Я залез в заначку, только меня накрыли. I crawled into a hiding place, but was discovered.

зануда, 'a bore.' Петров стал таким занудой, что я предпочитаю избегать его. Petrov has become such a bore that I prefer to avoid him.

западники, pl., 'westerners,' Ukrainian, Polish, and Jewish prisoners who had lived in the former Polish territories of Western Ukraine and Belorussia before 1939. В 1949-м году всех западников перевели в спецлагеря. In 1949 all the westerners were transferred to special camps. [AD, adherents to Westernism, a nineteenth-century intellectual movement opposed to Slavophilism]

заправлять арапа. *See* арап.

запретка, запретная зона. *See* зона 3.

запретный ⊂ 1. запретная зона. *See* зона 3. 2. запретная черта, 'forbidden line,' used to delimit a small, temporary work zone for a brigade, marked with small flags each day by the chief of the escort guards. A prisoner crossing the line can be shot as an attempted runaway. Когда бригада подошла к месту работы, начальник конвоя обозначил запретную черту рабочей зоны флажками. When the brigade approached the work site, the chief of the escort marked the forbidden line of the work zone with flags. *Cf.* зона 3.

зарядиться, pf., 'to get loaded, to get drunk.' Наш бригадир сегодня зарядился, и весь день дрыхнул в рабочей зоне. Our brigadier got loaded today and slept the entire day in the working zone. [AD, to be loaded (said of a gun)]

засилосовать, pf., 'to silo.' Слабосилка работала вчера на капусте. Белые листья заложили в чан, а зелёные засилосовали для з/к. Yesterday the weak contingent worked in the cabbage patch. They placed the white leaves in a vat, and they siloed the green ones for the prisoners. [AD]

засосать, pf., 'to have hunger pangs.' На второй день этапа у меня так засосало внутри, что я подумал, что все кишки повылезут. On the second day of the transport I got such hunger pangs that I thought all my guts would ooze out.

засы́паться, pf., 'to be caught red-handed.' Ко́лька зале́з в каптёрку и засы́пался. Kol'ka crept into the storeroom and was caught red-handed. [AD, pop.; F 178; To 388]

заткну́ть ⊂ заткну́ть плева́тельницу [плева́ло], 'to shut up (one's) trap.' Заткни́ плева́тельницу [плева́ло]! Shut your trap! [AD, плева́тельница 'cuspidor'; St 143]

заткну́ться, 'to be silent.' Заткни́сь [Закро́йся], а то тебе́ глаза́ вы́колю! Shut up, or I'll poke your eyes out! [AD, с. pop.; St 143] *Also* закры́ться.

затрудни́ть, затрудня́ть, 'to make use of, to employ.' ОКБ затрудни́ло деся́тки о́пытных архите́кторов. The ОКВ (organizational-construction bureau) employed dozens of experienced architects.

затру́ханный, 'done in, broken, a shadow.' Говоря́т, что, когда́ наш коменда́нт при́был эта́пом, он был совсе́м затру́ханный, а тепе́рь всей зо́ной воро́чает. It is said that when our barracks chief arrived with the transport he was completely done in, but now he bosses the whole camp.

заты́рить, pf., 'to hide.' Ва́ся суме́л заты́рить всё укра́денное так, что ни одна́ экспеди́ция не могла́ найти́ веще́й. Vasja managed to hide all the stolen goods so that not a single search party could find the things. [Tr; F 178; St 136]

затяну́ть, pf., 'to drag, to puff.' Дай хоть разо́чек затяну́ть. Let me take just one little drag. [AD, to suck in] *Also* пососа́ть.

‡ **захалты́рить, захалты́ривать,** 'to take away, to cheat out of.' Э́то потому́, что у тебя́ там администра́ция чемода́н захалты́рила и ты не хо́чешь быть объекти́вным. That's because the administration took away your suitcase, and you don't want to be objective. (В круге пе́рвом) Из пяти́ дней оди́н захалты́ривает нача́льство ... The authorities cheat you out of one day in five. (Один день Ивана Денисовича)

зацепи́ться. *See* приземли́ться.

зачёты, pl., 'bonuses,' given to prisoners for overfulfilling their quotas on a given day. They consist of one and a half, two, or three days of credit towards one's sentence, depending on the percentage of overfulfillment. The bonuses are often cancelled as punishment. Согла́сно зачётам я до́лжен был освободи́ться в 1942-м году́, то́лько, как война́ начала́сь, все мои́ зачёты пошли́ на сма́рку. Taking bonuses into account, I should have been freed in 1942, but as war had begun all my bonuses went down the drain.

зашмона́ть, pf., 'to take away illegally.' Во вре́мя инвентариза́ции по́пки зашмона́ли у меня́ шевио́товый пиджа́к. During the inventory the screws took away my woolen jacket.

зашухари́ть. *See* зашухе́рить.

зашухе́рить, pf., 'to inform on, to denounce.' Но́чью я пробра́лся в бара́к ко́нтриков и соба́ка днева́льный меня́ зашухе́рил [зашухари́л]. I had gone into the politicals' barracks in the night when that bastard of an orderly informed on me. [КК, зашу́херить] *Also* зашухари́ть.

зашухе́риться, pf., 'to be caught red-handed.' Из-за нело́вкого прыжка́ из окна́ бара́ка, я зашухе́рился. Because of a clumsy leap from the barracks window, I was caught red-handed. [Tr, зашухерова́ться]

зверю́га, 'beast, brute.' Комендо́нт зо́ны был настоя́щим зверю́гой; за мале́йшее противоре́чие избива́л до полусме́рти. The commandant was a real brute; he would beat you within an inch of your life for the slightest contradiction. [AD, pop.]

звоно́к ⊂ от звонка́ до звонка́ просиде́ть, 'to serve a sentence from the first day (lit., bell) to the last.' Арте́м просиде́л в лагеря́х от звонка́ до звонка́ — це́лых 15 лет. Artem served in camps from the first bell to the last—the whole 15 years.

зекс, indecl., 'watch, lookout.' Ко́ля зале́з в капте́рку, а я стоя́л на зекс [ата́нде, ата́се]. Kolja crept into the warehouse and I stood watch. [Tr; F 178; To 363; Lingo 244, zex] *Also* ата́нде, ата́се.

зелёный ⊂ зелёный прокуро́р. *See* прокуро́р 2.

земля́к, 'a fellow countryman,' a play on the word земля́ 'earth.' The name is frequently given prisoners, since most of them are employed at digging. Гей, земля́к [землячо́к], не волну́йся; нача́льник вручи́т тебе́ пятнадцатикилогра́ммовый каранда́ш, и бу́дешь иша́чить. Hey, fellow countryman, don't worry; the boss will entrust you with a 15-kilogram crowbar, and you'll work like a dog. [AD] *Also* землячо́к.

землячо́к, dim. of земля́к (q.v.).

зепа́ло, 'mouth.' Гей, братва́, предупрежда́ю: рази́нете зепа́ла — хана́ вам. I'm warning you, brothers; if you stand around gaping, you've had it. [D, зепь 'throat'; зепа́ла 'one who shouts']

з/к [ze-ká], заключённый, 'a prisoner.' The initials are the official form of address both in written statements and in spoken announcements. Гра́ждане з/к! Citizen prisoners! [KK]

змей. *See* оперуполномо́ченный.

зозу́ля, 'a whore.' Да́рья, э́та зозу́ля [кра́ля] из санча́сти, опя́ть прикати́лась в мужско́й бара́к. Dar'ja, that whore from the medical office, has arrived again at the men's barracks. [D, a drunkard] *Also* зазу́ля, кра́ля.

зо́на ⊂ **1.** 'compound,' a guarded area surrounded by barbed wire, which can vary in size from a single barracks for fewer than 100 prisoners to an enormous area containing 50,000 prisoners. Вчера́ Ма́ша отколо́ла тако́й но́мер в зо́не, что нача́льник режи́ма вы́нужден был прие́хать но́чью в зо́ну. Yesterday Maša behaved so strangely in the compound that the disciplinary officer had to come during the night. **2.** рабо́чая ———, 'working zone.' Рабо́чая зо́на была́ в одно́м оцепле́нии с жилзо́ной; жилзо́на была́ то́лько отгоро́жена колю́чей про́волокой от рабо́чей зо́ны. The working zone was in a single enclosure with the living zone; the latter was separated from the working zone only by barbed wire. **3.** запре́тная ———, 'forbidden zone,' 5 to 10 yards wide inside and outside the compound, surrounded by barbed wire and continuously raked so that footprints will show up better. Оди́н з/к зале́з случа́йно в запре́тную [огневу́ю] зо́ну [or в запре́тку], и по́пка на вы́шке его́ пристрели́л. A prisoner accidentally got in the forbidden [firing] zone and a screw in the tower shot him down. *Also* огнева́я зо́на 'firing zone,' запре́тка. **4.** жили́щная ———. *See* жилзо́на. **5.** промы́шленная ———. *See* промзо́на. **6.** огнева́я ———. *See* meaning 3.

зы́реть. *See* зы́рить.

зы́рить, impf., 'to see.' Свои́ми глаза́ми зы́рил [зы́рел], как Ма́ша поле́зла в мужску́ю зо́ну. I saw Maša climb into the men's compound with my own eyes. [D] *Also* зы́реть.

‡ **зэк.** *See* з/к.

зэ-ка́. *See* з/к.

‡ **зэ́ковский,** 'pert. to з/к (q.v.).' Ещё прове́рить у́тром на́до, не оде́т ли костю́м гражда́нский под зэ́ковский? In the morning they also had to check to see if anyone had on civilian clothes under his camp uniform. (Оди́н день Ива́на Денисо́вича)

И, и

изоли́рованный ⊂ вре́менно изоли́рованный, 'temporarily isolated.' *Cf.* изоля́ция.

изоля́тор, 'an isolator,' a camp building containing a number of cells. It is meant for prisoners under investigation for infractions of camp rules, but is often used for punishment as well. Оперуполномо́ченный распоряди́лся, что́бы Ва́ньку посади́ли в изоля́тор. The security officer saw to it that Van'ka was placed in the isolator. [AD, an isolation ward or room] *Cf.* ка́рцер.

изоля́ция ⊂ вре́менная изоля́ция, 'temporary isolation,' a term used by the authorities to describe the sentence of political prisoners, in order to motivate them to complete work norms. З/к, з/к: вы сове́тские гра́ждане во вре́менной изоля́ции. Вы должны́ искупи́ть свою́ вину́ пе́ред ро́диной самоотве́рженным трудо́м. Prisoners, prisoners: you are Soviet citizens in temporary isolation. You must atone for your guilt before your native land by selfless labor.

икра́ ⊂ мета́ть икру́. *See* мета́ть.

инвентариза́ция, 'an inventory,' which in camps includes a check of government-owned and personal clothing and bedding, a prisoner check (of provision, length of sentence, and prisoner number), and a search of the barracks for hidden, illegal articles. It is a painful procedure accompanied by humiliating body searches, long hours of standing in line, and the loss of many essential articles. Годова́я инвентариза́ция была́ одно́й из тя́жких мук в лагеря́х; на ка́ждом шагу́ ты чу́вствовал, что ты лишён прав. The annual inventory was one of the worst torments in the camps; you felt at every step that you were deprived of rights. [AD]

И́ндия, ' "India," ' jocular name of a special barracks for prisoners (usually criminals) who violate camp regulations. It is so-called because many of its inmates are stark naked, having lost their clothing playing cards. У́рки ра́довались, когда́ их направля́ли в « Индию ». Для фрайеро́в э́то была́ настоя́щая му́ка; они́ остава́лись на произво́л блатны́х. The criminals were glad when they were sent to "India." For the pigeons it was pure hell; they were at the mercy of the criminals.

‡ **исписа́ться**, pf., 'to commit suicide.' ([Ко́стя] отбега́ет, вспры́-гивает на му́сорный я́щик, выхва́тывает нож, обнажа́ет живо́т.) Не подходи́! Не подходи́! — испишу́сь! ([Kostja] runs to one side, jumps up on a trash bin, draws a knife, and bares his belly). Keep away! Stay back! I'll do myself in! (Оле́нь и шалашо́вка) А что́ ты, гад, — испи́шешься, а мне тебя́ лечи́ть? What do you think, you bastard? If you carve your-self up, am I supposed to sew you up? (Оле́нь и шалашо́вка) [AD, to be written out, to have used up one's inspiration]

ИТК [i-te-ká], исправи́тельно-трудова́я коло́ния, 'ITK,' cor-rective labor colony. [K] *See* трудколо́ния.

ИТЛ [i-te-él], исправи́тельно-трудово́й ла́герь, 'ITL,' cor-rective labor camp. Меня́ осуди́ли к десяти́ года́м ИТЛ. I was sentenced to 10 years of ITL. [K]

ИТРовец [i-te-éraɣic], инжене́рно-техни́ческий рабо́тник, 'an ITR,' an engineering-technical worker. В на́шем ла́гере бы́ло свы́ше ста ИТРовцев. There were more than 100 ITRs in our camp. [K, but without suffix]

ИТРовский [i-te-érafs̩kij], pertaining to ITR. *See* ИТРовец.

ишачить. *See* проиша́чить.

К, к

ка́лики-морга́лики, pl., 'drugs, narcotics.' Бригади́р, ви́дя что Фе́де всё мо́ре по коле́но, спроси́л: « Фе́дя, где зафасова́л ка́лики-морга́лики? » — « Обжа́л лепи́лу. Он у меня́ на крючке́ ». The brigadier, seeing that Fedja was high, asked, "Fedja, where did you get the drugs?" "I squeezed them out of the medic. I have my hooks in him."

калы́м, 'a bribe.' Продолжа́ть свою́ рабо́ту — э́то ве́рная смерть; я су́нул бригади́ру калы́м, и он перевёл меня́ на лёгкую рабо́ту. To continue my work would be certain death; I slipped the brigadier a bribe and he transferred me to easy work. [AD, bride price] *Also* магары́ч.

камса́, 'dried, jerked fish,' usually putrefied and hence loathed by the prisoners. Сно́ва привезли́ в каптёрку э́ту воню́чую камсу́ [хамсу́]. They've brought that stinking dried fish to the food storage again! [AD, fish of the herring family] *Also* хамса́.

канде́й. *See* конде́й.

кант. *See* канто́вка.

кантова́ться. *See* проканто́ва́ться.

канто́вка, 'shirking.' *Also* кант. *Cf.* проканто́ва́ться.

ка́пнуть, ка́пать. [Tr, To 390, ка́пать only] *See* настуча́ть.

каптёр, from завкаптёркой from заве́дующий каптёркой, 'supply clerk,' a prisoner manager of the storage area. Ко́лька залéз в каптёрку и засы́пался; каптёр и коменда́нт бы́ли внутри́, и они́ его́ накры́ли. Kol'ka slipped into the storeroom and was caught red-handed; the supply clerk and the barracks chief were inside, and they grabbed him.

каптёрка, 'supply,' storage area for food or clothing, or both, depending on the size of the camp. Пока́ уда́стся что́-нибудь получи́ть из каптёрки, э́то така́я воль́нка, что и оде́жде не рад. There's so much red tape before you finally get your clothing from supply that you can't really enjoy it.

каранда́ш, 'a crowbar' (lit., pencil). Не бо́йся, земляч́ок,

здесь дадýт тебé двадцатикилограммовый карандáш [каран-
дáшик], и пишѝ по карьéру. Never fear, fellow countryman,
here they will give you a 20-kilogram "pencil" and you can
"write" in the quarry. *Also* карандáшик, a dim. of карандáш.

карантѝн, 'quarantine,' obligatory for each incoming group of
prisoners. During quarantine criminals and barracks chiefs try
to steal everything they can from the newcomers. Как тóлько
нас вы́грузили из вагóнов, начáльник отпрáвил наш этáп в
карантѝн. As soon as we were unloaded from the cars, the
chief sent our transport into quarantine. [AD]

кармáнничать, impf., 'to pick pockets.' Карзýбый кармáн-
ничал всю своѝ жизнь; бóльшую часть своéй жѝзни он
провёл в тю́рьмах и лагеря́х. Karzubyj picked pockets his
entire life; most of his life he spent in prisons and camps. [D]

кармáнщик, 'a pickpocket.' Берегѝсь Николáя! Он ленин-
грáдский кармáнщик. Он тебя́ обрабóтает лýчше хирýрга.
Beware of Nikolaj! He's a Leningrad pickpocket. He'll work
you over [i.e., cut out your pocket] better than a surgeon.
[AD, pop.]

кáрцер, 'cooler,' a prison cell with especially severe conditions,
used for punishment. It is usually windowless, has a stone
floor and no bed. Several prisoners are sometimes crowded into
each such cell. Когдá я отказáлся подписáть заключѝтель-
ную статью́, стáрший слéдователь отпрáвил меня́ в кáрцер.
When I refused to sign the article of conclusion, the senior
interrogator sent me to the cooler. [AD, place for temporary
solitary confinement in prerevolutionary prisons] *Cf.* изоля́тор.

кассáция, кассациóнная жáлоба, 'an appeal' (of a sentence).
Соглáсно совéтским закóнам осуждённый имéл 72 часá,
чтóбы подáть кассáцию. According to Soviet law, the convict
had 72 hours to appeal his sentence. [AD, colloq.]

каталáжка, 'a jail.' Милѝция меня́ схватѝла и брóсила в
городскýю каталáжку. The militia caught me and threw me
into the city jail. [AD, pop. obs.]

катýшка, '25-year sentence' (lit., a spool), the longest in the
Soviet Union. Цéлая катýшка — э́то бы́ло обы́чное нака-
зáние для влáсовцев. A 25-year stretch was the usual punishment for Vlasovites. « Волóдя, тебé скóлько дáли? » —
« Я размáтываю пóлную катýшку ». "What did they give
you, Volodja?" "I'm unwinding a full spool." [KK]

катю́ша, 'flint and steel.' Гей, земля́к, вы́тащи свою́ катю́шу и разведи́ костёр. Погре́ться на́до. Hey, fellow countryman, get your flint and steel out and light the camp fire. We need to warm up. [AD, jocular, pet name for a rocket launcher]

кача́ть ⊂ кача́ть права́, 'to punish for violating the criminal code.' Му́рка нару́шила зако́н и паха́н пришёл к ней права́ кача́ть. Murka violated the code and the ringleader came to punish her. [aLi 84, правила качать 'to deal with according to criminal rules']

ка́ша ⊂ ка́ша ма́нная, 'semolina,' name ironically given a very poor quality wild millet cereal similar in appearance to semolina. Э́та « ка́ша ма́нная » так мне надое́ла, что проглоти́ть её не могу́. I'm so sick of this semolina that I can't even choke it down.

ка́шка ⊂ Лу́чше ка́шки не доло́жь, но рабо́той не трево́жь. 'Better not to increase the rations (lit., cereal), than to bother us with work,' an expression of the prisoners' readiness to forgo additional food rather than undertake additional work.

КВЖД [ka-ve-že-dé], Кита́йско-Восто́чная желе́зная доро́га, 'KVŽD,' Chinese Eastern Railroad, a popular camp and semi-official designation for the provision under which the former employees of the railroad were arrested after their return to the Soviet Union. Рабо́тников Кита́йско-Восто́чной желе́зной доро́ги арестова́ли и отпра́вили в лагеря́ по КВЖД. The employees of the Chinese Eastern Railroad were arrested and sent to camps under the KVŽD provision. [K]

КВЧ [ka-ve-čé], культу́рно-воспита́тельная часть, 'KVČ,' culture and education section. К годовщи́не Октя́брьской револю́ции КВЧ привезло́ кинокарти́ну в зо́ну. For the anniversary of the October revolution the KVČ brought a movie to the compound. [K]

кема́ть. [To 472, ке́мать, 473, хи́мать; St 139, 142, кема́ть]. *See* кима́рить.

ке́ря. *See* ко́реш.

кима́рить, 'to nap, doze.' Бригади́р наш по́сле устано́вки брига́ды и распределе́ния рабо́ты, пошёл в земля́нку кима́рить [кема́ть]. After arranging the brigade and assigning the work, our brigadier went to a dugout for a nap. [S 76, 79; St 139, 142] *Also* кема́ть.

ки́ровский ⊂ Ки́ровский набо́р, 'Kirov roundup,' a wave of arrests in 1934–1936 following the murder of Sergej Mironovič Kirov (1886–1934), party boss in Leningrad and believed to be a trusted aide of Stalin. Ани́сова посади́ли во вре́мя Ки́ровского набо́ра. Anisov was imprisoned during the Kirov round-up.

кирю́ха. *See* ко́реш.

кирю́шка. *See* ко́реш.

кича́, 'a prison.' Попа́л я в кичу́ [кича́н, кичма́н] в Соль-Иле́цк, а там одна́ ко́нтра сиди́т. I was put in prison in Sol'-Ileck, and only counter-revolutionaries are imprisoned there. [Tr; F 178; To 81; St 133, 142, ки́ча] *Also* кича́н, кичма́н.

кича́н. [KK] *See* кича́.

кичма́н. [To 81; St 142] *See* кича́.

кли́чка, 'nickname.' All "self-respecting" criminals have one or more nicknames which are made a part of their personal files. Сле́дователь заноси́л в де́ло все да́нные, включа́я кли́чки; э́то облегча́ло удостовере́ние ли́чности. The interrogator noted down in the file all data, including nicknames. This facilitated the identification. [AD]

кни́жка ⊂ армату́рная кни́жка. *See* армату́рный.

ковыря́лка **1.** 'a midwife-abortionist.' Ка́тя забере́менела от коменда́нта; она́ обрати́лась к изве́стной ковыря́лке в зо́не, чтобы сде́лать себе́ або́рт. The barracks chief got Katja pregnant; she went to a well-known midwife in the compound for an abortion. [KK, до́кторша ковыря́лка] **2.** 'female onanist.' Не тро́гай э́ту ковыря́лку; ведь вся зо́на смеётся над не́ю. Don't touch that masturbator; after all, the whole compound laughs at her.

ковыря́ться, impf., 'to masturbate' [used only of women]. Большинство́ лагпу́нктов тайше́тских лагере́й бы́ло исключи́тельное же́нское; большинство́ з/к в э́тих лагеря́х ковыря́лись. Most of the sections of the Tajšet camps were exclusively women's, and most of the prisoners there masturbated.

ко́готь ⊂ рвать ко́гти. [S 81; To 353, драть когти] *See* смахну́ть.

козырьки́, pl., 'louvers,' covering the cell windows, particularly in political prisons. На́ша ка́мера име́ла ма́ленькое око́шко под са́мым потолко́м; снару́жи око́шко э́то бы́ло закры́то козырька́ми так, что да́же в со́лнечные дни све́та бы́ло мáло. Our cell had a small window just under the ceiling. On the outside this window was covered with louvers so that even on sunny days there was little light. [AD sing., 'a small awning'] *Also* намóрдник, футля́р.

колёса, pl., 'boots.' Хрóмовые колёса бы́вшего румы́нского генерáла привлекáли внимáние всех у́рок нáшего барáка. The box-calf boots of a former Rumanian general attracted the attention of all the criminals in our barracks. [Tr; F 183; To 209]

коллéгия ⊂ Коллéгии ОГПУ, 'Collegia of OGPU,' the notorious judicial bodies whose functions were replaced by the OCO (q.v.) of the NKVD. Коллéгии ОГПУ называ́лись официа́льно Судéбные Коллéгии ОГПУ; в действи́тельности они́ ничегó óбщего с судóм не имéли. The Collegia of OGPU were officially called Judicial Collegia of OGPU, but in reality they had nothing in common with a court.

колóния. *See* трудколóния.

колóнна, 'a column,' the unit into which prisoners are divided according to their work speciality, construction site, etc., to facilitate rollcalls, dispatching work convoys, feeding, and the like. Barracks assignments are usually made on the basis of columns. Колóнна заключённых, окружённая конвóем и собáками, находи́лась примéрно вполпути́ до рабóчей зóны, когдá начался́ си́льный бурáн. A column of prisoners, surrounded by a convoy and by dogs, was about halfway to the work zone when a heavy blizzard came up. [AD]

колоту́шки, pl., 'playing cards.' Когдá бригади́р ушёл к начáльнику учáстка, вся бригáда сéла игрáть в колоту́шки. When the gang boss went to the camp commandant, the whole brigade sat down to play cards. [KK]

Колымá ⊂ Колымá, ах Колымá, чу́дная планéта,/Двенáдцать мéсяцев — зимá, а остальны́е — лéто. 'Kolyma, oh Kolyma, a wonderful planet,/Where winter lasts 12 months, and the rest is summer,' the words to a camp song. The Kolyma region, a gold mining center in eastern Siberia and a major center for forced labor, is noted for its extreme cold.

команди́р ⊂ команди́р взвóда, 'platoon commander,' usually a sergeant in charge of the guards in each section of the compound. Команди́р взвóда ежеднéвно приходи́л на вáхту, чтóбы смотрéть за развóдом. Every day the platoon commander would come to the guard shack to observe the marching off to work. [AD]

командиро́вка 1. 'a temporary project,' such as cutting hay, gathering wood, and the like. Сельхо́з был командиро́вкой кирпи́чного уча́стка. The agricultural area was a temporary project of the brick-making unit. 2. 'temporary duty assignment, TDY.' Я пое́хал в командиро́вку. I went out on TDY. [AD]

кома́р ⊂ кома́р начиха́л, 'a mosquito sneezed' [i.e., a trifle]. Вещкаптёр получи́л пять пар ва́ленок на всю зо́ну; э́то то́чно, что кома́р начиха́л. The clothing manager received five pairs of felt boots for the whole compound; it's exactly as if a mosquito sneezed.

комендáнт, 'barracks chief,' usually chosen from among the worst of the criminals. Комендáнт был хозя́ином твое́й жи́зни и́ли сме́рти; захо́чет, и доведёт тебя́. The barracks chief was the master of your life and death; if he wished, he would bring you down.

комиссова́ть, 'to come to a decision,' said of a commission. На Карабáс прие́хала специа́льная медици́нская коми́ссия, что́бы комиссова́ть всю слабоси́лку. A special medical commission came to Karabas to reach a decision on the entire weak contingent.

комиссо́вка, 'the work of a commission; the decision-making process of a commission.' Комиссо́вка начала́сь неме́дленно по́сле прие́зда нача́льника санотде́ла. The commission proceedings began immediately after the arrival of the head of the main medical office.

ко́мси-ко́мса, 'to split in half, to share.' The term comes from the language of one of the Asian minorities in the Soviet Union, and not from the French *comme ci, comme ça* as might be thought. It may derive from Arabic *khamséen* 'fifty' (50–50 ? ?), or it may be related to Turkish *kómşu* 'neighbor' (the neighborly thing to do is to share ? ?). Дава́й ёбнем си́дор у э́того фра́йера и ко́мси-ко́мса. Let's steal the parcel from that pigeon and split it.

конве́йерный ⊂ конве́йерный допро́с, 'conveyer-belt interrogation,' a continuous interrogation employed to break the will of a prisoner. Са́ша держа́лся кре́пко на сле́дствии; одна́ко, когда́ примени́ли конве́йерный допро́с, он расколо́лся, как це́лка, по́сле пе́рвых пяти́ су́ток. Saša was firm during the regular interrogation. However, when they applied the conveyer-belt interrogation, he broke like a hymen after only five days.

конве́рт ⊂ **1.** за мя́гкое ме́сто и в конве́рт [я́щик], 'by the ass (lit., soft spot) and into the envelope [box], arrested.' « Ивано́в, как в тюрьму́ попа́л? » — « Взя́ли за мя́гкое ме́сто и в конве́рт [я́щик] ». "Ivanov, how'd you land in prison?" "They grabbed me by the ass and here I am." **2.** за ши́ворот и в конве́рт [я́щик], 'by the collar and into the envelope [box], arrested.' В 1937-м году́, зна́ешь, кто́-то напи́шет на тебя́, тебя́ за ши́ворот и в конве́рт [я́щик]. In 1937, you know, someone had only to denounce you and you were arrested.

конвои́р, 'a member of the конво́й' (q.v.). [AD]

конво́й, 'convoy, escort,' which leads prisoners to work outside the camp and guards them there. Пе́ред съёмом нача́льник конво́я счита́л брига́ду и то́лько по́сле э́того разреша́л бойца́м оста́вить рабо́чую зо́ну. Before the signal to knock off work, the convoy chief counted the brigade and only after this allowed the soldiers to leave the work zone. [AD]

конде́й, 'cooler, punishment cell,' a term less frequently used than ка́рцер, изоля́тор (qq.v.). Васи́лий попыта́лся утащи́ть хлеб из хлеборе́зки, то́лько коменда́нт заме́тил э́то и повёл его́ в конде́й [канде́й]. Vasilij tried to swipe bread from the breadcutter's, but the barracks chief noticed and took him to the cooler. *Also* канде́й.

конто́ра-штаб, 'headquarters.' Конто́ра-штаб уча́стка находи́лся в ста шага́х от зо́ны. The section headquarters was 100 paces from the compound. [AD]

ко́нтра, coll., контрреволюционе́ры, 'counter-revolutionaries.' На Кайба́се одна́ ко́нтра собрала́сь; они́ занима́ют все лу́чшие рабо́ты. There were only counter-revolutionaries at the Kajbas camp section; they have all the best jobs. Таку́ю ко́нтру я сгною́ в изоля́торе. I'll let such counter-revolutionaries rot in the isolator. [AD, с. pop. 'a counter-revolutionary']

ко́нтрик, контрреволюционе́р, 'a counter-revolutionary.' У́рки до тако́й сте́пени издева́лись над ко́нтриками, что после́дние реши́ли организова́ться и раз навсегда́ распра́виться с ни́ми. The criminals tormented the counter-revolutionaries to such a degree that the latter decided to organize and deal with them once and for all. [KK]

концентра́шка, концентрацио́нный ла́герь. *See* ла́герь 7.

концла́герь, концентрацио́нный ла́герь. *See* ла́герь 7.

конча́ть ⊂ Конча́й ночева́ть! 'Rise and shine!' used to rouse prisoners in the morning and after a work break. Ребя́та! Конча́й ночева́ть! Подъём! Men! Rise and shine! Reveille!

копы́то ⊂ вы́тянуть копы́та. *See* вы́тянуть.

ко́реш, 'a fellow countryman.' Гей, ко́реш [ко́рыш, ко́риш, корешо́к, ке́ря, кирю́ха, кирю́шка]! Дава́й махнёмся боти́нками. Дам в прида́чу па́йку хле́ба. Hey, fellow countryman. Let's trade boots. I'll throw in a ration of bread. [aLi 56, ко́рыш] *Also* ко́рыш, ко́риш, корешо́к, ке́ря, кирю́ха, кирю́шка.

корешо́к 1. 'a cigarette butt.' Во вре́мя прогу́лки оди́н из заключённых по́днял корешо́к с земли́. During the exercise period one of the prisoners picked up a cigarette butt from the ground. **2.** dim. of ко́реш (q.v.). [AD, pop.; S 80; St 142]

коридо́р ⊂ гуля́ш по коридо́ру. *See* гуля́ш.

ко́риш. *See* ко́реш.

корм ⊂ подно́жный корм, 'pasturage,' a term applied to the various roots and berries gathered by the prisoners to eat during the summer. Как то́лько бригади́р объяви́л переку́р, вся брига́да пусти́лась на подно́жный корм. Собира́ли и е́ли все съедо́бные ко́рни и расте́ния. As soon as the brigadier announced the break, the whole brigade set out to look for pasturage. They gathered and ate all kinds of edible roots and plants. [AD]

кормёжка, 'the suckling of infants' (by their prisoner mothers). Два́жды в день води́ли ма́мки че́рез ва́хту для кормёжки в деткомбина́т. Twice daily the mothers were led through the guard shack to the nursery to suckle the infants. [AD, colloq. 'feeding']

корму́шка, 'food hatch,' a small square opening in the door of a cell through which prisoners receive their meals. С утра́ корму́шка [откидна́я фо́рточка] в тюре́мной две́ри откры́лась и па́ечка залете́ла. In the morning the food hatch in the prison door opened and the bread ration flew in. [AD, feeding trough] *Also* фо́рточка 2.

корпусно́й, 'a chief warder,' an officer in charge of guards in a prison. Во вну́тренних тю́рьмах то́лько корпусно́й име́л пра́во открыва́ть ка́меру. Only the chief warder had the right to open a cell in inner prisons. [AD, adj. pert. to corps] *Cf.* старшо́й.

ко́рыш. *See* кореш.

косану́ть, pf., 'to finagle, to get by guile.' Ва́ська ло́вко косану́л бу́лку хле́ба из хлеборе́зки. Vas'ka skillfully finagled a loaf of bread from the breadcutter's. *Cf.* закоси́ть.

коси́ть. *See* закоси́ть.

‡ **косты́ль,** 'bread ration.' « А — па́йка вам поло́жена? » — « Да. Косты́ль — пе́рвый. А бала́нду на́шу мо́жешь рабо-тя́гам отдава́ть ... ». "And do you get a bread ration?" "Oh, sure. We get a bread ration. But you can give our gruel to the hard workers." (Олень и шалашовка)

кость ⊂ Была́ бы кость, а шку́ра нараста́ет. 'If the bone is left, the hide will grow back,' an expression used by inmates to cheer each other up. It was popular during the war and post-war years when malnutrition was common in the camps. [DPos 399, 693, 850, for similar proverbs]

котёл. *See* прива́рок.

ко́шка ⊂ живу́чая, как ко́шка, 'having nine lives, like a cat,' a phrase used to describe the great physical and mental resistance of female prisoners to the hardships of camp life. Ка́ждая ба́ба, живу́чая как ко́шка; все они́ выжива́ли лу́чше, чем мужчи́ны в лагеря́х. Every woman had nine lives; they all survived better in the camps than the men. [DPos 289]

КПЗ [ka-pe-zé], ка́мера предвари́тельного заключе́ния, 'a KPZ,' a preliminary detention cell, found in all police stations. Ско́ро по́сле аре́ста Петро́ва перевели́ из КПЗ [пред-вари́лки] во вну́треннюю тюрьму́. Soon after his arrest Petrov was transferred from the KPZ to the inner prison. *Also* предвари́лка.

КПЧ [ka-pe-čé], координацио́нно-пла́новая часть, 'КРČ,' co-ordination planning section, usually found only on the main compound. It is responsible for presenting an annual production plan to the main administration. КПЧ распоряжа́лось всей рабси́лой ла́геря. The КРČ was in charge of the entire work force in the camp. *See* ППЧ, ОКБ.

КР [ka-ér] 1. контрреволюционе́р, 'a KR,' a counter-revolu-tionary. Нача́льник уча́стка отобра́л одни́х КРов [ka-éraf], что́бы отпра́вить на сеноко́с. The camp commandant selected only KR's for the haymowing. **2.** контрреволюцио́нный, 'counter-revolutionary.' « Кака́я статья́? » — « КР ». "What's your provision?" "KR." **3.** копа́й и руби́, 'dig and chop,' a jocular reinterpretation of the Russian abbreviation (see meaning 2). Digging and chopping are the chief work open to political prisoners in the camps. « Кака́я статья́? » — « Копа́й и руби́ ». "What's your provision?" "Digging and chopping." [KK]

КРА [ka-er-á], контрреволюцио́нная агита́ция, 'KRA,' counter-revolutionary agitation, a reference to article 58.10 of the Soviet Criminal Code of 1926. Васи́льев был осуждён к 10 года́м ИТЛ за КРА. Vasil'ev was sentenced to 10 years of ITL (corrective labor camps) for KRA.

кра́ля. *See* зозу́ля.

кра́сненький. *See* цветно́й, блатно́й 1.

краснопого́нник, 'a red epaulet,' a soldier belonging to a secret service unit, so named for the red epaulets (кра́сные пого́ны) worn on the shoulders. Наш эта́п охраня́лся четырьмя́ краснопого́нниками. Our transport was guarded by four red epaulets.

КРГ [ka-er-gé], контрреволюцио́нная группиро́вка, 'KRG,' counter-revolutionary group, a reference to article 58.11 of the Soviet Criminal Code of 1926. Рамзи́нская гру́ппа в основно́м суди́лась по КРГ. For the most part, the Ramzin group was sentenced for KRG.

КРД [ka-er-dé], контрреволюцио́нная де́ятельность, 'KRD,' counter-revolutionary activity, a popular camp and semiofficial designation for any activity defined in article 58 of the Soviet Criminal Code of 1926. « Ивано́в, кака́я у тебя́ статья́? » — « КРД ». "Ivanov, what article are you in for?" "KRD."

Кресты́, pl., 'Kresty,' a famous prison in Leningrad. Меня́ арестова́ли в Ленингра́де и я отфуя́рил в Креста́х бо́льше го́да. I was arrested in Leningrad and served more than a year in Kresty prison.

крохобо́р, 'a crumb snatcher,' a prisoner who steals petty items from his fellows, held in contempt by "real" thieves. Он настоя́щий крохобо́р — ведь вчера́ полпа́йки хле́ба утащи́л у меня́. He's a real crumb snatcher; why, yesterday he stole half a ration of bread from me. [AD; Tr]

КРТД [ka-er-te-dé], контрреволюцио́нная троцки́стская де́я-тельность, 'Trotskyite KRD,' an expanded form of КРД (q.v.).

кру́гленькая. [AD, кру́гленькая су́мма 'significant sum'] *See* ха́зерлах.

кружо́к ⊂ кружо́к самоде́ятельности, 'a circle of amateurs,' which performs in camp and sometimes, under heavy guard, in surrounding cities. Сосе́д по на́ре наха́льно записа́лся в кружо́к самоде́ятельности, чтобы облегчи́ть себе́ рабо́ту. My bunk neighbor brazenly signed up with a circle of amateurs in order to lighten his work. [AD]

кры́шка, 'the end.' Когда́ Си́дорова посади́ли в изоля́тор, он ду́мал, что ему́ кры́шка. When Sidorov was put in the isolator, he thought his end had come. [AD, pop.] *Also* луна́, пизде́ц.

крючо́к ⊂ быть на крючке́, 'to be on (someone's) hook,' to be blackmailable. За связь с заключёнными каптёр, вольня́га, был у меня́ на крючке́; вы́нужден был пуля́ть мне табачо́к, когда́ сиде́л в БУ́Ре. The supply clerk, a free employee, was on my hook for fraternizing with the prisoners. He had to send me tobacco while I was in the BUR (strict discipline barracks). [AD]

кси́ва **1.** 'a forged or stolen document, passport.' Я суме́л пробра́ться через запре́тную зо́ну. За зо́ной друзья́ мой ожида́ли меня́ с кси́вой. I managed to make my way through the forbidden zone. Outside the compound my friends were waiting with a forged passport. [Tr] **2.** 'a secret note.' Я бро́сил ему́ кси́ву. I threw him a secret note. [F 178; To 159]

КТР [ka-te-ér], каторжа́нин, 'KTR,' official term for a prisoner at hard labor. Во вре́мя пове́рки днева́льный доложи́л, что в бара́ке чи́слится 90 КТР [ka-te-éraf], налицо́ 62, за зо́ной 28. During the checkup the orderly reported that there were 90 KTR's in the barracks, 62 present and 28 outside the compound.

КТРовец [ka-te-érayic], 'male prisoner at hard labor.' *See* КТР.

КТРовка [ka-te-érafka], 'female prisoner at hard labor.' *See* КТР.

‡ **кубло́,** ' "family," ' a collective term used to describe the *priduroks* (приду́рок, q.v.). Я — норма́льно. Ну, немно́жко хрено́во. С кубло́м разошёлся. I'm the same as always. Well,

a bit screwed up. I had a falling out with the "family." (Оле́нь и шалашо́вка) [D, a nest]

кула́к, 'kulak,' a well-to-do peasant. The word became a term of abuse for those who refused to join collective farms, and millions were deported to labor camps or special settlements. Эта́п кулако́в с Украи́ны привезли́ в Карла́г. A transport of kulaks from the Ukraine was brought to Karlag (the Karaganda camp). [AD]

кум 1. *See* оперуполномо́ченный. 2. ——— королю́, 'like a king' (lit., godparent to a king). Капте́р в на́шей зо́не име́л прекра́сную житу́ху. Кум королю́, сыт, оде́т и в ус не дул. The storage manager in our compound had an excellent life. He lived like a king, was satisfied, well dressed, and without a care.

ку́мпол, 'head.' Дай ему́ по ку́мполу и пусть отвя́жется. Hit him on the head and make him let me be. [To 322; St 142]

‡ **куро́чить.** *See* раскуро́чить.

кусо́к, '1000 rubles.' Дава́й пуля́й два куска́ и сапо́жки твой. Pay me 2000 rubles and the boots are yours.

Л, л

Ла́герь   **1.** 'camp,' a general term. A camp complex is composed of a number of camp districts, each of which is itself composed of a number of camp sections and subsections. [AD] *See* уча́сток, отделе́ние 1, пункт 1.   **2.** закры́тый ———, 'closed camp,' the designation for camps where important foes of the regime were sent during the Great Purge. No word was ever received from these prisoners, and the especially hard conditions were presumably designed to kill them. This term was used interchangeably by prisoners with those given in meanings 3, 4, and 5 (qq.v.). Во вре́мя ежо́вщины крупне́йшие враги́ наро́да поса́жены бы́ли в закры́тые лагеря́. Никто́ из бли́зких не узна́л о их судьбе́. During the Ežov purge the more important "enemies of the people" were put in closed camps. None of the families found out their fate.   **3.** ——— без пра́ва перепи́ски, 'a camp without the right to correspond.' Закры́тые лагеря́ и спецлагеря́ счита́лись лагеря́ми без пра́ва перепи́ски, хотя́ в спецлагеря́х разреша́лось 1–2 ра́за в год. Closed camps and special camps were considered camps without the right to correspond, although it was permitted once or twice per year in special camps. *Cf.* meaning 2.   **4.** специа́льный ———, 'special camp,' name of camps established after World War II for Vlasovites, Banderites, and other alleged traitors. Prisoners in these camps had a limited right to correspond. По́сле войны́ всех вла́совцев и дома́новцев убра́ли из о́бщих лагере́й; говоря́т, что их загна́ли в специа́льные лагеря́ [спецлагеря́]. After the war all Vlasovites and Domanovites were removed from the general camps; it is said that they were driven to special camps. *Also* (and more commonly) спецла́герь. *Cf.* meaning 2.   **5.** осо́бый ———, 'camp of special designation,' name of camps established after the Revolution for clergy, members of the bourgeoisie, and other important opponents of the regime. В двадца́тых года́х Соловки́ счита́лись осо́бым ла́герем [особла́гом]. В них изоли́ровали буржу́ев и духове́нство. In the 1920s, Solovki was considered a special camp. The bourgeoisie and clergy were isolated there. *Also* особла́г. *Cf.* meaning 2. **6.** ка́торжный ———, 'hard labor camp,' introduced during World War II for alleged collaborators with the Germans, for recidivists, and for prisoners convicted of serious crimes. По́сле тре́тьего уби́йства нача́льство реши́ло отпра́вить Воло́дьку в ка́торжные лагеря́. After his third murder the authorities decided to send Volod'ka to a hard labor camp. **7.** концентрацио́нный ———, 'concentration camp,' the official designation for German camps, applied unofficially to Russian camps. Всю хе́вру из Лубя́нки этапи́ровали в концентрацио́нный ла́герь [концентра́шку, концла́герь]. The whole gang was shipped from Lubjanka to a concentration camp. *Also* концентра́шка, концла́герь. **8.** откры́тый ———, 'open camp,' with the right of limited correspondence with the outside world. По́сле сме́рти Ста́лина наш ла́герь объяви́ли откры́тым, и я сра́зу суме́л связа́ться со свое́й семьёй. After Stalin's death our camp was declared open, and I was at once able to get in touch with my family. **9.** штрафно́й ———, 'penalty camp,' a special camp for punishing prisoners for infractions of camp discipline. За многокра́тный отка́з от рабо́ты з/к направля́лись в штрафны́е лагеря́ [в штрафняки́]. For multiple refusals to work, prisoners were shipped to penalty camps. *Also* штрафня́к. **10.** Тюрьма́ и ла́герь, э́то на́ши родны́е. *See* тюрьма́ 4.

лагпу́нкт, ла́герный пункт. *See* уча́сток.

ла́па, 'a bribe.' Семён дал ла́пу наря́дчику и тот перевёл его́ на лёгкую рабо́ту. Semen gave the work assigner a bribe and was assigned to easy work. [To 445]

ларёк ⊂ ларёк з/к, 'prisoners' commissary,' where extra food can be purchased to supplement the food ration. С нача́лом войны́ закры́ты ларьки́ з/к; их вновь откры́ли в 1946-м году́. With the start of the war the prisoners' commissaries were closed; they were reopened in 1946. [AD]

ларёчник, 'a prisoner manager of the commissary.' Initially, the job was given only to criminals, but later political prisoners were permitted to hold the job because of stealing by the criminal managers. Наш ларёчник нажива́лся на кра́йней нужде́ заключённых. Освободи́вшись, он увёз с собо́й ку́чу де́нег. Our commissary manager made a fortune on the extreme poverty of the prisoners. On being released he took a pile of money with him. [AD, colloq.]

лата́ть, 'to scurry away.' Заха́р зале́з в же́нский бара́к, где заме́тил нача́льника режи́ма, и пришло́сь ему́ лата́ть. Zaxar entered the women's barracks where he spied the disciplinary officer and had to scurry away. [AD, pop. зада́ть лататы́; Sm, лататы; Tr, латата́]

лафа́, 'good luck, good fortune.' Вчера́, когда́ но́вый эта́п пришёл, так мы име́ли лафу́; всего́ от пу́за. Yesterday when the new transport arrived, we had good luck: everything in abundance. [D]

ла́хи, pl., 'belongings.' *See* мана́тки.

лаху́дра, 'trash,' applied to men or women. Ты лаху́дра, тебя́ ма́ло лупи́ли вчера́ но́чью. You trash, they didn't beat you enough last night. [D, worse than a prostitute]

лега́вый. [AD, pop.] *See* ляга́вый.

лезть ⊂ лезть в буты́лку [пузырёк], 'to become angry without cause.' Ва́ня, не лезь в буты́лку [пузырёк], а то бригади́р набьёт тебе́ мо́рду. Vanja, don't get angry over nothing, or the brigadier will smash your ugly mug. [AD, pop.]

лейтена́нт, 'a "lieutenant," ' a jocular term for someone in the first stage of syphilis. Ко́лька всё вре́мя блядова́л без вся́ких мер осторо́жности; вчера́ лекпо́м сказа́л мне, что он уже́ « лейтена́нт ». Kol'ka whored around without taking any precautions whatever; yesterday the medic told me that he was already a "lieutenant." *Cf.* генера́л, полко́вник.

лекпо́м, ле́карский помо́щник. [AD, colloq.] *See* лепи́ла.

леопа́рд, 'an underage criminal.' Нача́льник уча́стка стара́лся организова́ть брига́ду из одни́х леопа́рдов, чтобы приучи́ть их к рабо́те, то́лько неуда́чно. The commandant tried to organize a gang entirely of juveniles to train them to work, but without success. [aLi 66, a completely degraded thief]

ле́пень. [D, a shawl] *See* лепёха.

лепёха, 'a suit of clothes.' Са́ша-У́рка долбану́л лепёху [ле́пень] от одного́ из фрайеро́в из вновь прибы́вшего эта́па. Saša-Urka swiped a suit from one of the pigeons in the newly arrived transport. *Also* ле́пень.

лепи́ла, 'medic, a physician's aide.' Я су́нул шерстяну́ю руба́шку лепи́ле [лекпо́му] и он дал мне освобожде́ние с рабо́ты на пять дней. I slipped a wool shirt to the medic and he freed me from work for five days. *Also* лекпо́м.

лепя́нка, 'a clay building, barracks,' built mostly in dry climates. В Карла́ге да́же не́которые вольнонаёмные жи́ли в лепя́нках. In Karlag (the Karaganda camp) even some of the free workers lived in clay buildings.

лесозагото́вка. [AD] *See* лесопова́л.

лесопова́л, 'logging,' a specialty of many far-northern camps. Such camps are dreaded by the prisoners because of the extremely severe conditions and the unlikelihood of survival. Копыло́в отфуя́рил на лесопова́ле [лесозагото́вке] пять лет, где дошёл до тако́й сте́пени, что, как инвали́да, отпра́вили в инвали́дный ла́герь. Kopylov spent five years at logging where he was reduced to such a state that he was sent to an invalid camp. *Also* лесозагото́вка.

ле́циха, 'a broad,' a mildly derogatory term for a woman. Посмотри́ на э́ту ле́циху, как ве́ртит буфера́ми. Хоте́лось бы проспа́ть с ней одну́ ночь. Look at that broad wiggling her tits. I'd like to spend a night with her.

ли́па 1. 'padding,' false, inflated data used in work reports. Наш бригади́р включи́л в рабо́чий наря́д одну́ ли́пу, и вся брига́да получи́ла монта́жный котёл. Our brigadier included only padding in the work report and the whole brigade received the special construction ration. 2. 'a false document.' Ивано́в пе́ред побе́гом добы́л ли́пу. Ivanov obtained false papers before his escape. [AD, c. pop. 'something false, counterfeit'; Tr; F 182, ли́повый 'false'; To 164]

липа́ч, 'a counterfeiter.' В Сове́тском Сою́зе липаче́й почти́ нет. Почти́ всех ухло́пали. There are almost no counterfeiters in the Soviet Union. Almost all were shot.

ли́тер, 'travel warrant.' If a prisoner lacks funds, the warrant can be exchanged for a ticket to his destination. Когда́ Ивано́в освободи́лся, у него́ бы́ло ме́ньше 500 рубле́й на лицево́м счету́, и поэ́тому нача́льство вы́дало ему́ ли́тер до ме́ста назначе́ния. When Ivanov was released, he had less than 500 rubles in his personal account so the authorities issued him a travel warrant to his destination. [AD, colloq.]

лишёнец 'a deprived citizen,' a free citizen without many rights of citizenship. Although this term has lacked official status since the adoption of the 1936 Constitution, it continued to be applied to the deprived citizens who resided around the camps. Вокру́г ла́геря бы́ло мно́го лише́нцев, кото́рые рабо́тали как вольнонаёмные, то́лько без пра́ва переселе́ния в другу́ю ме́стность. There were many deprived citizens around the camp who worked as free employees, only without the right to move to another locality. [S 172]

ло́жка ⊂ Дорога́ ло́жка к обе́ду. 'A spoon is valuable at dinner time,' a popular expression in camps, indicating that the value of a thing is determined by its usefulness, rather than by its intrinsic worth. [Ž]

ло́пать. *See* сло́пать.

ло́шадь ⊂ От рабо́ты ло́шади до́хнут. 'Work has killed many a horse,' a camp warning to avoid work, or perish. Воло́дя, не торопи́сь с рабо́той, а то — от рабо́ты ло́шади до́хнут. Volodja, don't hurry with the work—work has killed many a horse.

л/п [el-pé], ла́герный пункт. *See* уча́сток.

Лубя́нка, 'Lubjanka,' a famous inner prison in Moscow. До ла́геря я просиде́л год сле́дственным в Лубя́нке. I spent a year under investigation in Lubjanka before going to labor camp.

луна́ 1. 'the end.' Ка́жется, что на́шему агроно́му луна́; у ку́ма име́ются доказа́тельства про́тив него́. I think our agronomist has had it; the security agent has evidence against him. *Also* кры́шка, пизде́ц. 2. 'execution.' Генера́л Вла́сов просиде́л два го́да сле́дственным в Москве́, и в конце́ посла́ли на луну́. General Vlasov was under investigation in Moscow for two years and in the end was executed (lit., sent to the moon). [D, death]

лупа́ло, 'an eye.' Чего́ лупа́ла вы́ставил? What are you sticking your eyeballs out for? [D, лу́пала 'one who winks, blinks']

лу́паться, impf., 'to gaze, stare.' Чего́ лу́паешься? What are you staring at? [D, лу́пать глаза́ми 'to wink']

лупи́ть. *See* отлупи́ть, вы́лупить.

ЛФТ [el-ef-té], лёгкий физи́ческий труд, 'LFT,' light physical work, assigned to prisoners with impaired health. После́дняя комиссо́вка дала́ мне ЛФТ и меня́ перевели́ в сельскохозяй-ственную брига́ду, где труд счита́лся лёгким. The last decision of the medical commission gave me LFT and I was moved to an agricultural brigade where the work was considered easy. *Cf.* ТФТ, труд 1.

лы́биться, impf., 'to smirk, grin.' Чего́ ты лы́бишься, как проститу́тка? Why are you smirking like a prostitute? [D]

лю́ра, 'gruel,' derogatory name for watery camp soup, not so common a term as бала́нда (q.v.). Опя́ть настря́пали лю́ру из зелёных ли́стьев капу́сты и камсы́. They've cooked up gruel again from green cabbage leaves and dried fish. *Cf.* ю́шка.

ляга́вый, 'a dick,' a derogatory name for a detective or an informer. Я уже́ был гото́в оста́вить кварти́ру, как оди́н ляга́вый [лега́вый] накры́л меня́ и я никуда́ не мог де́ться. I was just about to leave the apartment when a dick discovered me and I couldn't hide anywhere. [Tr; F 179; To 113] *Also* лега́вый.

ляга́ш, 'a dick, a detective.' Му́ра, что тебя́ заста́вило связа́ться с лягаша́ми и пойти́ рабо́тать в губчека́? Mura, what made you deal with the dicks and go to work for the provincial Cheka? [aLi 63]

ля́рва, 'whore.' Э́та ля́рва опя́ть поле́зла в мужско́й бара́к. That whore has crawled into the men's barracks again. [Tr; S 76]

М, м

магáр. *See* магáра.

магáра, 'magara,' a weed of the millet family, the seeds of which are used for cereal in the camps. Проглотнýть не могý э́ту магáру, так онá мне надоéла [э́тот магáр, так он мне надоéл]. I can't swallow this magara, I'm so sick of it. *Also* магáр.

магарь́ч, 'a bribe.' Я сýнул бригадúру магарь́ч и он меня́ перевёл на легчáйшую рабóту. I slipped the brigadier a bribe and he transferred me to an easier job. [AD, pop.] *Also* каль́м.

мáйка, 'a sleeveless undershirt,' issued prisoners for the summer upon return of the winter shirt issue. Since the shirt becomes completely worn out, only the collar has to be returned at the end of the season. Веснóй я получúл мáйку и трусь́; э́то бь́ло моё едúнственное бельё за лéто. In the spring I received an undershirt and a pair of shorts; it was my only underwear for the summer. [AD]

мáйхер, 'a dagger.' Вáська вь́тянул мáйхер из-за голенúща и пригрозúл, что зарéжет кáждого, кто трóнется с нар. Vas'ka took a dagger from his boot top and threatened to cut the throat of anyone who budged from his bunk.

Макáр ⊂ кудá Макáр теля́т не гоня́л, 'where Makar did not drive his calves,' a designation for the far-northern camps. Этáп длúлся 25 дней. Наконéц вь́грузили нас, кудá Макáр теля́т не гоня́л. The transport lasted 25 days. At last they unloaded us where Makar did not drive his calves. [DPos 222, ... не гоняет]

малúна 1. 'a meeting place for criminals.' Мы пошлú в малúну, чтóбы приготóвить план дéйствия. We went to the meeting place to prepare a plan of action. [Tr; To 91; St 136] 2. 'an excellent life.' В нáшем лáгере э́то не жизнь, а малúна. In our camp it isn't a life, but a good life. [AD, pop. 'something very pleasant'] 3. 'a place to hide stolen goods.' Я зать́рил все манáтки в малúну. I put all my belongings in a hiding place.

малолётка   **1.** 'a teenager.' They are assigned to special camps, but frequently serve part of their sentences with regular prisoners. В нашем лагере хуже всех были малолётки; на каждом шагу они нападали на нас и отнимали последнюю даже крошку табаку. In our camp the teenagers were worst of all; they jumped us at every turn and took away every last crumb of tobacco. [AD, pop. 'child'; Sm, малолеток 'apprentice swindler'; F 181, малолеток 'teenager']   **2.** 'a short-timer,' a prisoner with a short sentence. Копылов не захочет рискнуть побегом; ведь он малолётка. Kopylov won't risk an escape; he's a short-timer.

малосрочный, 'a short-timer,' a prisoner with a short sentence. В ИТК преимущественно содержались малосрочные. For the most part, short-timers were kept in ITK's (corrective labor colonies).

мамáн, indecl., 'mother.' После пяти лет в заключении я увидел мамáн и папáн в первый раз. After five years in prison I saw mama and papa for the first time.

манáтки, pl., 'belongings.' Сидоров, собери свои манáтки [шмóтки] и в этáп! Sidorov, gather up your belongings and (get ready) to be transported. [AD, pop.] *Also* шмóтки, лáхи.

мандá, 'cunt,' often used as a term of abuse. Ах, мандá ты! Ты кусóк мандьí! Ah, you cunt, you piece of a cunt! [D]

мандёж ⊂ сухóй мандёж, 'nonsense, rubbish.' Вáся, э́то для меня́ сухóй мандёж. Vasja, this is nonsense to me. [D, мандá]

мандовóха, 'a cunt louse, a crab,' a strong derogatory term applied to males and females. Ах, ты мандовóха [мандовóшка]: опя́ть нос суёшь, кудá не слéдует. Ah, you cunt louse; you're horning in again where you shouldn't. *Also* мандовóшка.

мандовóшка, dim. of мандовóха (q.v.).

манкирáнт, 'a shirker.' Сидоров э́то такóй манкирáнт, что на рабóту выхóдит, тóлько на рабóте пáльцем о пáлец не удáрит. Sidorov is such a shirker: he goes out to work, but doesn't lift a finger.

манкировать, pf. and impf., 'to shirk.' На э́том учáстке манкировать не придётся, тóлько ишáчить. No shirking allowed in this camp section; you must work like a dog. [AD, bookish]

‡ **мантỳлить,** impf., 'to slave away, to work like a dog.' Носѝлки забирáй, другѝм давáй, пусть мантỳлят. Take the wheelbarrows and give them to someone else. Let them slave away. (Олень и шалашовка) [D, to be a plate licker]

Маркс ⊂ Маркс — теóрия, а Ежóв — прáктика. 'Marx is the theory, Ežov is the practice,' a frequent, cynical response of a party member to a critic of the Soviet order. « Соглáсно Мáрксу все бýдут получáть по потрéбности ». — « Что нам Маркс? Маркс — теóрия, а Ежóв — прáктика ». "According to Marx, everyone will receive according to his need." "What is Marx to us? Marx is the theory; Ežov is the practice."

марỳха, 'mistress, wife.' Былá у меня хорóшая марỳха в лáгере, так её в этáп отпрáвили. I had a good mistress in camp, but she was shipped away. Былá у меня хорóшая марỳха на вóле. In free life I had a good wife. [Sm; Tr; To 35]

маслѝна, 'a bullet' (lit., an olive). Конвóйр запустѝл емý маслѝну в икрý. The escort fired a bullet into the calf of his leg. [F 183; To 169, мáслина; aLi 78]

мастỳрка ⊂ сдéлать мастỳрку, 'to produce an infection.' Ефѝм чýвствовал, что дохóдит окончáтельно; сдéлал себé мастỳрку [мостỳрку] в нóгу игóлкой и химѝческим карандашóм, чтóбы вýзвать гангрéну и быть освобождённым от рабóты. Efim felt he was finally on his last legs; he infected his leg with a needle and an indelible pencil in order to cause gangrene and be relieved of work. *Also* мостỳрка.

мастỳрщик, 'one who causes an infection (мастỳрка, q.v.).' Кóстя слáвился в зóне, как сáмый искýсный мастỳрщик; ни санчáсть ни начáльство не моглѝ доказáть симуляций. Он бóльше припухáл на нáрах, чем рабóтал. Kostja was renowned in the compound for his skill at causing infections; neither the medical office nor the camp authorities could prove wrongdoing. He spent more time on the bed boards than at work. *Also* мостỳрщик.

мат ⊂ крыть мáтом, 'to use the oath "you mother-fucker."' Наш бригадѝр рéдко ругáлся; тóлько, когдá начнёт крыть мáтом, так лýчше берегѝсь. Our brigadier rarely swore, but when he began to scream "you mother-fucker," you'd better watch out! [F 188, мат 'swearing, using the word "mother" in a vile way'; *cf.* AD, pop. крыть благи́м ма́том 'to scream bloody murder']

матери́нщик, 'a foul-mouth,' one addicted to cursing, especially to the expression "you mother-fucker." Ивано́в — э́то тако́й матери́нщик, что Бо́же упаси́. Ivanov is such a foul-mouth—God help us.

матери́ться, impf., 'to curse,' usually using the expression "you mother-fucker." Наш бригади́р был о́чень споко́йный; то́лько, как уже́ начнёт матери́ться [матюга́ться, матюко́м руга́ться], так береги́сь. Our brigadier was very even tempered; but when he began to use "you mother-fucker," then watch out! [AD, pop.] *Also* матюга́ться, матюко́м руга́ться, по-матюга́ться.

‡ **матерну́ть, матери́ть,** 'to curse,' usually using the expression "you mother-fucker." Нога́ми кому́-то в коле́на ткну́лся, его́ по́ боку огре́ли, матерну́ли па́ру раз, а уж он проныря́л ... He kicked somebody on the knee. They hit him in the side and swore at him a couple of times, but he got through. (Оди́н день Ива́на Дени́совича)

мать ⊂ **1.** мать твою́ за́ ногу, 'your mother by the leg,' a euphemism for ёб твою́ мать 'you mother-fucker.' Гей, мать твою́ за́ ногу [ёлки-па́лки зелёные], встава́й на рабо́ту. Hey, your mother by the leg—get to work. *See* ёлка. **2.** мать-герои́ня, 'mother-heroine,' an ironic designation for mothers in camps, taken from the government decoration awarded mothers of many children. Днева́льная Ма́ша, она́ мать-герои́ня; вчера́ родила́ ребёнка. The barracks orderly Maša is a mother-heroine; yesterday she gave birth to a child.

мать-перема́ть, 'mother,' a euphemism for ёб твою́ мать 'you mother-fucker.' Мать-перема́ть! Опя́ть мне всучи́ли три́ста грамм. The mothers! They've stuck me with 300 grams [i.e., a penalty ration] again.

матюга́ться. [D] *See* матери́ться.

‡ **матюгну́ться,** pf., 'to utter an oath,' usually the expression "you mother-fucker." Отдыша́вшись, узна́л Оле́г, что ожида́ются не то да́мские ко́фточки, не то сви́теры. Он матюгну́лся шёпотом и отошёл. When he caught his breath Oleg discovered they were waiting either for women's blouses or sweaters. He whispered an obscene oath and walked away. (Ра́ковый ко́рпус)

матю́к ⊂ матюко́м руга́ться. *See* матери́ться.

махно́вец, 'Maxnoite,' a free-lance criminal who lives outside the code covering the organized criminals (блатны́е, q.v.) and who is a bitter foe of the latter. Many Maxnoites are former members of the organized criminal world who have cooperated with the camp authorities for a time (as a gang leader, for example) and hence cannot rejoin the organization. Maxnoites are generally feared more than the other criminals because their behavior is completely unpredictable. The name comes from N. I. Maxno (1889–1935), a Ukrainian anarchist leader who fought both the Red and White sides during the civil war. Когда́ в на́шем ла́гере начала́сь резня́ ме́жду блатны́ми и су́ками, махно́вцы стоя́ли в стороне́ и ра́довались. When the fight between the criminals and the stoolies began in our barracks, the Maxnoites stood aside and cheered. [S 171] *Cf.* блатно́й 1, зако́н 1.

махну́ть, pf. **1.** 'to escape.' Ивано́в махну́л из рабо́чей зо́ны, то́лько в не сполна́ час конво́й привёл его́ обра́тно в нару́чниках. Ivanov escaped from the work zone, but in less than an hour the convoy brought him back in handcuffs. [AD, pop. 'to be off'] ‡ **2.** 'to swap.' Я говорю́: для сы́на миллионе́ра у меня́ есть запасны́е, немно́жко рва́ные, махнём на сви́тер, не гля́дя? Махну́ли. I say that for the son of a millionaire I have a spare pair [of shorts], torn a little, and would he like to swap them sight unseen for the sweater? So we swapped. (Оле́нь и шалашо́вка)

махну́ться, pf., 'to barter, exchange.' Гей, мужи́к, дава́й махнёмся боти́нками; дам в прида́чу па́йку. Hey, fellow, let's trade boots. I'll throw in a ration of bread besides.

МГБ [em-ge-bé], Министе́рство госуда́рственной безопа́сности, 'MGB,' Ministry of State Security (1946–1953). [K] *See* Чека́.

медвежа́тник **1.** 'a safecracker.' В блатно́м ми́ре взло́мщики се́йфов называ́лись медвежа́тниками [шнифера́ми], и они́ представля́ли собо́й аристокра́тию блатно́го ми́ра. Among the criminals, safe specialists were called safecrackers and they were the aristocracy of the criminal underworld. [KK] *Also* шни́фер. **2.** 'a safe.' У нача́льницы санча́сти де́ньги и драгоце́нности храни́лись в медвежа́тнике. The head of the medical section kept her money and valuables in a safe. [aLi 80, медвежо́нок 'safe']

мéльница ⊂ Водá мéльницы ломáет. *See* водá 1.

мент. [Tr; To 129] *See* мильтóн.

менять ⊂ менять червóнец. *See* червóнец 2.

мéра ⊂ мéра социáльной защиты, 'measure of social defense,' an expression used for some years after the Revolution by Russian courts instead of "punishment." Захáру дáли три гóда ИТЛ, как мéру социáльной защиты. Zaxar was given three years of ITL (corrective labor camps) as a measure of social defense.

мерзóтина, 'filthy, disgusting person.' Ах, ты мерзóтина на подóбие человéка, стой подáльше от меня. Ah, you filthy beast in the shape of a man—stand farther away from me.

мертвéцкая, 'morgue.' Дневáльный и егó помóщник вынесли в мертвéцкую доходягу, котóрый умер на нáрах нóчью. The orderly and his assistant carried to the morgue a goner who died on the bed boards during the night. [AD, colloq.]

мертвяк, 'a corpse.' Суки подрáлись с урками, и в результáте двух мертвякóв вынесли из барáка. The stooles got into a fight with the criminals and as a result two corpses were carried out of the barracks. [D, a hopeless, dying person, or a spiritually dead person]

метáть ⊂ метáть икру, 'to be scared shitless, to be extremely scared.' Пóсле убийства Кирова вся нáша кáмера икру метáла, что всех ухлóпают. After Kirov's murder, all the prisoners in our cell were scared shitless that they would be shot. [Fraz, c. pop. 'to raise a ruckus, usually over a trifle']

мильтóн, 'a cop.' Вася сидéл за убийство мильтóна [мéнта], котóрый пытáлся егó задержáть. Vasja was doing time for murdering the cop who tried to arrest him. [S 77, 79; To 119] *Also* мент.

минéтка ⊂ минéтку сдéлать, 'to commit fellatio.' Вчерá Мáша полéзла ко мне на нáры, и самá напросилась, чтóбы ей сдéлать минéтку. Yesterday Maša crawled onto the bed boards with me, and she herself asked to suck my cock. [To 42, минетка 'prostitute']

мозг ⊂ впрáвить мозги, 'to set (someone's) brains aright,' to instill correct thinking. Не волнýйтесь: Совéтская власть впрáвит вам мозги, наýчит вас плáкать по-рýсски. Don't worry; the Soviet government will straighten out your brains and teach you to weep in Russian. [AD, pop.]

мозгоеба́тель, 'a brain-fucker,' a tiresome, insistent bore. Не обраща́й внима́ния на э́того мозгоеба́теля; он тебе́ го́лову заморо́чит. Don't pay any attention to that brain-fucker; he'll give you a headache. *Cf.* поеба́ть 2.

мозгоеба́ть, impf., 'to brain fuck, to bug, to bore, to annoy.' Брось мозгоеба́ть, и дава́й возьмёмся за де́ло. Cut out the bullshit and let's get to work.

мо́йка, 'a razor blade,' used for picking pockets. Воло́дя был изве́стным карма́нщиком в Ленингра́де; он специализи́ровался в ре́зке карма́нов мо́йкой гла́вным о́бразом в трамва́е. Volodja was a famous pickpocket in Leningrad. He specialized in cutting out pockets with a razor blade in streetcars.

мокру́шник, 'a robber and murderer.' Наш коменда́нт э́то бы́вший мокру́шник. У него́ в про́шлом три уби́йства с грабежа́ми. Our barracks chief is a murderer. He has in his past three robberies with murder. [To 12; aLi 76]

молча́ть в тря́почку. *See* тря́почка.

морг, 'morgue,' a special barracks in each camp close to the hospital. В про́шлую ночь два деся́тка заключённых у́мерло в сангородке́. С утра́ тру́пы перевезли́ в морг. Last night 20 prisoners died in the hospital-medical block. In the morning the corpses were taken to the morgue. [AD]

мори́ловка, 'a killer camp.' Китла́г был настоя́щей мори́ловкой во вре́мя войны́; з/к па́дали, как му́хи. Kitlag (the Kitoj camp) was a real killer camp during the war; the prisoners died like flies.

Москва́ ⊂ Москва́ слеза́м не ве́рит. 'Moscow does not heed tears,' an expression implying that no one will pay any attention to complaints, appeals, and the like. Напра́сно вре́мя тра́тишь. Москва́ слеза́м не ве́рит. You're wasting your time. Moscow does not heed tears. [Ž]

москви́чка, 'an overcoat,' coveted by criminals more than any other object. Когда́ я вы́скочил из ла́геря, я сра́зу же приобрёл москви́чку и сапо́жки, и не подходи́ ко мне. When I escaped the camp I immediately got myself an overcoat and some shoes and I really cut a figure! [KK]

мосты́рка. *See* масты́рка.

мосты́рщик. *See* масты́рщик.

муда́к, 'a nut, a fool.' От тако́го мудака́ и ожида́ть бо́льше не́чего. From such a nut you can't expect anything else. [D, мудо́ 'testicle']

муж ⊂ ла́герный муж, 'camp husband.' Ма́ша меня́ла ла́герных муже́й, как перча́тки. Maša used to change her camp husbands like gloves.

мы́ться ⊂ мы́ться от ба́ни до ба́ни, 'to wash only at bath time,' since soap and hot water are generally not obtainable. На на́шем уча́стке с водо́й бы́ло пло́хо — все мы́лись от ба́ни до ба́ни. In our compound the water situation was bad— everyone washed only at bath time.

Н, н

наблаты́каться, pf., 'to absorb criminal mores and speech habits.' Смотри́, как Петро́в перемени́лся. Как прие́хал из эта́па, он был о́чень сми́рненький, а тепе́рь наблаты́кался так, что от уро́к не отличи́шь. See how Petrov has changed. When he came from the transport he was very quiet, but now he has so thoroughly absorbed criminal ways that you can't distinguish him from them.

наблюда́тель ⊂ америка́нский наблюда́тель, 'American observer,' a name given by work supervisors to fellow prisoners who try to avoid work. Чего́ стои́шь, как америка́нский наблюда́тель? Why are you standing around like an American observer?

нава́р, 'profit.' Во всех сде́лках са́мый лу́чший нава́р отла́мывался барь́ге. In all transactions the best profit went to the fence. [AD, fat]

наве́сить, pf., 'to hang (a provision on someone), to charge under a Criminal Code article.' Мой сле́дователь пыта́лся наве́сить мне статью́, то́лько она́ не приставала ко мне. My interrogator tried to hang the charge on me, only it didn't stick.

наво́дчик, 'a caser,' a criminal's assistant, often a juvenile, who surveys a place with a view to robbing it. Бригади́р Анти́п рассказа́л брига́де, что в во́зрасте двена́дцати лет на́чал рабо́тать наво́дчиком и постепе́нно дошёл до медвежа́тника. The brigadier Antip told the brigade that at the age of 12 he began to work as a caser and gradually worked up to safecracking. [Tr]

навора́чивать, impf., 'to eat.' Про́хор по́сле сангородка́ так навора́чивал, что я боя́лся, что у него́ за́ворот кишо́к полу́чится. After returning from the hospital-medical block, Proxor ate so much that I was afraid he would get an intestinal twist. [AD]

надзира́тель, 'a supervisor.' Ежедне́вно надзира́тель де́лал обхо́д зо́ны и принима́л жа́лобы от заключённых. Every day the supervisor used to make the rounds of the compound and hear complaints of the prisoners. Для безопа́сности тюре́мным надзира́телям не разреша́лось носи́ть ору́жье. For security reasons prison supervisors were forbidden to bear arms.

надзорслу́жба, надзо́рная слу́жба, 'the camp supervisory staff.' Когда́ у́рки разбушева́лись, вся надзорслу́жба удрала́ из зо́ны. When the criminals went on a rampage, the entire supervisory staff ran out of the compound.

нады́бать, pf., 'to spot,' to discover in order to steal. Блатны́е сра́зу нады́бали си́дор у Козло́ва и но́чью утащи́ли у него́. The criminals immediately spotted Kozlov's parcel and during the night stole it from him. [D, to find, search out]

наеба́ть, pf., 'to pound, to punch.' Я наёб ему́ мо́рду, что он подня́ться не мог. I pounded his ugly mug until he couldn't get up. *Also* наебну́ть.

наеба́ться, pf., **1.** *See* нахуя́риться. **2.** 'to fuck.' Воло́дя пролежа́л всю ночь с Ма́шей и наёбся, как пау́к. Volodja spent the whole night with Maša and fucked like a mink (lit., a spider).

наебну́ть. *See* наеба́ть.

нажа́ть, нажима́ть 1. 'to strain' (to fulfill a quota). Вся брига́да, как оди́н, нажима́ла во весь пар, чтобы зарабо́тать монта́жный котёл. The whole brigade, as one man, strained with all its strength in order to earn the construction ration. [AD, pop.] **2.** 'to stuff, to gulp down, to eat greedily.' Вме́сто хле́ба Ива́н нажима́л на бала́нду; это его́ довело́. Instead of bread Ivan stuffed himself on gruel; it made him a goner.

наказа́ние ⊂ де́тское наказа́ние. *See* де́тский.

‡ **нака́кать,** pf., 'to shit.' Полкопе́йки — это уваже́ние к челове́ку, а шестьдеся́т копе́ек с рубля́ не сдаю́т — это зна́чит, нака́кать тебе́ на́ голову. Half a kopek is respect for a man, but they don't even give you sixty kopeks change for a ruble. In other words, they shit on your head. (В круге пе́рвом) [D, ка́ка 'a nursery word for excrement']

‡ **нака́пать,** pf., 'to squeal, to act as an informer.' Нача́льника ла́геря ждут, чтоб на вас нака́пать. They're waiting for the camp commandant to return in order to squeal on you. (Оле́нь и шалашо́вка) *Cf.* ка́пнуть.

наломáть ⊂ наломáть спи́ну 1. 'to beat.' Вáня залéз в чужóй барáк; там емý так спи́ну наломáли, что недéлю на рабóту не выходи́л. Vanja crept into another barracks; there he was beaten so badly that he couldn't work for a week. [AD, pop. наломáть шéю, бóка] 2. 'to work prodigiously.' Сегóдня на рабóте пришлóсь так наломáть спи́ну, что нóчью все спáли, как уби́тые. We had to work so hard today that during the night everyone slept like the dead. [AD, pop.]

намáтывать. *See* намотáть.

намóрдник 1. 'a louver,' covering the windows of inner prisons. Все óкна во внýтренних тю́рьмах бы́ли покры́ты намóрдниками. All windows in inner prisons were covered with louvers. [AD, muzzle] *Also* козырьки́, футля́р. 2. 'disfranchisement,' a less common term than по рогáм (*See* рог). Кóстя получи́л дéсять лет и намóрдник на пять лет. Kostja was sentenced to ten years plus five-years disfranchisement. ‡ 3. дорóжный ———, 'face cloth.' Намóрдник дорóжный, тря́почка, за дорóгу вся отмóкла от дыхáния и кóй-гдé морóзом прихвати́лась, кóркой стáла ледянóй. The rag of a face cloth had gotten all wet from his breath on the way and was frozen here and there into an icy crust. (Один день Ивана Денисовича)

намотáть, намáтывать, 'to pin a sentence (on someone).' Кум намотáл мне срок за чепухý. The security officer pinned a sentence on me for a trifle. [AD, wind up] *Cf.* размотáть.

напáрник, 'a fellow worker.' Мой напáрник в бригáде был óчень добросóвестный мужи́к. My fellow worker in the brigade was a very honest man. [AD, colloq.]

нáра 1. *See* вагóнка. 2. нáры, pl., 'bed boards,' the continuous wooden shelves used instead of bunks. Бурáн шалéл весь день и вся зóна провалялась на нáрах. The blizzard roared all day and everybody in camp lolled about on the bed boards. [AD] 3. загнáть под нáры, 'to drive under the bed boards,' considered a great dishonor by the criminals. Замолчи́, а то загоню́ тебя́ под нáры. Shut up, or I'll drive you under the bed boards. [F 184; Lingo 80, Get under the bed!]

наркóм, 'a drug addict.' The word owes its effectiveness to the phonetic similarity of наркомáн 'drug addict' and наркóм 'people's commissar' (нарóдный комиссáр). Наш лекпóм оказáлся наркóмом; он пропи́л все лекáрства, содержáщие наркоти́ческие сре́дства, и поэ́тому его́ сня́ли с рабо́ты и на о́бщие. Our medic proved to be a drug addict. He used up all the medicines containing narcotics, and therefore he was fired and sent out on general labor.

наря́д 1. 'work sheet,' prepared by the work assigner. It contains quotas to be fulfilled and, when turned in, reports the work actually done. Бригади́р закры́л наря́д за после́днюю неде́лю и понёс в конто́ру. The brigadier closed the work sheet for the last week and took it to the office. [AD] *Also* наря́дка. **2.** 'assignment of work to columns and brigades.' Нача́льник коло́нны получи́л наря́д на строи́тельные рабо́ты в жилгородке́, и ему́ ну́жно бы́ло распредели́ть брига́ды согла́сно э́той разнаря́дке. The column chief received a construction assignment at the housing zone and he had to distribute the brigades according to the assignment. *Also* наря́дка. **3.** 'an order.' Пришёл наря́д из Карла́га на сто заключённых. An order for 100 prisoners came from Karlag (the Karaganda camps). [AD] *Also* наря́дка. **4.** наря́д-повремёнка, 'per diem assignment of work,' made when it is awkward to determine a quota. Ввиду́ того́, что зимо́й строи́тельные рабо́ты приостанови́лись, нача́льник перевёл на́шу брига́ду на наря́д-повремёнку. Because construction jobs were suspended in the winter, the commandant transferred our brigade to per diem assignments. **5.** специа́льный ———, 'a special order.' Монта́жника Ивано́ва этапи́ровали в Москву́ по специа́льному наря́ду [по спецнаря́ду]. The fitter Ivanov was transported to Moscow by a special order. *Also* спецнаря́д.

наряди́ть ⊂ наряди́ть на рабо́ту, 'to assign to work,' usually done by the compound chief, the work superintendent, and the work-assigner. Нача́льник уча́стка наряди́л на́шу брига́ду на сельскохозя́йственные рабо́ты. The compound chief put our gang on agricultural labor. [AD]

наря́дка. *See* наря́д 1, 2, 3.

наря́дчик, 'work-assigner,' a prisoner who helps the compound chief assign work. In large compounds, each column has its own work-assigner. Наря́дчик ежедне́вно выходи́л на ва́хту, что́бы наблюда́ть за выполне́нием разнаря́дки. Every day the work-assigner would go to the guard shack to supervise the carrying out of the work distribution. [AD]

наря́дчица, fem. form of наря́дчик (q.v.).

наса́дка. *See* насе́дка.

насе́дка, 'a plant,' an informer placed in a cell or barracks to spy on prisoners, or to persuade them to confess. В нача́ле сле́дствия я был в одино́чке. По́сле э́того сле́дователь подбро́сил мне насе́дку [наса́дку, подсы́пку] в ка́меру. At the beginning of the interrogation I was in solitary. Later the interrogator put a plant in my cell. [aLi 80, police agent] *Also* наса́дка, подсы́пка, подки́дыш.

настуча́ть, стуча́ть, 'to squeal, to act as an informer.' Си́доров настуча́л [ка́пнул, ду́нул] на Ивано́ва. Sidorov squealed on Ivanov. *Also* ка́пнуть, ду́нуть.

научи́ть ⊂ научи́ть пла́кать по-ру́сски, 'to teach (someone) to cry in Russian,' an ironic expression applied to prisoners who don't understand Russian. Не горю́й — здесь нау́чат тебя́ пла́кать по-ру́сски. Don't worry. Here they'll teach you to cry in Russian.

нафуя́рить, pf., 'to sentence.' Добромы́слов был год в неме́цком плену́; когда́ верну́лся на ро́дину, его́ посади́ли и нафуя́рили ему́ по́лную кату́шку. Dobromyslov was in a German prison camp for a year; when he returned home he was imprisoned and sentenced to a full 25-year stretch. « Гей, Копы́лов, ско́лько нафуя́рили? » — « Пять лет » — « Э́то чепуха́, э́то де́тское наказа́ние ». "Hey, Kopylov, how much did they give you?" "Five years." "That's a trifle, a child's punishment."

‡ **нахлеба́й,** 'a hanger-on, a parasite.' Пото́м я хочу́ предста́вить вам сокраще́ние вдво́е хозобслу́ги ла́геря — э́тих нахлеба́ев! Then I want to propose to you a reduction in camp administrative personnel by half—all those hangers-on! (Олень и шалашовка) [D]

нахомута́ть, хомута́ть, 'to pin (lit., to harness or yoke) a provision on someone, to accuse under a provision.' Кум пыта́лся нахомута́ть Си́дорову 58-у́ю статью́, но областно́й суд суди́л его́ то́лько за попы́тку перехо́да госграни́цы. The security officer tried to pin article 58 (dealing with political offenses) on Sidorov, but the district court only tried him for attempting to cross the state border. [AD, pop.]

нахуя́риться, pf., 'to work very hard.' Я сего́дня нахуя́рился [наёбся], что тепе́рь и пи́ще не рад. Today I worked so hard that I don't even feel like eating. *Also* наеба́ться.

нача́льник   **1.** 'thief' (lit., boss, chief). Since persons in authority have the best opportunity to steal, this word has become synonymous with "thief" in the camps. Гей, нача́льник! Hey, thief!   **2.** ——— карау́ла, 'chief of the camp guards.' On alternate days he might serve as chief of the escort guards (нача́льник конво́я). Наш нача́льник карау́ла [начка́р] был на ре́дкость сочу́вственный мужи́к. Our chief of guards was an unusually understanding guy. *Also* начка́р.   **3.** ——— коло́нны, 'column chief,' a position filled by a prisoner. Нача́льник коло́нны ежедне́вно по́сле разво́да уходи́л в конто́ру, что́бы пригото́вить разнаря́дку для его́ брига́д на сле́дующий день. Every day after the march off to work, the column chief went to the office to prepare the work distribution for his brigades for the next day.   **4.** ——— конво́я, 'chief of the escort guards.' *See* meaning 2.   **5.** ——— ла́геря, 'camp commandant,' usually from the military. Нача́льник ла́геря обеща́л уси́лить пита́ние трактори́стам, то́лько зна́ешь, жди у мо́ря пого́ды. The camp commandant promised to increase the tractor operators' rations, but you know, it's like waiting for kingdom come.   **6.** ——— режи́ма, 'disciplinary officer,' a free man, supervisor of platoon and convoy commanders. Нача́льник режи́ма на́шего отделе́ния был лейтена́нтом. The disciplinary officer in our district was a lieutenant.   **7.** ——— уча́стка, 'camp section commandant.' Нача́льник уча́стка отпра́вил Воло́дьку, как зло́стного прогу́льщика, на штрафну́ю командиро́вку. The camp section commandant shipped Volod'ka to a penalty camp as a malicious shirker.

начка́р, нача́льник карау́ла. *See* нача́льник 2.

нашко́дничать, шко́дничать, 'to be a pest, to be a trouble maker.' Ра́зве Карзу́бый вор? Он то́лько шко́дничает всю доро́гу. Is Karzubyj really a thief? He only makes trouble all the time.

НКВД [en-ka-ve-dé], Наро́дный комиссариа́т вну́тренних дел, 'NKVD,' People's Commissariat for Internal Affairs (1934–1943). [K] *See* Чека́.

нормиро́вщик, 'norm-setter,' an employee of the coordination-planning section. Воло́дя име́л сре́днее техни́ческое образова́ние; когда́ он попа́л в заключе́ние, оди́н знако́мый с

во́ли помо́г ему́ устро́иться нормиро́вщиком; приспосо́бился
к э́той рабо́те, где прорабо́тал бо́льше пяти́ лет. Volodja
had a secondary technical education. When he was imprisoned,
an acquaintance from outside helped him get a job as a norm-
setter. He got accustomed to this work and did it for more
than five years. [AD]

О, о

обвини́ловка, 'a conclusion to indict,' camp term for the official wording, обвини́тельное заключе́ние. Обвини́тельный акт is also commonly (and erroneously) used in camps and prisons. It is a detailed formulation of the accusation, prepared by the investigator and approved by the court, after which a copy is supposed to be sent to the prisoner at least three days before his court appearance. In the event that the case is to be decided by the ОСО or a тро́йка (qq.v.), the prisoner receives no conclusion to indict and often learns of his fate only after serving several years in camps. Во́ронову предъяви́ли обвини́ловку, то́лько он отказа́лся подписа́ть. Voronov was presented with the conclusion to indict, but he refused to sign.

обвини́тельный ⊂ обвини́тельный акт, обвини́тельное заключе́ние. *See* обвини́ловка.

обжа́ть, обжима́ть, 'to rob, to extort.' Три малоле́тки обступи́ли меня́, когда́ вы́шел из бара́ка, и обжа́ли на два стака́на табаку́. Three teenagers surrounded me when I left the barracks and robbed me of two glasses of tobacco. [AD, to wring (wet clothes)]

обрабо́тать, pf.,   **1.** 'to clean out, to steal.' Воло́дя получи́л посы́лку от жены́; но́чью его́ обрабо́тали на́чисто. Volodja received a parcel from his wife; during the night he was completely cleaned out. **2.** 'to disinfect.' Ба́нщик не успе́л обрабо́тать весь бара́к; втору́ю полови́ну оста́вили на за́втра. The bathhouse manager didn't have enough time to disinfect the whole barracks; the second half was postponed until tomorrow. [AD, to treat, process, persuade]

обрабо́тка, 'a clean-out, a heist, a robbery.' У́рки реши́ли, что по́лночь — э́то са́мое удо́бное вре́мя для обрабо́тки но́вого эта́па. The criminals decided that midnight was the most convenient time for a clean-out of the new transport.

обхо́д ⊂ ночно́й обхо́д, 'bed check,' conducted several times during the night, and sometimes followed by a roll call. Ввиду́ того, что надзиратель не досчитался двух заключённых во время ночного обхода, он приказал общую перекличку во всех бараках. Because the supervisor was two prisoners short at bed check, he ordered a general roll call in all the barracks. [AD]

объект, 'a work construction site.' На объекте № 5 три бригады работали круглый год. Three brigades worked year round at site No. 5. [AD]

обыск, 'a search,' common in prisons and, especially in camps, where, regardless of the weather, each prisoner is searched when going to or returning from work. Надзиратель и три бойца ворвались в барак; заключённые зашевелились, ибо чувствовали, что это пахнет обыском. The supervisor and three soldiers burst into the barracks; the prisoners began to stir for they sensed that it meant a search. [AD]

обыскать, обыскивать, 'to search.' В нашей зоне командир взвода лично обыскивал з/к; это не входило в его обязанности, только попросту любил поиздеваться. In our compound the platoon commander used to search the prisoners personally; this wasn't included in his duties, but he simply liked to torment them. [AD]

обязательство ⊂ Дал слово — сдержи; взял обязательство — выполни. *See* слово.

ОГПУ [o-ge-pe-ú] **1.** Объединённое государственное политическое управление при Совете Народных Комиссаров СССР, 'OGPU,' Unified State Political Administration of the Council of People's Commissars of the USSR (1922–1934). [K] *See* ГПУ, Чека. **2.** О, Господи, помоги удрать! 'Oh Lord, help me escape!' a jocular reinterpretation of the initials.

одиночка, одиночная камера, 'a solitary prison cell,' used to isolate a prisoner during his investigation. Сидоров был подследственным в течение шести месяцев; всё это время он просидел в одиночке. Sidorov was under investigation for six months. All that time he was in a solitary cell. [AD, colloq.]

одноделец, 'accomplice,' partner in the same venture. Все мои однедельцы попали в разные лагеря. All my accomplices went to various camps. *Also* подельник.

однокамерник, 'a cellmate.' На Воркуте я встретился с моим однокамерником из Лубянки. In the Vorkuta camps I met a cellmate from Lubjanka prison.

одноэта́пник, 'a fellow prisoner from the same transport.' Карзу́бый был мои́м одноэта́пником из Ворку́ты. Karzubyj was my fellow prisoner on the transport from Vorkuta.

ОКБ [o-ka-bé], организацио́нно-констру́кторское бюро́, 'OKB,' organizational-construction bureau, found in the larger camps. Its tasks are similar to those of the КПЧ and ППЧ (qq.v.), but on a higher echelon. It might, for example, be in charge of planning for a number of camps. ОКБ актю́бинского ла́геря затрудня́ло деся́тки о́пытных архите́кторов и инжене́ров, попа́вших в заключе́ние. The ОКВ of the Aktjubinsk camp employed dozens of experienced architects and engineers who had been imprisoned.

око́нщик. *See* фо́рточник.

окруже́нец, 'ex-prisoner of war,' later arrested by the Soviets and charged with having accepted a special mission for the Germans. По́сле войны́ окруже́нцы, как ненадёжный элеме́нт, бы́ли переведены́ из о́бщих лагере́й в спецлагеря́ вме́сте с вла́совцами, банде́ровцами и др. After the war, ex-prisoners of war, considered an unreliable element, were transferred from general to special camps along with the Vlasovites, Banderites, and others. [KK]

‡ **оле́нь,** 'an innocent, an easy dupe.' Вот ты ещё … оле́нь! Ты ещё ничего́ не понима́ешь. Why, you're still … a dupe, an innocent! You don't understand anything at all. (Олень и шалашовка) [AD, a deer]

ОЛП [ol-pé], отделе́ние ла́герного пу́нкта or отде́льный ла́герный пункт. *See* пункт 1.

ООС [o-ós], отде́л осо́бого снабже́ния, 'OOS,' department of special supply, providing food, clothing, repairs, and the like to a number of compounds and to the free population. Брига́да тракгори́стов снабжа́лась от ООС близлежа́щего уча́стка. A brigade of tractor operators was supplied by the OOS of a nearby camp section.

ОП [o-pé], оздорови́тельный пункт, 'OP,' rehabilitation point, a barracks for the least hopeless of the goners, who, after a term on a special ration to improve their health, might be returned to work. Медици́нская коми́ссия вы́брала 50 заключённых в ОП; всех перевели́ в специа́льные бара́ки. The medical commission selected 50 prisoners for OP. All were transferred to special barracks.

о́пер. *See* оперуполномо́ченный.

операти́вник. *See* оперуполномо́ченный.

оперуполномо́ченный, операти́вный уполномо́ченный, 'security officer,' the representative of the security police and the law enforcement officer in camp. Оперуполномо́ченный [Кум, О́пер, Операти́вник, Змей] на́шего отделе́ния был о́чень жёстким челове́ком. Все, включа́я нача́льство, боя́лись его́, как огня́. The security officer of our district was a very hard man. Everyone, including the other officials, feared him like fire. [КК] *Also* кум, о́пер, операти́вник, змей.

опра́вка, 'latrine call.' In prison and during transport, prisoners are taken to the latrine once a day. Пара́ши находи́лись во всех ка́мерах в тюрьме́; то́лько оди́н раз в день заключённые выводи́лись из ка́меры на опра́вку, где возмо́жно бы́ло опоро́жнить и вы́мыть пара́шу. Latrine pails were located in all cells in prison; only once a day prisoners were taken from their cells for latrine call, when it was possible to empty the pail and wash it.

осведоми́тель, 'collaborator, informer.' Тре́тья часть вербова́ла осведоми́телей среди́ бы́вших рабо́тников мили́ции. The third section recruited informers among former employees of the militia. [AD]

освобожде́ние ⊂ досро́чное освобожде́ние, 'early release,' for good behavior on recommendation of the authorities. It could happen after two thirds of the sentence was completed, and was discontinued with the beginning of World War II. The term was frequently used ironically to imply "owing to death." Серге́й всё вре́мя мечта́л о досро́чном освобожде́нии. За после́днее вре́мя на́чал доходи́ть, а вчера́ но́чью он « освободи́лся досро́чно ». Sergej dreamed about an early release all the time. Lately, he began to fail, and last night he got his "early release."

основа́ния ⊂ о́бщие основа́ния, pl., 'general, physical labor,' as opposed to office and administrative work. Большинство́ з/к в Воркуте́ находи́лось на о́бщих основа́ниях [рабо́тах; на о́бщем режи́ме]; жизнь у них была́ о́чень тяжёлая. Most of the prisoners in Vorkuta were on general labor; they had a very hard life. *Also* о́бщая рабо́та, о́бщий режи́м.

ОСО [o-só], Осо́бое совеща́ние, 'OSO,' Special Commission, a quasi-judicial organ of the NKVD, abolished in 1956. It imposed summary judgments (including death sentences) and was a main instrument of Stalin's terror. In camps, the terms ОСО and тройка (q.v.) were used interchangeably, with the latter term becoming much less common during World War II. Антонов решением ОСО был приговорён к 10 годам ИТЛ. Antonov was sentenced to 10 years of ITL (corrective labor camp) by a decision of the OSO.

особлаг, особый лагерь. *See* лагерь 5.

отбивные ⊂ отбивные по рёбрам, 'a very severe beating,' resulting in broken ribs, from отбивные '[pork] chops.' Знать не хочу! Выеби, и скажи « нашёл », иначе отбивные по рёбрам получишь. I don't want to know anything, just do it, or I'll break your ribs.

отбой, 'the signal for going to bed.' Из-за отсутствия воды нас продержали в бане до самого отбоя. Because of the lack of water we were kept in the bathhouse right up to bed time. [AD, signal for the end of something]

отбухать, pf., 'to serve a sentence.' Артём отбухал целых 15 лет. Artem served the whole 15 years. [D, to separate, or cut off]

отбыть, pf., 'to fulfill an obligation requiring a stay someplace,' as army service, or a penal sentence. Артём отбыл от звонка до звонка. Artem served his sentence from the first bell to the last. [AD]

отвалить ⊂ отвалить беду, 'to get one's gun off, to satisfy one's lust, to achieve orgasm.' Ваня вчера отвалил беду за одну баланду. Yesterday Vanja got his gun off in exchange for a bowl of gruel.

отделение   **1.** 'camp district,' composed of a number of camp sections, grouped together for geographical, administrative, and economic reasons. The central camp section of a camp district has more facilities than the other camp sections: a hospital, the main supply for the district, and central administrative offices. Врач, бывший заключённый, был начальником санчасти нашего отделения. The physician, a former prisoner, was the head of the central medical office for our camp district.   **2.** ——— лагерного пункта. *See* пункт 1.

отказ   **1.** 'refusal to go out to work.' If repeated several times, it can result in an additional sentence. Во время войны отказ считался саботажем, и з/к судили по 58.14. During the war refusal to work was considered sabotage, and prisoners were sentenced under article 58.14. **2.** 'the report prepared in cases of refusal to work.' Оттого́ что Ивано́в страда́л а́стмой, лепи́ла отказа́лся подписа́ть отка́з на него́. Because Ivanov suffered from asthma, the medic would not sign the report about his refusal to go to work. [AD, a refusal]

отка́зчик, 'a shirker.' Нача́льство призна́ло Кругло́ва зло́стным отка́зчиком и реши́ло суди́ть его́ за отка́з. The camp authorities found Kruglov a malicious shirker and decided to try him for refusal to work. [D, one who refuses anything]

отлома́ться, отла́мываться, 'to fall to someone's share.' Во всех сде́лках са́мый лу́чший нава́р отла́мывался бары́ге. In all transactions the best profit went to the fence.

отлупи́ть, лупи́ть, 'to beat.' Сего́дня бригади́р отлупи́л Его́ра за невы́ход на рабо́ту. Today the brigadier beat Egor for missing work. Я́шку Свистуна́ лупи́ли ка́ждый бо́жий день. Jaška Svistun was beaten every blessed day. [AD, pop.]

отлу́чка, 'AWOL,' absence without leave. Ефи́ма посади́ли в ка́рцер за отлу́чку; он ушёл к ла́герной жене́ на друго́м уча́стке. Efim was put in the cooler for being AWOL; he visited his camp wife in another compound. [AD, temporary absence]

отмахну́ть, pf., 'to serve a sentence.' Артём отмахну́л це́лых 15 лет в лагеря́х. Artem served the whole 15 years in labor camps.

отпе́тый ⊂ отпе́тый наро́д, 'lost causes,' prisoners regarded as incorrigible by the government. На известко́вом исключи́тельно отпе́тый наро́д. All the prisoners on the lime compound are lost causes. [AD, colloq.]

оттяну́ть, pf., 'to bully.' Нача́льник уча́стка оттяну́л норми́ровщика за опозда́ние в подгото́вке наря́дов. The camp section commandant bullied the norm-setter for the delay in preparing the work sheets.

оття́пать, pf., 'to beat up.' Сего́дня бригади́р оття́пал Его́ра за невы́ход на рабо́ту. Today the brigadier beat Egor for missing work. [AD, pop. 'to chop off']

отфуя́рить, pf., 'to serve a sentence.' Артём отфуя́рил по́лную кату́шку. Artem served a full 25-year stretch.

отштукату́рить, pf., 'to clean with fingers and tongue.' Си́доров дошёл до тако́й сте́пени, что он не мог воздержа́ться, чтобы не отштукату́рить ми́ску от ка́ши до бле́ска.

Sidorov wasted away to such a degree that he couldn't help licking his bowl until it shone. [AD, colloq. 'to plaster']

охвати́ть, pf., 'to fulfill.' Дава́й охва́тим но́рму до обе́да. Let's fulfill the quota before noon. [AD, to enfold, to embrace]

‡ **охоботи́ть, охоба́чивать,** 'to run through, to wear out.' Ско́лько Ефре́м э́тих баб охоба́чивал — предста́вить себе́ нельзя́. How many of these women Efrem had gone through he could not imagine. (Ра́ковый ко́рпус) [D, to whip into shape; to eat greedily]

‡ **О́ХРА, охра́на,** 'camp garrison.' *See* во́хра.

охра́нник, 'a guard,' either from the camp garrison, or a prisoner guard. Охра́нники окружи́ли всю коло́нну и на́чали обы́скивать всех поодино́чке. The guards surrounded the entire column and began to search everybody one by one. [AD, colloq.]

оцепле́ние, 'a work zone,' formed by the convoy at a detached work site, marked off by pennants and even containing a forbidden zone. The prisoners' work at the site is done within this zone. Как то́лько брига́да останови́лась, нача́льник конво́я установи́л бойцо́в в угла́х оцепле́ния и указа́л брига́де грани́цы зо́ны. As soon as the brigade stopped, the convoy chief stationed soldiers at the corners of a work zone and showed the boundaries to the brigade. [AD]

очки́ втере́ть очки́, 'to pull a fast one, hoodwink, deceive.' Наш бригади́р уме́л втира́ть очки́ и всегда́ выходи́л с хоро́шей вы́работкой. Our brigadier knew how to pull a fast one and always came out with a good output. [AD; F 180; St 137]

очковтира́тельство, 'hoodwinking, padding,' superficial execution of a work assignment only to be rid of it. Наш бригади́р не терпе́л очковтира́тельства, то́лько ча́сто приходи́лось ему́ по́льзоваться э́тим, что́бы прокорми́ть брига́ду. Our brigadier wouldn't tolerate work padding, but he frequently had to resort to it in order to feed the brigade. [AD, colloq.]

‡ **ошара́шиться,** pf., 'to get used to the *šaraška* (шара́шка, q.v.)' Спаси́бо, стари́к, но ты так ошара́шился, что забы́л ла́герные поря́дки. Thanks, old man, but you've gotten so used to the *šaraška* that you've forgotten the camp rules. (В кру́ге пе́рвом)

П, п

па́даль, 'carrion,' a strong abusive term. Береги́сь э́той па́дали, ведь он стука́ч, ведь он рабо́тает для ку́ма. Beware of that carrion, he's a squealer; he works for the security officer, you know. [AD, abusive sense not indicated]

па́дла, 'carrion,' a strong abusive term. Я бы уби́л э́ту па́длу [э́то па́дло]. I could murder that carrion! [D, abusive sense not indicated] *Also* па́дло.

па́дло. [D; KK] *See* па́дла.

паёк 1. 'the food ration,' consisting of a bread share and various amounts of cereal, meat, vegetables, and fats, depending on output, work category, and state of health of the prisoner. [AD] *See* па́йка, прива́рок. **2.** кро́вный ———, 'legal (lit., blood) ration,' the basic ration of food given to all prisoners. Ах, ты проститу́тка, чего́ глаза́ вы́лупил? Это же мой кро́вный [зако́нный] паёк. Ah, you whore! What are you staring at? This is my legal ration. *Also* зако́нный паёк. **3.** зако́нный ———. *See* meaning 2. **4.** больни́чный ———, 'hospital ration,' somewhat better quality food with a higher fat content. It is intended for the sick, but is also given for bribes to prisoner officials. Смотри́, все э́ти приду́рки получа́ют больни́чный паёк! Look! All those *priduroks* are getting the hospital ration. **5.** цинго́тный ———, 'scurvy ration,' a special dish for prisoners suffering from vitamin C deficiency. Во вре́мя войны́ почти́ всем заключённым необходи́мо бы́ло вы́писать цинго́тный паёк. During the war it was necessary to prescribe the scurvy ration for almost all the prisoners. **6.** уси́ленный ———, 'fortified ration,' prescribed by the medical commission for prisoners in danger of losing their ability to work. Степа́нову комиссо́вка вы́писала уси́ленный паёк. A decision of the medical commission prescribed a fortified ration for Stepanov. **7.** монта́жный ———, 'construction ration,' given prisoners working in construction camps for heavy industry. It consists of a spoonful of cereal and oil with a piece of meat.

На́шу брига́ду перевели́ на стро́йку ферроспла́вного це́ха; вся брига́да начала́ получа́ть монта́жный паёк. Our brigade was transferred to work on the construction of a ferroalloy shop; the entire brigade began to receive the construction ration. **8.** стаха́новский ———, 'Stakhanovite ration,' a special meat ration given to prisoners who exceed their quotas. This term, taken from free life, replaces the official designation, реко́рдный паёк, in camp usage. Си́доров вы́полнил но́рму на две́сти проце́нтов и получи́л стаха́новский паёк. Sidorov exceeded his norm by 200 percent and received the Stakhanovite ration. **9.** реко́рдный ———. *See* meaning 8. **10.** штрафно́й ———, 'penalty ration,' for prisoners who break camp rules. The bread portion is less than the guaranteed ration and the cooked food is less nutritious. Нача́льник посади́л Копыло́ва на штрафно́й паёк за отка́з от рабо́ты. The commandant put Kopylov on the penalty ration for refusal to work. **11.** сухо́й ———, 'dry ration,' cereal, flour, vegetables, salt, etc., issued to a prisoner or brigade working too far from camp for it to be convenient for the kitchen to deliver cooked food. Брига́да строи́телей рабо́тала далеко́ от зо́ны, и поэ́тому обе́д получа́ла сухи́м пайко́м. The construction brigade worked far from the compound and hence received a dry ration for lunch.

па́йка, 'bread share,' the bread portion of the food ration. Since prisoners frequently receive only bread (e.g., when being transported), this term is often loosely used for the food ration in general. Наш бригади́р закоси́л сто у́тренних па́ек хле́ба. Our brigadier finagled 100 morning shares of bread. [Tr] *Also* гаранти́йка, горбу́ша 2, пти́чка, горбы́ль. *See* паёк.

папа́н, indecl., 'the old man, father.' Он никогда́ не ви́дел своего́ папа́н. He never saw his old man. [AD, pop. 'папа́ня']

пара́ша 1. 'latrine pail.' Подтёлков просиде́л три го́да в тюрьме́, три го́да с воню́чей пара́шей под но́сом. Podtelkov was in prison for three years, three years with a stinking latrine pail under his nose. [AD, pop.; Tr] **2.** на пара́ше просиде́ть, 'to serve while sitting on the latrine pail,' said of a trifling sentence. Си́доров получи́л три го́да. Тако́й срок мо́жно на пара́ше просиде́ть. Sidorov got three years. Such a sentence can be served sitting on the latrine pail. **3.** 'scuttlebutt, gossip, rumor.' С нача́ла войны́ пошли́ пара́ши, что больша́я амни́стия бу́дет объя́влена к два́дцать пя́той годовщи́не

Октября́. At the beginning of the war the scuttlebutt was that a great amnesty would be announced in connection with the 25th anniversary of the October revolution. [KK]

пара́шник, 'rumormonger.' Не обраща́й внима́ния на э́того пара́шника. Don't pay any attention to that rumormonger. [D, one who cleans the latrine pail]

‡ **пара́шный,** 'latrine,'adj. И бара́ка что́-то не шли отпира́ть, и не слыха́ть бы́ло, что́бы днева́льные бра́ли бо́чку пара́шную на па́лки — выноси́ть. For some reason nobody came to open the barracks, and you couldn't hear the orderlies putting the latrine tank on poles to carry it out. (Оди́н день Ива́на Дени́совича)

парашюти́ст, ' "parachutist, " ' a prisoner who sleeps next to the latrine pail, пара́ша, in a crowded prison cell. The phonetic word play involved here cannot be translated into English. Гей, « парашюти́ст », отодви́нься немно́го. Мне ну́жно опра́виться. Hey, "parachutist," move over a bit. I have to use the latrine.

пари́лка, 'the steamer,' a very hot penalty cell, often used to break the spirit of new prisoners. Пе́рвые три дня в тюрьме́ я пробы́л в пари́лке, где така́я жари́ща была́, что мо́жно бы́ло подо́хнуть. I spent my first three days in prison in the steamer, where one could croak. [AD, pop. 'steam room']

па́спорт ⊂ па́спорт с ограниче́нием, 'restricted passport.' Various restrictions as to place of habitation and kinds of employment apply to different categories of citizens. The passports of ex-political prisoners and criminals are so marked as to identify them to the militia and security organs. При освобожде́нии большинство́ заключённых получа́ло па́спорт с ме́ньшим или бо́льшим ограниче́нием. Upon release most of the prisoners received a passport with a major or minor restriction.

паха́н, 'father; ringleader of a group of thieves,' who has attained the position by seniority and experience, and not necessarily by greater skill. The term is often used by prisoners to refer to Stalin. Паха́на [Поха́на] мо́жно бы́ло отличи́ть по лу́чшей оде́жде и разгово́ру. One could distinguish the ringleader by his better clothing and conversation. *Also* поха́н. [St 142, поха́н] *Cf.* жега́н.

пацáн, 'a teenager.' По́здно ве́чером вы́шел я из бара́ка;

гру́ппа пацано́в вы́скочила из-за угла́, обыска́ла меня́ и отняла́ после́днее. Late in the evening I stepped outside the barracks; a group of teenagers jumped me from behind the corner, searched me, and took everything. [AD, c. pop.; S 79; St 142]

паца́нка, fem. form of паца́н (q.v.).

пая́ть. *See* припая́ть.

пердя́чий ⊂ пердя́чим па́ром, 'by farting steam.' Во вре́мя войны́ те́хника в сове́тских лагеря́х стоя́ла на высо́ком у́ровне; рабо́ты производи́лись пердя́чим па́ром. During the war technology in Soviet camps stood at a high level; work was carried on by farting steam. В 1943-м году́ бара́ки в на́шей зо́не не ота́пливались; они́ обогрева́лись пердя́чим па́ром. In 1943 the barracks in our compound were unheated; they were warmed by farting steam. [D, перде́ть 'to fart loudly']

перевоспита́ние, 'reeducation,' an expression used by the Soviet authorities to describe the purpose of their prisons, in contrast to those of capitalistic countries. Первонача́льная цель лагере́й в Сове́тском Сою́зе была́ о́чень гума́нная; вла́сти ду́мали о перевоспита́нии [переко́вке] престу́пников и враго́в Сове́тского стро́я. The original purpose of camps in the Soviet Union was very humane; the authorities thought of the reeducation of criminals and enemies of the Soviet system. [AD] *Also* переко́вка.

перегна́ть ⊂ Догна́ть и перегна́ть капиталисти́ческие стра́ны. *See* догна́ть.

переда́ча, 'food or clothing parcel.' По́сле оконча́ния сле́дствия Си́доров получи́л от сле́дователя разреше́ние на переда́чи. After the conclusion of the investigation Sidorov got the interrogator's permission to receive parcels. [AD]

передо́к ⊂ слаба́ на передо́к, 'an easy lay, a willing sexual partner.' Зна́ешь, Ма́ша хоро́шая же́нщина, то́лько слаба́ на передо́к. You know, Maša is a good woman, but an easy lay. [D, the front part of something]

переки́нуться, pf., 'to die.' Си́доров на́чал доходи́ть и вся брига́да ду́мала, что он ско́ро переки́нется, но он вы́тянул благодаря́ посы́лкам от до́чери. Sidorov started to fail and the entire gang thought he would soon die. He pulled through thanks to the parcels his daughter sent him.

перекли́чка, 'roll call,' made on the job, in barracks, sometimes during the night. The prisoner is required to answer with his name and the provision under which he has been sentenced. Ве́чером надзира́тель вме́сте с коменда́нтом зашли́ в бара́к, веле́ли всем постро́иться и сде́лали перекли́чку. In the evening the supervisor and the barracks chief entered the barracks and ordered everyone to line up for a roll call. [AD]

переко́вка. [KK] *See* перевоспита́ние.

переку́р ⊂ переку́р с дремо́той, 'smoke break with a nap,' a camp expression for a longer-than-usual break, taken whenever the opportunity presented itself. Брига́да воспо́льзовалась моме́нтом, что бригади́р ушёл в конто́ру, что́бы сдать наря́ды, и все как оди́н легли́ на переку́р с дремо́той. The brigade took advantage of the moment that the brigadier went to the office to hand in the work sheet and the whole bunch lay down for a nap. [AD, colloq. переку́р]

переселе́ние ⊂ во́льное переселе́ние, 'a free settlement,' an expression often used ironically for a special settlement (спец-переселе́ние, q.v.), but, possibly, an official term for a special category of migrants enjoying somewhat more freedom than special settlers. За́ городом нахо́дится во́льное переселе́ние чече́нов. Outside town there is a free settlement of Chechens. [AD, переселе́ние 'a resettlement']

переси́дчик, '*peresídčik*,' a prisoner who completes his term, but is forced to remain in camp "until further notice." Большинство́ полити́ческих заключённых, срок кото́рых конча́лся в 1941-м году́, бы́ли оста́влены в лагеря́х, как переси́дчики, до специа́льного распоряже́ния. Most of the political prisoners whose terms ended in 1941 were left in camps as *peresídčiks* "until further notice."

пересле́дствие, 'a reinvestigation.' Ивано́ва вы́звали на пересле́дствие. Ivanov was called back for reinvestigation.

пересу́д, 'a retrial.' Ивано́ва вы́звали на пересу́д. Ivanov was called up for retrial. [AD, pop.]

пересы́лка. [AD, pop. obs.] *See* перпу́нкт.

перо́, 'a knife, a blade.' У́рки перо́м перехвати́ли гло́тку коменда́нту. The criminals cut the barracks chief's throat with a knife. [D, shank or butt of a dagger; Tr; F 183; To 200]

перпу́нкт, пересы́льный пункт, 'transit camp or prison.' Конво́й повёл нас со ста́нции на перпу́нкт [пересы́лку]. А convoy led us from the station to the transit camp. *Also* пере-сы́лка.

пёс. *See* соба́ка 2, су́ка 1.

петушо́к ⊂ быть по петушка́м, 'to be bosom friends.' Снача́ла наш бригади́р и наря́дчик бы́ли по петушка́м, а пото́м подра́лись из-за двуство́лки. At first our gang boss and the work allocator were bosom friends, but then they quarreled over a broad.

петь ⊂ кто пля́шет и поёт. *See* пляса́ть.

пизда́ ⊂ **1.** Где ра́ньше была́ со́весть, там пизда́ вы́росла. 'Where I once had a conscience, now a cunt has grown,' an expression indicating that civilizing luxuries, such as a conscience, have had to be sacrificed in order to survive in camp. « Как тебе́ не со́вестно заряжа́ть туфту́? » — « Где ра́ньше была́ со́весть, там пизда́ вы́росла ». "Why aren't you ashamed to pad your output?" "Where I once had a conscience, now a cunt has grown." **2.** ⊂ пиздо́й накры́ться, 'to drop dead.' Ивано́в иша́чил весь срок, пока́ пиздо́й не накры́лся. Ivanov worked like a dog his whole life until he dropped dead. **3.** Из пизды́ сда́чи нет. 'A cunt makes no change.' Ма́ша днева́льная поссо́рилась со свои́м еба́рём. После́дний потре́бовал обра́тно пода́ренные ей сапо́жки. Ма́ша отре́зала: « Из пизды́ сда́чи нет! » The orderly Maša had a quarrel with her lover. He demanded the return of the boots he had given her, but Maša snapped, "A cunt makes no change!" **4.** в пизду́ на переде́лку, 'unfit.' Смотри́ на э́того доходя́гу Ко́лю. Когда́-то рабо́тал молотобо́йцем, а тепе́рь хоть в пизду́ на переде́лку. Look at that goner Kolja. He used to work as a blacksmith's helper, but now he's completely unfit. **5.** пизда́-разбо́йница, 'a cunt' (lit., a cunt-bandit), a derogatory name for a woman. Ма́ша днева́льная — э́то настоя́щая пизда́-разбо́йница; она́ до тако́й сте́пени очертене́ла, что ни стыда́, ни со́вести не́ту в ней. The orderly Maša is a real cunt; she has become so possessed that she shows neither shame nor conscience. [D]

пиздёть. *See* пизди́ть.

пиздёц, 'the end.' Когда́ Ивано́ва посади́ли в изоля́тор, он сдре́фил и ду́мал, что ему́ пиздёц. When Ivanov was put in the isolator he was afraid because he thought his end had come. *Also* кры́шка, луна́.

пизди́ть, impf., 'to tell a lie.' Слу́шай, Ивано́в, не пизди́; и так зна́ю, кто утащи́л. Listen, Ivanov, don't lie; I know who stole it anyway. *Also* пиздéть.

пиздорва́нец. *See* пиздорва́нка.

пиздорва́нка, 'a cunt-ripper,' a derogatory term for both males and females. (Пиздорва́нец, by contrast, is applied only to males). Смотри́, э́та пиздорва́нка опя́ть нашко́дничала в бара́ке. Look, that cunt-ripper has made a nuisance of himself in the barracks again.

пиздю́лька, dim. of пиздю́ля (q.v.).

пиздю́ля 1. 'a runt, a pip-squeak,' an expression of contempt. Э́та пиздю́ля [пиздю́лька] из четвёртого бара́ка опя́ть побежа́ла к о́перу стуча́ть. That runt from the fourth barracks has squealed to the security officer again. Поду́маешь, э́та пиздю́ля [пиздю́лька] хоте́ла кома́ндовать мно́ю! Imagine, that runt wanted to boss me around! *Also* пиздю́лька. **2.** пиздю́лей наве́сить, 'to beat.' Клю́шкину наве́сили таки́х пиздю́лей, что весь день проваля́лся на на́рах. Kljuškin was beaten so badly that he stayed on the bed boards all day.

пи́ща ⊂ По́вар у нас замеча́тельный — пи́ща была́ горя́чая. *See* по́вар.

плева́ло. *See* заткну́ть.

плева́тельница. *See* заткну́ть.

площа́дка ⊂ прогу́лочная площа́дка, 'prison exercise ground,' divided into small sections and fenced so that prisoners cannot see from one to another. Надзира́тель вы́вел на́шу ка́меру на прогу́лочную площа́дку вну́тренней тюрьмы́. The supervisor led our cell to the exercise ground of the inner prison.

пляса́ть ⊂ кто пля́шет и поёт, 'who dance(s) and sing(s),' a phrase frequently said of the criminals since it very aptly describes their carefree life as compared to that of the political prisoners. [AD]

побе́г, 'escape.' Побе́ги в ла́гере удава́лись о́чень ре́дко. Escapes from camp were very rarely successful. [AD]

по́вар ⊂ По́вар у нас замеча́тельный — пи́ща была́ горя́чая. 'Our cook was excellent—the food was hot.' This expression signifies that the chief value of camp food is that it is hot.

пове́рка, 'a prisoner count.' Ежедне́вно пове́рка де́лалась во всех бара́ках лагере́й. Every day a prisoner count was made in all barracks in the camps. [AD]

погоре́ть, pf., 'to be caught red-handed.' Са́ша погоре́л и вследствие э́того получи́л пять лет. Saša was caught red-handed and as a result got five years. [AD, pop.]

поде́льник, 'accomplice.' Меня́ отпра́вили в Ни́жний Таги́л, а моего́ поде́льника в Карла́г. I was sent to Nižnij Tagil, and my accomplice was sent to Karlag (the Karaganda camp). *Also* однодéлец.

подкалы́мить, pf., 'to earn illegally.' Ва́ська пошёл помо́чь хлеборе́зу и подкалы́мил две бу́лки хле́ба. Vas'ka went to help the breadcutter and illegally earned two loaves of bread.

подки́дыш, 'a plant, an informer.' Из разгово́ра с сока́мерником я скуме́кал, что он подки́дыш. From talking with my cellmate, I gathered that he was a plant. [AD, abandoned child] *Also* наса́дка, насе́дка, подсы́пка.

подлю́га, 'carrion.' Карзу́бый был таки́м крохобо́ром, что в со́бственной брига́де таска́л; бригади́р предупреди́л его́: « Придушу́, подлю́га, е́сли хоть одну́ па́йку ута́щишь в брига́де ». Karzubyj was such a crumb snatcher that he would steal from his own gang. The brigadier warned him, "I'll smother you, you carrion, if you steal so much as one bread ration from this gang." [AD, pop. abusive 'scoundrel']

подмахну́ть, pf., 1. 'to sign a document without reading it.' Короле́нко так был истощён шестимеся́чным сле́дствием, что, не чита́я протоко́лов допро́са, подмахну́л все докуме́нты. Korolenko was so exhausted by the six-month-long investigation that, without reading the investigation records, he carelessly signed all the documents. [AD, colloq.] 2. 'to permit to have intercourse.' Ма́ша подмахну́ла вещстолу́ и он вы́писал ей но́вое бельё. Maša gave herself to the clothing clerk and he signed out new underwear for her.

подна́чить, подна́чивать, 'to egg on, to encourage.' Брига́да подна́чивала обо́их доходя́г так, что после́дние перешли́ из ссо́ры в дра́ку. The brigade egged on both goners until they finally came to blows. [AD, с. pop.; Tr]

подо́нки, pl., 'the dregs of the camp soup.' Копыло́в ждал под око́шком ку́хни, что́бы получи́ть подо́нки от своего́ земляка́-по́вара. Kopylov waited at the kitchen window to receive the dregs from his fellow countryman, the cook. [AD]

подо́хнуть, до́хнуть ⊂ 1. Подо́хни [Умри́] ты сего́дня, а я за́втра! 'Croak [Die] today if you wish, but I'll wait till tomorrow,' an expression of the prisoners' desire to outlive one another, even by a day. [DPos 613, Дай Бог умереть хоть сегодня, только не нам] **2. Привы́кнешь!** — а не привы́кнешь, подóхнешь. *See* привы́кнуть 1. [AD, to die (of animals); pf. only c. pop. 'to die (of people)'] **3.** impf. only, 'to be crapped out' [i.e., asleep]. Смотри́, Васю́к, там фрáйер на нáрах дóхнет — нáдо егó обрабóтать. Look, Vasjuk, there's a pigeon crapped out on the bed boards. We must clean him out.

подрубáть, рубáть. [KK, impf. only] *See* пошáмать.

подслéдственный, 'a prisoner under investigation.' Мнóгие подслéдственные в лагеря́х выходи́ли на рабóту в бригáдах уси́ленного режи́ма. Many prisoners under investigation in the camps went to work in strict discipline brigades. [AD]

подстрели́ть, подстрельну́ть, both pf., **стреля́ть,** 'to hit up for something, to finagle, to get by guile.' Ники́та подстрельну́л оку́рок от начáльника конвóя и пригласи́л своегó лу́чшего дру́га Петрóва, чтóбы покури́ть. Nikita hit up the convoy chief for a butt and invited his best friend Petrov to have a smoke. Вáнька никогдá табаку́ не покупáл; он всё врéмя стреля́л табачóк. Van'ka never bought tobacco; he finagled butts all the time. [AD, impf. only, pop. 'to beg'; S 79, to beg; St 135, to steal]

подсы́пка. *See* насéдка.

подфарти́ть, pf., 'to be lucky.' Волóде подфарти́ло [пофарти́ло] сегóдня; он сви́стнул си́дор у нацмéна из нóвого этáпа. Volodja had good luck today; he stole a parcel from an Asiatic (lit., a member of any national minority) who came with the last transport. *Also* пофарти́ть.

подхали́м. [AD] *See* жóпочник.

подхалимáж, 'toadyism, brown-nosing.' И́горь вы́жил 15 лет в лагеря́х подхалимáжем. Igor' survived 15 years in camps by toadyism. [AD, colloq.]

подхалту́рить, халту́рить, 'to moonlight, to work at an additional job.' Кóля халту́рил на сторонé; в свобóдное врéмя ходи́л помогáть хлеборéзу рéзать пáйки. Kolja was moonlighting; in his free time he used to help the breadcutter cut the bread shares. [AD, colloq. impf. only]

подшухéрить, pf., 'to swipe, to steal.' Ефи́м подшухéрил одея́ло из каптёрки и срáзу прóдал егó за две пáйки хлéба.

Efim swiped a blanket from the clothing warehouse and sold it at once for two shares of bread.

подъём 1. 'reveille, signal to fall in' (at the end of a break). Са́мый стра́шный моме́нт в мое́й ла́герной жи́зни — э́то был подъём. The most terrifying moment in camp life was reveille. [AD] **2.** Подъём бу́дет, не буди́. / Развод бу́дет, не буди́. / Обе́д бу́дет, два ра́за буди́. 'Reveille will come, don't wake me. / Time to work will come, don't wake me. / When it's dinner time, wake me twice,' a saying which expresses the desire of the prisoners to be awakened to eat, but not to work.

поеба́ть, еба́ть 1. 'to mistreat, to fuck.' « Кака́я житу́ха в Китла́ге? » — « Лу́чше не спра́шивай — ебу́т в хвост и в гри́ву ». "What's it like in Kitlag (the Kitoj camp)?" "Better not ask—you are fucked at every turn." **2.** —— мозги́, 'to bug, to annoy with tedious questions' (lit., to brain-fuck). Не еби́ мозги́! Don't bug me! *Cf.* мозгоеба́тель. [D, see his ети́]

показу́ха 1. 'a braggart.' Си́доров был таки́м показу́хой, что в брига́де никто́ не ве́рил ни одному́ сло́ву его́. Sidorov was such a braggart that no one in the brigade believed a word he said. **2.** 'a front.' А всё э́то показу́ха, не обраща́й внима́ния на э́то. All that is a front—don't pay any attention to it. [KK]

покури́ть, pf., 'to take a break' (lit., to have a smoke). The word is so used in camps even though tobacco often is not to be had. Дава́й поку́рим! Let's take a break! [AD]

полко́вник, 'a "colonel,"' someone in the second stage of syphilis. Ма́ша, остерега́йся Си́дорова, лекпо́м сказа́л мне, что он « полко́вник ». Maša, watch out for Sidorov; the medic told me that he's a "colonel." *Cf.* лейтена́нт, генера́л.

положе́ние ⊂ положе́ние о паспорта́х, 'passport statute.' Passports of ex-political prisoners are so marked as to identify them to the militia and other security organs. На основа́нии положе́ния о паспорта́х я был лишён пра́ва прожива́ть в областны́х города́х Сове́тского Сою́за. On the basis of the passport statute I was deprived of the right to reside in the district capitals of the Soviet Union. [AD]

полти́нники, pl. **1.** 'eyes.' Гей, хе́вра, держи́ полти́нники [бля́хи] откры́тыми! Hey, gang, keep your eyes open! [aLi 79] **2.** —— разу́ть, 'to gape, to gawk.' Гей, фра́йер, чего́ полти́нники [бля́хи] разу́л? Hey, pigeon, what are you gawking at? [AD, colloq. полти́нник 'fifty kopeks'] *Also* бля́хи.

‡ **полуцвéт,** 'a would-be, or self-styled criminal.' Пéрвым таки́м лез какóй-то бесновáтый кривля́ка, котóрого незнáющий человéк при́нял бы за психопáта … но Олéг за э́тим психопáтом срáзу узнáл полуцвéта с э́той обы́чной для них манéрой пугáть. The first such [line breaker] was a raving fellow whom an ignorant person would take for a psychopath … but Oleg immediately recognized him as a would-be criminal playing his usual role to frighten people. (Рáковый кóрпус) *Cf.* блатнóй 1, цветнóй

‡ **полуцветнóй,** 'self-styled criminal,' pertaining to полуцвéт (q.v.). Дешёвка полуцветнáя, лечи́ть я егó бýду! The cheap, phony crook! Am I supposed to treat him!? (Олéнь и шалашóвка)

поматюгáться, матюгáться. [D] *See* матери́ться.

поми́лование 1. 'pardon, mercy.' В слýчае пригóвора к вы́сшей мéре наказáния заключённый имéл тóлько прáво проси́ть о поми́ловании. In the event of a death sentence the prisoner had only the right to ask for a pardon. [AD] **2.** 'an appeal for a pardon,' loosely used by prisoners for прóсьба о поми́ловании. Он написáл поми́лование. He wrote an appeal for a pardon.

‡ **помóечник,** 'slop swiller.' Сýка позóрная. Помóечник воню́чий! Не подходи́! Пéрвого зарéжу! Испишýсь! You shameless bastard, you stinking slop swiller, stay back! I'll cut your throat first, then kill myself! (Олéнь и шалашóвка)

помóйщик, 'garbage-picker,' usually a goner who searches through garbage and refuse heaps for peels, rinds, and other scraps. Смотри́ на э́того помóйщика; говоря́т, что он был уважáемым учи́телем в Москвé. Look at that garbage-picker; they say he was a respected teacher in Moscow.

помóщник ⊂ помóщник прокурóра, ' "prosecutor's assistant," ' ironic name for a defense lawyer, so-called because he aids the prosecutor more than the defendant out of fear of being accused of disloyalty to the state. Судéбные óрганы предложи́ли мне взять « помóщника прокурóра », но я отказáлся, потомý что из своегó óпыта знал, что лýчше бýду без негó. The court offered me a "prosecutor's assistant," but I refused because I knew from experience that I would be better off without one.

помпобы́т, помóщник по бы́ту, 'a column chief's deputy,' in charge of food and clothing. Помпобы́т колóнны смотрéл за вещевы́м и проду́ктовым снабже́нием коло́нны. The deputy column chief looked after the clothing and food supply of the column.

поно́сник, 'a diarrhetic,' a derogatory name frequently applied to goners, since diarrhea is a common symptom among them. Смотри́! Брига́ду поно́сников повели́ в сельхо́з. Look! They've led a gang of diarrhetics to the agricultural zone.

‡ **поно́сница,** 'fem. form of поно́сник (q.v.).' (Оле́нь и шала́шовка)

понт 1. ⊂ взять на понт. *See* взять 2. ‡ **2.** 'a bluff, a pretense.' Вы́шел из двере́й Це́зарь, жмётся — с по́нтом больно́й. Cezar' came out of the door all bent over, trying to look sick. (Оди́н день Ива́на Дени́совича)

по́пка, 'a screw,' a derogatory name for a guard. Как то́лько мы вы́шли за ва́хту, по́пки [вертуха́и, попуга́и] окружи́ли нас и повели́ к ме́сту рабо́ты. As soon as we got past the guard shack, the screws surrounded us and led us to the work site. [aLi 80, police agent] *Also* вертуха́й, попуга́й.

попроша́йка, 'a scrounge,' usually a goner who is unable to resist begging, even though knowing he will receive only a blow for his efforts. Э́тот попроша́йка опя́ть подошёл к стола́м, чтобы умоля́ть ка́ждого о подо́нках. The scrounge again went up to the tables to beg everyone for the dregs. [AD, colloq.]

попуга́й. *See* по́пка.

попыха́йло, 'a work pusher,' an assistant to the gang boss responsible for pushing the prisoners to greater effort. Попыха́йло [Попыха́ч] на́шего бригади́ра был зверь-зверём, ху́же самого́ бригади́ра Воло́ди. Our work pusher was a real beast, worse than the brigadier Volodja himself. *Also* попыха́ч.

попыха́ч. *See* попыха́йло.

портя́нка, 'a foot cloth,' never washed, but disinfected from time to time. Мои́ портя́нки рассы́пались, а до разда́чи но́вой оде́жды остава́лось бо́льше трёх ме́сяцев. My foot cloths were in tatters, and it was more than three months until a new clothing issue. [AD]

пору́ка ⊂ кругова́я пору́ка, 'a mutual guarantee,' wherein the members of the group are responsible for each other's actions. З/к пе́ред отпра́вкой на сеноко́с вы́нуждены бы́ли подписа́ть кругову́ю пору́ку. Before being sent to the hay harvest prisoners had to sign a mutual-responsibility declaration. [AD]

поселе́ние ⊂ во́льное поселе́ние, 'a free settlement,' for free employees and ex-prisoners who work in a camp. В каки́х-нибудь 300 шага́х от зо́ны начина́лись постро́йки во́льного поселе́ния [посёлка]. Some 300 paces from the compound the buildings of the free settlement began. *Also* во́льный посёлок.

посёлок ⊂ во́льный посёлок. [AD] *See* поселе́ние.

пососа́ть, pf., 'to finish smoking a cigarette butt' (by sucking the last tiny bit through the fingers). Дай хоть пососа́ть табачо́к. Let me just finish up the butt. [AD, to suck for a while] *Also* затяну́ть.

потаску́ха, 'a whore.' Э́та потаску́ха опя́ть поле́зла на ночь в мужску́ю зо́ну. That whore has again gone to the men's compound for the night. [AD, pop., with contemptuous shade]

пофарти́ть. *See* подфарти́ть.

поха́н. *See* паха́н.

пошака́лить, шака́лить 1. 'to scavenge, to scrounge.' Невзира́я на то, что Орло́в на́чал получа́ть посы́лки из до́ма, он продолжа́л шака́лить по помо́йкам. In spite of the fact that Orlov started to receive parcels from home, he continued to scavenge in the trash heaps. **2.** 'to pillage, to rob.' Са́мое ужа́сное в жилзо́не бы́ли малоле́тки, кото́рые шака́лили на одино́чных з/к, выходи́вших на опра́вку; отнима́ли после́дний табачо́к, па́йку или ма́йку. The most appalling thing about the living zone was the presence of the teenagers. They would rob prisoners going to the latrine alone and take their tobacco, bread ration, or their undershirt.

пошама́ть, ша́мать, 'to eat.' Ивано́в получи́л продово́льственную посы́лку от свое́й ма́тери. Полови́ну проду́ктов он пошама́л [подруба́л] в пе́рвый же ве́чер. Ivanov received a food parcel from his mother. He ate half the food on the very first evening. [AD, с. pop.; S 75; To 399] *Also* подруба́ть.

пошуруди́ть. *See* шуруди́ть.

ППЧ [pe-pe-čé], произво́дственно-пла́новая часть, 'PPČ,' the production planning section, responsible for preparing annual production plans. In some camps, this office is called КПЧ (q.v.). На́ше ППЧ получи́ло вы́говор за опозда́ние в приготовле́нии произво́дственного пла́на. Our PPČ was reprimanded for a delay in the preparation of a production plan.

правилка, 'a vest,' symbol of authority among the criminals. «Кто у вас пахан?» — «Тот в правилке». "Who's ringleader here?" "The one in the vest."

правосудие ⊂ советское правосудие [*also* пролетарское], 'Soviet [proletarian] justice.' Советское [Пролетарское] правосудие решило заменить тебе смертный приговор 25 годами. Soviet [Proletarian] justice has decided to commute your death sentence to 25-years' imprisonment.

предварилка. [AD, pop. obs.] *See* КПЗ.

премвознаграждение, премиальное вознаграждение, 'a premium,' awarded for exceeding one's labor quota. For fulfilling less than 100 percent, a prisoner receives nothing. В 1942-м году только за один месяц начислили мне премвознаграждение в сумме двадцати рублей. In 1942 for one month only I was credited with a premium in the amount of 20 rubles.

преступление ⊂ Человек должен только существовать, а преступление найдётся. *See* человек 2.

приварок, 'cooked food,' the portion of the food ration received from the kitchen. This part of the ration is also referred to by the terms каша, баланда, and котёл. Пайка в Карлаге была такая самая, только приварок—куда лучше. The bread ration in Karlag (the Karaganda camp) was the same, but the cooked food was far superior. [AD, pop. tech.] *See* паёк.

привыкнуть, привыкать ⊂ 1. Привыкнешь! — а не привыкнешь, подохнешь. 'You'll get used to it, and if not, then you'll croak,' advice given to a fellow prisoner to adapt to camp conditions or perish. 2. Первых пять лет трудновато, а потом привыкаешь. 'The first five years are rather hard, but then you get used to it,' an ironic response to the question, "How is it in camp?"

придуриваться, impf., 'to be on an easy job.' Мой шурин придуривался весь срок; сначала работал каптёром, а потом приземлился в культбригаде. My brother-in-law had it easy his whole term; at first he worked as a supply clerk and later he landed a job in the entertainment brigade.

‡ **придурня,** coll., '*priduroks* (придурок, q.v.).' Но спорить с ними было бесполезно: у придурни меж собой спайка и с надзирателями тоже. The *priduroks* were as thick as thieves and were in good with the overseers too. (Один день Ивана Денисовича)

придýрок, '*pridurok*,' a prisoner who has landed an easy job by camp standards, such as cook, orderly, breadcutter, cafeteria manager, barber, and the like. На нáшем учáстке все придýрки получáли больнúчный котёл. In our section all the *priduroks* received the hospital ration.

приземлúться, pf., 'to land a job.' Моемý шýрину повезлó в лагеря́х; он приземлúлся [зацепúлся] в хлеборéзке. My brother-in-law was lucky in camp; he landed a job at the breadcutter's. [AD, aviation, sports 'to land on earth'; KK] *Also* зацепúться.

принудúловка, принудúтельные рабóты, 'forced labor.' Шýра ожидáл освобождéния, а емý суд вкатúл пять лет принудúловки. Šura expected to go free, but the court sentenced him to five years of forced labor. [AD, pop. 'forced labor without loss of liberty']

припая́ть, пая́ть, 'to pin (a provision on someone), to accuse under a provision.' Бéдному Иванóву припая́ли 58.6 и дáли емý пóлную катýшку. They pinned article 58.6 on poor Ivanov and gave him a full 25-year stretch. [AD, pop. 'to solder'; KK]

припýхнуть, припухáть 1. 'to sleep, to rest.' Во врéмя войны́ выходны́е давáлись рéдко в лагеря́х; я был до такóй стéпени измóтан, что весь выходнóй день припухáл на нáрах. During the war days off were a rarity in camps. I was so exhausted that I would sleep the whole day through on the bed boards. Волóдя, хвáтит ишáчить, давáй припýхнем! Volodja, that's enough working like a dog; let's rest a little. **2.** impf. only, 'to be a goner; to wait idly by on a very low ration.' Я припухáл пять лет на Воркýте и éле вы́рвался оттýда живьём. I was a goner for five years in Vorkuta and I just managed to escape from there alive. Два мéсяца мы припухáли на пересы́лке. We idled away two months at the transit camp on a goner's ration.

приспúчить, pf., 'to pin (a provision on someone), to accuse under a provision.' Прокурóр приспúчил Иванóву измéну рóдине. The prosecutor pinned treason on Ivanov.

причáпать, чáпать, 'to creep.' Алёша тóлько причáпал на бан, и тут егó ляга́вые накры́ли. Aleša had just crept up to the station when the dicks caught him. Что ты чáпаешь, как мёртвый? Why do you creep around like a dead man?

пришúть, pf. 1. 'to pin (a provision on someone), to accuse under a provision.' Сле́дователь приши́л Си́дорову сабота́ж. The interrogator pinned sabotage on Sidorov. [AD, c. pop. 'to stitch'; Tr, приши́ть кого́ 'to implicate falsely'] **2.** ——— перо́м, 'to stab.' Но́чью у́рки приши́ли перо́м коменда́нта БУ́Ра. The criminals stabbed the BUR (strict discipline barracks) commandant during the night. [AD, c. pop. 'to kill'; F 180, пришить в доску 'to kill'; To 418, to kill] **3.** ——— запла́ту обра́тно, 'to add to a sentence a portion of it already served.' Борду́лин получи́л 15 лет. По́сле трёх лет ла́герный суд приши́л ему́ обра́тно запла́ту. Bordulin was sentenced to 15 years. After three years a camp court added the three years already served onto his sentence.

пришпо́рить, pf., 'to pin (a provision on someone), to accuse under a provision.' О́пер пришпо́рил Фроло́ву антисове́т-скую агита́цию. The security officer pinned anti-Soviet agitation on Frolov. [AD, to spur]

прове́рка, 'a special prisoner count,' carried out at irregular intervals, as, for example, when the regular check reveals a discrepancy, after an escape, or during an inventory. Но́чью побе́г из зо́ны случи́лся. Надзира́тель вы́строил всех в бара́ке и сде́лал прове́рку. During the night there was an escape from the compound. The supervisor got everybody in the barracks up and conducted a special count. [AD, verification]

проглотну́ть ⊂ проглотну́ть язы́к, 'to hold (lit., swallow) one's tongue.' Сове́тую тебе́ проглотну́ть язы́к, а то кры́шка. I advise you to hold your tongue, or it's curtains for you. [AD, проглоти́ть язы́к]

прогу́л, 'absenteeism' (or excessive tardiness). Си́дорову припая́ли два го́да за прогу́л. They pinned two years on Sidorov for absenteeism. [AD]

прогу́льщик, 'an absentee.' Воло́дя отказа́лся рабо́тать; по́сле бесполе́зных угово́ров нача́льник уча́стка отпра́вил его́, как зло́стного прогу́льщика, на штрафну́ю командиро́вку. Volodja refused to work; when the commandant couldn't persuade him to change his mind, he was shipped to a penalty assignment as a malicious absentee. [AD]

продкапте́р, from заве́дующий продкапте́ркой, 'food clerk,' a prisoner in charge of the food storage. Ивано́в по́сле рабо́ты халту́рил; помога́л продкапте́рку па́йки ре́зать. Ivanov used to moonlight after work; he helped the food clerk cut the bread shares.

продкаптёрка, продовóльственная каптёрка, 'food supply.' Орлóв прúнял продкаптёрку, и чéрез два мéсяца посадúли егó за недостáчу. Orlov took over the food supply and in two months was imprisoned for a shortage.

продстóл 1. продовóльственный стол, 'food distribution desk,' office where the list of food due each prisoner is prepared. This list goes to the food storage, where the cook picks up a portion to be cooked, and where the gang boss or orderly picks up the bread for the gang. Наш продстóл помещáлся в контóре учáстка. Our food distribution desk was located in the section office. **2.** from начáльник продстолá, 'food distribution clerk,' a prisoner in charge of the food distribution desk, a most desirable job in camp, since it is possible to steal food there. Продстóл вúписал бригадúру трúдцать восемсóток и три пятьсóтки. The food distribution clerk signed out to the brigadier thirty 800-gram rations of bread and three 500-gram rations.

прожáрка, 'the disinfection of clothing.' Заключённые дрожáли от хóлода, дожидáясь вещéй из прожáрки. The prisoners shivered from cold while waiting for their clothing to be disinfected. [AD, colloq.]

прожúть ⊂ Не украдёшь, не проживёшь. *See* укрáсть.

произвóл, 'criminal justice,' domination by criminals, resulting from the indifference and inaction of the camp garrison. Одúн произвóл был в Китлáге в 1948-м годý. In 1948 there was only criminal justice in Kitlag (the Kitoj camp). [AD]

проишáчить, ишáчить, 'to work like a dog' (lit., ass). Иванóв проишáчил цéлый день, а вéчером éле нóги волочúл домóй. Ivanov worked like a dog the whole day, and in the evening could scarcely drag himself home. Идú рабóтать; ведь тебé на лбу напúсано « ишáчить ». Get to work. After all, "Work like a dog" is writ large on your face. [AD, pop. ишáчить only]

прокантовáться, кантовáться, 'to shirk, to goof off.' Иванóв кантовáлся всю зúму в зóне. The whole winter Ivanov goofed off in camp.

прокурóр 1. ⊂ Прокурóр медвéдь, а хозяин черпáк. 'The prosecutor is a bear, but the ladle is your master.' This proverb describes the contrast between the prosecutor or other duly constituted authority on the one hand and the necessity of adapting oneself to unwritten camp rules on the other. Survival in camps means an unceasing struggle for enough to eat (the ladle). **2.** зелёный прокуро́р, 'green prosecutor,' a term used for nature in the spring and summer. The term may imply that, although conditions are difficult, it is preferable to take one's chances with nature than to remain in camp. Фе́дя Косо́й сорва́лся к зелёному прокуро́ру. Fedja Kosoj (the squint-eyed) escaped to the green prosecutor.

промзо́на, промы́шленная зо́на, 'industrial zone,' the work zone in an industrial camp. В актю́бинском ла́гере большинство́ з/к рабо́тало в промзо́не. In the Aktjubinsk camp most of the prisoners worked in the industrial zone.

промо́т, 'illegal sale, or loss, of government property.' Си́дорова суди́ли за промо́т; доба́вили ему́ три го́да. Sidorov was tried for selling government property; he was given an additional three years. [D, squandering, wasting]

промота́ть, pf., 'to sell illegally, or lose, government property.' Ко́ля промота́л казённую гимнастёрку и одея́ло; он получи́л за э́то три па́йки хле́ба. Kolja sold a government-issue blouse and blanket; he got three shares of bread for them. [AD, colloq. 'to squander, to waste']

промо́тчик, '*promotčik*,' one who sells illegally, or loses, government property. Нача́льник реши́л всех промо́тчиков отда́ть под суд. The commandant decided to bring all *promotčiks* to trial. [D, one who squanders, wastes]

пропа́длина, 'carrion,' derogatory name often used for someone who serves as an informer for the authorities. It is a somewhat stronger term than па́дла (q.v.). Си́доров пропа́длина опя́ть настуча́л на Ивано́ва. That carrion Sidorov squealed on Ivanov again.

про́пуск ⊂ про́пуск на рабо́те, 'absenteeism.' Ивано́в за про́пуск на рабо́те был приговорён к трём года́м лише́ния свобо́ды. Ivanov was sentenced to three years' deprivation of liberty for absenteeism. [AD]

пропусти́ть ⊂ пропусти́ть хо́ром, 'to gang-bang,' to rape by a group of men. Повари́ха привезла́ обе́д к брига́де тракто-ри́стов, и вся брига́да пропусти́ла её хо́ром. The cook took lunch out to a gang of tractor operators, and the whole brigade gang-banged her.

прора́б, производи́тель рабо́т, 'work superintendent,' a prisoner, often a well-known architect, responsible for a construction project. Прора́б был о́чень взволно́ван, потому́ что ни одна́ брига́да не вы́полнила но́рмы. The work superintendent was very disturbed because not a single gang fulfilled its norm. [AD]

‡ **прора́бской,** 'pert. to прора́б (q.v.).' Ко́мнат в конто́ре две. Второ́й, прора́бской, дверь недоприкры́та, и отту́да го́лос прора́ба греми́т. There were two rooms in the office. The second one, the work superintendent's, had the door ajar and you could hear the superintendent shouting in there. (Один день Ивана Денисовича)

просиде́ть, сиде́ть, 'to serve a term as punishment.' [AD]

прохоря́, pl., 'leather boots.' Чече́н из после́днего эта́па так кре́пко спал но́чью, что я суме́л стяну́ть его́ прохоря́ и он да́же не просну́лся. A Chechen from the last transport slept so soundly last night that I was able to pull his boots off and he didn't even wake up.

‡ **процентова́ть,** pf. and impf., 'to set a work quota.' Това́рищ прора́б. Как же мне люде́й процентова́ть? Я тогда́ акт простоя́ соста́влю. Comrade work superintendent. How can I set a work quota for these people? I'll just make out a report that there's no work for them. (Олень и шалашовка)

проценто́вка, 'percentage of work,' the fulfillment of which is the basis for determining the prisoners' ration. Наш бригади́р закры́л наря́д наш с о́чень ни́зкой проценто́вкой. Our brigadier closed our work assignment with a very low percentage.

прошмона́ть, шмона́ть, 'to frisk, to search.' Ежедне́вно два́жды шмона́ли брига́ды, раз при разво́де, а второ́й раз, когда́ работя́ги возвраща́лись в зо́ну. The brigades were frisked twice each day, once at the march off to work and a second time when the workers were returning to the compound. *Cf.* прошмони́ть, шмони́ть, шмоня́ть.

‡ **прошмони́ть, прошма́нивать,** 'to frisk.' По ме́ре того́, как этапи́руемых ареста́нтов сгоня́ли в штаб тюрьмы́, — их шмони́ли, а по ме́ре того́, как их прошма́нивали — их перегоня́ли в запасну́ю пусту́ю ко́мнату. As those being transported were rounded up in prison headquarters, they were frisked. And when they had been frisked they were taken into an empty spare room. (В круге пе́рвом) *Cf.* прошмона́ть, шмони́ть, шмоня́ть.

проштра́фиться, pf., 'to commit a misdemeanor.' In camps, this can result in having one's bonuses cancelled, or in incarceration in the isolator. Салтыко́в проштра́фился на убо́рке карто́феля и его́ отпра́вили на кирпи́чный заво́д, где рабо́та была́ непоси́льная. Saltykov committed a misdemeanor during the potato harvest and was transferred to the brick yard, where the labor was beyond his strength. [AD, colloq.]

псих, 'a psycho,' a psychopath or a neurotic. In camps, criminals would often pretend to be crazy in order to terrorize and intimidate camp newcomers. Карзу́бый притворя́лся пси́хом всю доро́гу, и таки́м о́бразом терроризи́ровал фра́йеро́в. Karzubyj pretended to be psycho the whole way and thus terrorized the pigeons. [AD, pop. 'mentally unbalanced person']

психова́ть, 'to pretend to be psycho.' Чума́, чтобы напуга́ть фра́йеро́в, ча́сто психова́л. Все боя́лись его́, как огня́. Čuma, in order to frighten the pigeons, often pretended to be psycho. Everyone feared him like fire. [AD, pop. 'to be nervous']

пти́чка, 'the bread ration.' Надзира́тель откры́л корму́шку и пти́чки [птю́шки] на́чали залета́ть в ка́меру. The supervisor opened the food hatch and the bread rations began to fly into the cell. *Also* птю́шка. *See* па́йка.

ПТЧ [pe-te-čé], произво́дственно-техни́ческая часть, 'РТČ,' production technical section, found only in industrial camps, responsible for highly technical planning. Са́шка прорабо́тал три го́да в ПТЧ. Saška worked in the PTČ for three years.

птю́шка. *See* пти́чка.

пу́зо ⊂ 1. Чем добру́ пропада́ть, лу́чше пусть пу́зо ло́пнет. *See* добро́. 2. нае́сться от пу́за, 'to overeat.' Серко́в сра́зу, как получи́л посы́лку от жены́, нае́лся от пу́за, а но́чью пришло́сь вы́звать лекпо́ма, чтобы спасти́ его́. As soon as he got the parcel from his wife, Serkov overate, and during the night the medic had to be called to save his life. [AD, pop. 'belly']

пузырёк ⊂ лезть в пузырёк. [S 76] *See* лезть.

пуля́ть, impf., 'to slip, to pass, to pay.' Нача́льник уча́стка дал поня́ть капте́ру, чтобы пуля́л два куска́; в проти́вном слу́чае он угрожа́л ему́ сня́тием с рабо́ты. The camp section commandant let the supply clerk know that he wanted to be slipped 2000 rubles. Otherwise he threatened to fire him. [AD, pop. 'to shoot; to throw']

пункт 1. отде́льный ла́герный ———, 'camp sub-section,' a part of a camp section, detached from the rest for economic or other reasons. Наш отде́льный ла́герный пункт [ОЛП, отделе́ние ла́герного пу́нкта] находи́лся в двадцати́ киломе́трах от центра́льного уча́стка, и мы снабжа́лись от центра́льного уча́стка. Our camp sub-section was 20 kilometers from the central camp section, and we were supplied from there. *Also* ОЛП, отделе́ние ла́герного пу́нкта. **2.** ла́герный ———. *See* уча́сток.

пусти́ть ⊂ пусти́ть в расхо́д, 'to liquidate.' Генера́ла Вла́сова суди́ли в Москве́ и пусти́ли в расхо́д. General Vlasov was tried in Moscow and liquidated. [AD, pop.]

п/я, почто́вый я́щик, 'POB,' post office box. [K]

пятачо́к 1. 'a gold five-ruble coin' (in gold smugglers' argot). Ивано́в ослу́шался прика́за прави́тельства о сда́че зо́лота госуда́рству. В 1937-м году́, во вре́мя о́быска, обнару́жили у него́ не́сколько деся́тков пятачко́в. Ivanov disobeyed the government's order to turn in gold. In 1937, during a search, several dozen gold five-ruble coins were found in his possession. [AD, colloq. 'a five-kopek coin'] **2.** всё на пятачке́, 'everything is perfect, fine.' « Как у вас дела́? » — « Всё на пятачке́ ». "How are things?" "Fine."

пя́тушки ⊂ дава́й по пя́тушкам, 'let's shake on it, let's shake hands.' Бригади́р и наря́дчик поспо́рили из-за Ма́ши; в конце́ наря́дчик сказа́л: « Слу́шай, Воло́дя, из-за пизды́ дра́ться не бу́дем. Дава́й по пя́тушкам ». The gang boss and the work assigner got into an argument over Maša. Finally the work assigner said, "Listen, Volodja, let's not fight over a cunt. Let's shake hands." [AD, пять 'five']

Р, р

рабóта 1. вспомогáтельная ———, 'auxiliary work,' for which no quotas can be established. This category includes the maintenance crew and such staff workers as orderlies, cooks, clerks, barbers, bathhouse managers, and the like. Когдá объявúли зачёты, все, дáже доходя́ги, старáлись перейтú с вспомогáтельных на основнúе рабóты. When bonuses were announced, everyone, even the goners, tried to switch from auxiliary to basic work. *Cf.* meaning 2. **2.** основнáя ———, 'basic work,' for which quotas can be established. Мой шýрин был год на основнúх рабóтах, и получúл зачёты по два с половúной дня за день. My brother-in-law spent a year at basic work and received bonuses of two and a half days per day. *Cf.* meaning 1. **3.** с вúводом на рабóту, 'with work as usual,' a phrase usually added to sentences to periods in the penalty cells. Бородýлин попáлся с ножóм во врéмя шмóна. Егó посадúли в кáрцер с вúводом на рабóту. A knife was found on Borodulin during a frisk. He was put in the cooler with work as usual. **4.** óбщая ———. *See* основáния. **5.** Дурáк рабóту лю́бит, и рабóта дуракá лю́бит. *See* дурáк 1. **6.** Лýчше кáшки не долóжь, но рабóтой не тревóжь. *See* кáшка. **7.** От рабóты лóшади дóхнут. *See* лóшадь. **8.** взять в рабóту. *See* взять 1. **9.** рабóта не бей лежáчего, 'light work, a soft job.' Я приземлúлся дневáльным у начáльника учáстка — рабóта не бей лежáчего. I landed a job as an orderly in the camp commandant's office—a soft job with nothing to do. [DPos 171, Лежáчего не бьют; Ž 206] **10.** рабóта на измóр, 'killing, exhausting work.' На Колымé нам достáлась рабóта на измóр; за три мéсяца вся бригáда дошлá. We were assigned very exhausting work at Kolyma. In three months the entire gang was on its last legs. **11.** Кáждый знáет, что в суббóту / Мы не хóдим на рабóту, / А у нас суббóта кáждый день. 'Everybody knows we don't work on Saturday, and to us every day is Saturday,' a part of a popular criminals' song.

работя́га, 'a hard worker,' one on general labor. Копыло́в — э́то был настоя́щий работя́га. Он иша́чил до тех пор, пока́ но́ги не вы́тянул. Kopylov was a real hard worker. He worked like a dog until he dropped. [AD, colloq.]

рабси́ла, рабо́чая си́ла, 'work force.' В Феврале́ нача́льник реши́л подкорми́ть з/к, что́бы подгото́вить рабси́лу к посевно́й. In February the commandant decided to fatten up the prisoners in order to prepare the work force for the sowing campaign. [KK]

разбаза́рить, pf., 'to sell something belonging to the state' (sometimes considered sabotage). Си́доров вме́сте с нача́льником уча́стка разбаза́рил всю вещкаптёрку. Си́дорова суди́ли, а нача́льника сня́ли с рабо́ты. Sidorov and the commandant sold the entire clothing stock. Sidorov was tried and the commandant was removed from his post. [AD, colloq. 'to squander, waste'; KK]

развод, 'the march off to work,' including roll calls, signing out with guards, and the assigning of escorts. На на́шем уча́стке нача́льник во́хры кома́ндовал разво́дом. In our camp section the chief of the camp garrison took command of the march off to work. [AD, posting (of guards); a conducting to various places]

разводя́щий, 'a corporal of the guard.' Разводя́щий приво́дит сме́ну бойцо́в и расставля́ет их по вы́шкам; э́то происхо́дит ка́ждые четы́ре часа́. The corporal of the guard brings up the relief and posts them on the watch towers; this happens every four hours. [AD]

раздави́ть ⊂ раздави́ть пол-ли́тра [поллитро́вку], 'to kill [i.e., drink] a bottle (lit., a half-liter) of vodka.' Вольня́жка суме́л пронести́ для меня́ че́рез ва́хту поллитро́вку [пол-ли́тра], и я её в миг раздави́л. A free employee was able to bring a bottle of vodka past the guard shack for me and I killed it in a jiffy. [AD, pop.]

‡ **разменя́ть,** pf., 'to serve (a sentence).' Ды́рсин же разменя́л после́дний год. Dyrsin was finishing up his last year. (В кру́ге пе́рвом)

‡ **размо́т,** 'an unwinding.' А ино́й раз поду́маешь — дух сопрёт: срок-то всё же конча́ется, кату́шка-то на размо́те ... Го́споди! At other times you get to thinking and you choke up: your term really is ending, your 25-year term (lit., spool) is unwinding ... Lord! (Один день Ивана Денисовича)

размота́ть, разма́тывать, 'to serve (lit., to unwind).' Дне-ва́льный конто́ры разма́тывал по́лную кату́шку. На восьмо́й год он ду́баря дал и бедня́жка оста́лся в долгу́ госуда́рству. The office orderly was serving a 25-year sentence (lit., was unwinding a full spool). The poor wretch died in the eighth year in debt to the state. [AD] *Cf.* намота́ть.

разнаря́дка 1. 'work allocation,' daily distribution of work to columns and brigades, arranged on the preceding evening by the work assigner. Согла́сно разнаря́дке на́ша брига́да должна́ была́ за́втра вы́йти в жилгородо́к. According to the work allocation, our brigade had to go out to the housing construction zone tomorrow. [AD, tech.] **2.** 'daily production staff meeting.' Нача́льник уча́стка назна́чил разнаря́дку на де́вять часо́в ве́чера у себя́ в конто́ре. The commandant set the production staff meeting for 9 P.M. in his office.

‡ **разнаряжа́ть,** impf., 'to assign work.' И не проверя́я и не пересчи́тывая, потому́ что никто́ у Тю́рина никуда́ уйти́ не мог, он бы́стро стал разнаряжа́ть. And without checking or counting, because none of Tjurin's men could go anywhere, he quickly began to give them their work orders. (Оди́н день Ива́на Дени́совича)

разу́ть полти́нники. *See* полти́нники 2.

рак ⊂ ра́ком поста́вить, 'to put in a standing position, bent forward (for intercourse).' Встре́тил я Ма́шу в рабо́чей зо́не; ложи́ться бы́ло не́куда. Понево́ле пришло́сь Ма́шу поста́вить ра́ком и вы́ебать. I met Maša at the work site; there was no place to lie down, so I had to bend Maša over and fuck her standing up. [AD, рак 'crayfish']

ракло́, 'a small-time crook,' not associated with the organized criminal world. Карзу́бый на во́ле был ракло́м; то́лько в лагеря́х он связа́лся с блатны́ми и стал пахано́м. Outside Karzubyj was a small-time, independent crook; in the camps he joined the criminal element and became a ringleader. [AD, рака́лия pop. obs. abusive 'scoundrel, villain'; D, рака́лия meaning as in AD; St 145, ракло 'vagabond']

рамзи́нский ⊂ рамзи́нская гру́ппа, 'Ramzin group,' from Prof. Leonid K. Ramzin (1887–1948), alleged and confessed (in 1930) head of an organization whose purported object was to undermine the Soviet regime by industrial sabotage. Я попа́л в лагеря́ с рамзи́нской гру́ппой. I got into camps with the Ramzin group.

расколо́ться, pf. 1. 'to crack, to fold,' to admit to crimes under the pressure of investigation. У Крыло́ва сла́бый позвоно́чник; сле́дователь нажа́л на него́ немно́жко, и он сра́зу расколо́лся. Krylov has no backbone; the interrogator pressed him a little and he cracked. **2.** ——, как це́лочка. *See* це́лочка 2. [AD, dissolve, fall to pieces]

расконвои́рованный. *See* бесконво́йный.

расконвои́ровать, 'to make (someone) a trusty.' « Гей, нача́льник, когда́ ду́маете расконвои́ровать меня́? » — « Когда́ рак сви́стнет ». "Hey, boss, when do you intend to make me a trusty?" "When the crayfish whistles."

‡ **раскуро́чить, куро́чить,** 'to clean out, to steal blind.' Вы слы́шали, господа́? — говоря́т, блатны́х прижа́ли и да́же на Кра́сной Пре́сне уже́ не куро́чат. Did you hear, gentlemen? They say they've cracked down on the criminals and even at Krasnaja Presnja they don't steal you blind any more. (В кру́ге пе́рвом)

расписа́ть, pf., 'to bloody' (lit., to paint). — Поло́жь па́йку на ме́сто, ина́че ха́рю распишу́, — бригади́р сказа́л Ми́шке, когда́ узна́л, что па́йка исче́зла из нар. "Put that bread ration back or I'll bloody your ugly mug," said the brigadier to Miška, when he found out that a share was missing from the bed boards. [AD]

распоряже́ние ⊂ до осо́бого распоряже́ния, 'until further notice,' a phrase used in statements to prisoners who have finished their terms to the effect that they must stay on until a special order from above is received. Когда́ Гольц отсиде́л свой срок, его́ вы́звали в конто́ру ла́геря, что́бы расписа́ться за « до осо́бого распоряже́ния ». When Holz had served his time, he was called into the camp office to be registered for "until further notice."

расхло́пать, pf., 'to shoot.' С нача́ла войны́ всех ко́нтриков в лагеря́х пограни́чной полосы́ расхло́пали. At the beginning of the war all counter-revolutionaries in border-area camps were shot.

рвать ⊂ рвать ко́гти. *See* смахну́ть.

режи́м ⊂ о́бщий режи́м. *See* основа́ния.

режи́мный ⊂ режи́мные города́, 'off-limits cities' (to holders of certain restricted passports). Столи́цы сою́зных респу́блик счита́лись режи́мными города́ми; в них нельзя́ бы́ло прожива́ть бы́вшим з/к, в осо́бенности [тем, кого́ забра́ли по] 39-ой статье́. The capitals of the Union republics were considered off-limits cities; ex-prisoners and particularly those with the 39th article of the passport statute could not reside in them.

ре́заться, impf., 'to play recklessly, noisily.' Всю ночь усну́ть не мог — у́рки ре́зались в штос. I couldn't get to sleep all night—the criminals were playing a wild game of stuss. [AD, colloq.]

рези́нщик, 'a stretcher, a prolonger,' an official or worker who prolongs his work more than necessary. Наш бригади́р был хоро́ший рези́нщик [волы́нщик]; когда́ мо́жно бы́ло, он растя́гивал рабо́ту. То́лько, когда́ ну́жно бы́ло, уме́л нажа́ть на брига́ду. Our brigadier was a good stretcher; when it was possible, he stretched out the work, but when necessary he could push the brigade. *Also* волы́нщик.

рекорди́ст. [AD] *See* стаха́новец.

рецидиви́ст, 'a repeater, recidivist,' assigned to special camps or closed prisons in the 1950s. Нача́льство ГУЛА́Га реши́ло отпра́вить всех рецидиви́стов в спецлагеря́. The GULAG leadership decided to send all recidivists to special camps. [AD]

рог ⊂ по рога́м, 'disfranchisement' (lit., on the horns). The expression is used instead of the official wording, пораже́ние в права́х. Копыло́ву да́ли черво́нец и пять по рога́м. Kopylov was sentenced to a ten-year stretch and five years' disfranchisement.

романи́ст, 'a story teller, a liar.'

ротату́й ⊂ суп ротату́й, 'slop, a thin watery soup.' Сего́дня на ку́хне раздава́ли оди́н суп ротату́й. Ни жи́ра ни мя́са, одна́ зелёная капу́ста пла́вала в зелёной води́чке. They're only serving slop in the mess today—no meat, no fat, just cabbage swimming in green water.

руба́ть. *See* подруба́ть.

руба́шка ⊂ смири́тельная руба́шка, 'a strait jacket.' Смири́тельные руба́шки в сове́тских тю́рьмах отлича́лись от таковы́х в дома́х для умалишённых. Тюре́мная смири́тельная руба́шка затя́гивалась до остано́вки кровообраще́ния, что приво́дит к поте́ре созна́ния. Применя́лась под наблюде́нием врача́. Prison strait jackets differed from those in mental hospitals. Prison strait jackets were tightened until the blood circulation stopped and loss of consciousness resulted. They were used under the observation of a doctor. [AD]

рубль ⊂ длинный рубль, 'a fast (lit., long) ruble, one obtained easily and unscrupulously.' После войны многие советские граждане погнались за длинным рублём, и им пришлось искупить их жадность в советских лагерях. After the war many Soviet citizens tried to make a fast ruble and had to atone for their greed in Soviet camps. [AD, pop.]

ругать ⊂ ругать по всем швам, 'to chew out, to scold harshly.' Сегодня комендант ругал нашего дневального по всем швам. Today the barracks chief really chewed out our orderly.

рыжики, pl., 'gold wristwatch.' Думаю, как свистнуть рыжики из руки этого фрайера. I'm thinking of how to steal a gold wristwatch out of the hand of that pigeon. [Tr, рыжий 'golden'; To 190, рыжик 'something golden'; KK]

С, с

сакти́ровать, акти́ровать, 'to write off.' *See* актиро́вка.

самоотопле́ние, 'self-heating,' the heating of barracks and prison cells solely by the body heat of the inmates. Из-за отсу́тствия то́плива бара́к, где посели́ли но́вый эта́п, не ота́пливался. Нача́льство рассчи́тывало на самоотопле́ние. Because of the fuel shortage, the barracks where the new shipment of prisoners resided was not heated. The command relied on self-heating. *Cf.* пердя́чий.

самоохра́на, 'the prisoner-guard,' often made up of former employees of the militia or the secret police. Команди́р взво́да стара́лся вы́ловить з/к из ка́ждого эта́па для рабо́ты в самоохра́не, потому́ что во́льных стрелко́в бы́ло недоста́точно для охра́ны заключённых. The platoon commander tried to fish out prisoners from each transport to work as prisoner-guards, because he was understaffed with free guards.

самоохра́нник, 'a prisoner-guard.' Самоохра́нник повёл брига́ду тракитори́стов в по́ле. A prisoner-guard led the tractor brigade to the field.

самору́б, 'a self-mutilator,' a prisoner who maims himself in order to avoid hard labor and possible death from exhaustion. Ивано́в наро́чно отруби́л себе́ ладо́нь на лесопова́ле. Он самору́б. Ему́ доба́вили статью́: членовреди́тельство. Ivanov deliberately chopped off his hand at the lumber camp. He's a self-mutilator. They added self-mutilation to his sentence. [KK]

самоса́д, 'crude, home-grown or wild tobacco.' Прода́й мне полстака́на самоса́да. Sell me half a glass of tobacco. [AD]

самости́йник, 'an independent,' a name given Banderites and other Ukrainians because of their dream of an independent Ukraine. Вчера́ самости́йники опя́ть разгуля́лись в бара́ке и запе́ли украи́нские националисти́ческие пе́сни. Yesterday the independents went on a spree in the barracks and started to sing Ukrainian nationalistic songs.

сангородо́к, санита́рный городо́к, 'hospital-medical block,' an area of the camp containing the hospital, convalescent barracks, the morgue, sometimes a separate kitchen, and a medical staff office. Си́доров пролежа́л не́сколько дней в стациона́ре, и по́сле э́того его́ отпра́вили в сангородо́к. Sidorov lay in the infirmary for several days and then was sent to the hospital-medical block.

САНО́, санита́рный отде́л. *See* санотде́л.

санобрабо́тка, санита́рная обрабо́тка, 'sanitary treatment,' which includes disinfection of clothing and, often, a cold water bath. Что́бы не теря́ть рабо́чее вре́мя, нача́льник уча́стка распоряди́лся, что́бы санобрабо́тка производи́лась по́сле съёма. In order not to lose work time, the commandant arranged for the sanitary treatment to be carried out after knocking off from work. [KK]

санотде́л, санита́рный отде́л, 'main medical office for an entire camp system,' supervising the work of a number of camp districts, each of which has its own medical office. Санотде́л [САНО́] Карла́га проводи́л ку́рсы для подгото́вки лекпо́мов и медици́нских сестёр. The main medical office in Karlag (the Karaganda camp) arranged courses for training medics and nurses. *Also* САНО́. *Cf.* санча́сть.

санпропускни́к, санита́рный пропускни́к, 'disinfecting chamber.' Санпропускни́к находи́лся [Дезка́мера находи́лась] в двухста́х ме́трах от зо́ны, и заключённые вы́нуждены бы́ли ходи́ть в ба́ню под конво́ем. The disinfecting chamber was 200 meters from the compound and the prisoners had to go to their bath under escort. [AD] *Also* дезка́мера.

санча́сть, санита́рная часть, 'central medical office for a camp district,' serving five or six camp sections. Врач, бы́вший з/к, был нача́льником санча́сти на́шего отделе́ния. A physician, a former prisoner, was the head of the central medical office for our district. Душа́ боли́т за произво́дство, а но́ги тя́нут в санча́сть. 'The soul suffers for the enterprise, but the legs long for the dispensary (lit., the central medical office),' an ironic commentary by the prisoners on the state of their health. [AD] *Cf.* санотде́л.

сбо́ндить, pf., 'to snatch, to swipe, to steal.' Карзу́бый поле́з в сосе́дний бара́к и сбо́ндил су́мку с проду́ктами. Karzubyj crept into the next barracks and swiped a bag of food. [D; St 143]

свúстнуть, pf., 'to steal.' Иванóв свúстнул пáйку из нар. Ivanov stole a bread share from the bed boards. [AD, pop.; St 143, свиснуть (*sic*); aLi 62, свистнуть]

свистоплáска, 'lying, beating around the bush.' Пóсле мéсяца под слéдствием слéдователь заорáл на меня: « Брось э́ту свистоплáску, давáй расскáзывать! » After a month the investigator bawled at me, "Stop beating around the bush and start talking!" [AD, colloq. 'a complete muddle']

свояк. [AD, wife's brother or brother-in-law] *See* шурáк.

СВЭ [es-ve-é], социáльно-врéдный элемéнт, 'SVÈ,' socially harmful element, a popular camp and semiofficial designation for people considered harmful to the state (the homeless, prostitutes, tramps, etc.). Дневáльного нáшего барáка посадúли по СВЭ. Что э́та статья́ представля́ла собóй, он не имéл поня́тия. Our barracks orderly was imprisoned as an SVÈ. He had no idea what this provision was. *Cf.* СОЭ.

связь ⊂ связь с заключёнными, 'fraternizing with prisoners.' В нáшем лáгере двух стрелкóв сня́ли с рабóты за связь с заключёнными. Two guards were removed for fraternizing with prisoners in our camp. [AD]

сдрéфить, дрéфить, 'to be afraid.' Когдá Иванóва посадúли в изоля́тор, он сдрéфил и дýмал, что емý пиздéц. When Ivanov was put in the isolator, he was afraid, because he thought his end had come. [AD, сдрéйфить; S 93, (с)дрейфить and (с)дрефить; St 137, здрефить]

сексóт, секрéтный сотрýдник, 'a prisoner informer, a collaborator,' used as a term of abuse for anyone. Э́тот сексóт опя́ть настучáл на Баранóвского и егó увелú в шизó. That collaborator informed on Baranovskij again and he was taken to the penalty isolator. [KK]

сексóтничать, impf., 'to squeal, to collaborate with the authorities.' Все в нáшем барáке знáли, что наш дневáльный сексóтничит, тóлько нé было комý гóлову емý отрубúть. Everybody in the barracks knew our orderly was squealing, but nobody dared to cut off his head.

сельхóз, сéльское хозя́йство, 'agricultural area,' a sub-unit of an industrial camp, as opposed to a separate agricultural camp. Всех доходя́г начáльник веснóй напрáвил в сельхóз. The commandant sent all the goners to the agricultural area in the spring.

сесть ⊂ На мне далекó не уéдешь, / Где сядешь, там и слéзешь. *See* уéхать.

сидéть. *See* просидéть.

‡ **сидка,** 'imprisonment.' И хотя ничегó он за собóй запрещённого не пóмнил сегóдня, но насторóженность восьми лет сидки вошла в привычку. And although today he didn't remember doing anything forbidden, the caution bred of eight years' imprisonment had become a habit. (Один день Ивана Денисовича)

сидор, 'a food or clothing parcel.' Вчера Ваня надыбал сидор у одногó казáха под подушкой и нóчью сука утащил. Yesterday Vanja spotted a parcel under the pillow of one of the Kazakhs and during the night the bastard stole it. [To 154, сидр]

силос, 'silage,' derogatory term for the green leaves of cabbage used to feed prisoners. It is prepared like silage for cattle, chopped coarsely and allowed to ferment for several weeks. Веснóй питáние ухудшилось в лáгере; три рáза в день кормили з/к силосом так, что и мочá была зелёная. In the spring the chow worsened in camp; the prisoners were fed three times a day with silage so that even their urine turned green. [AD]

система ⊂ вагóнная система, 'a four-place bunk arrangement.' Each unit, with two upper and two lower bunks, is moveable and can stand without support of the wall. The system provides somewhat more privacy than the continuous bed boards which it replaces. Руковóдство лáгеря решило передéлать сплошные нáры в вагóнную систéму. The camp leadership decided to remake the continuous bed board system into a four-place system.

сифóн, 'syph, syphilis.' Кóля проспáл ночь с Мáшей и подцепил сифóн. Kolja slept with Maša one night and caught the syph. [KK]

скакáрь. [Tr; To 7 скóкарь] *See* домушник.

скрипушник. *See* скрыпушник.

скрыпушник, 'a train thief,' one specializing in stealing baggage and parcels in trains and stations. Вáня скрыпушник попáлся на линии Москвá-Ленингрáд. Vanja the train thief was caught on the Moscow-Leningrad line. *Also* скрипушник.

скӳрвиться 1. 'to turn informer.' Все урки избегáли Кóльку; узнáли, что пóсле послéднего визита у óпера он скӳрвился.

All the criminals avoided Kol'ka; they found out that, after his last visit to the security officer, he had turned informer. [KK] ‡ 2. 'to become a whore.' Потóм был óтчим, хоть не лáсковый, но справедлúвый, с ним вполнé мóжно бы́ло бы жить, но мать ... скýрвилась. Óтчим брóсил её и прáвильно сдéлал. Then he had a stepfather, who was just if not affectionate. It would have been quite possible to live with him, but his mother became . . . a whore. His stepfather left her, and rightly so. (Рáковый кóрпус)

слабáк, 'a member of the слабосúлка (q.v.).'

слабкомáнда, слáбая комáнда, 'weak contingent.' Данúла вы́писали из сангородкá и напрáвили в слабкомáнду. Danilo was discharged from the hospital-medical block and sent to a weak contingent.

слабосúлка, слабосúльная комáнда, 'weak contingent,' the official term for ailing prisoners and goners, who live apart, who do light work, and thus eat less than the hard workers. Слабосúлка зимóй совсéм не рабóтала; тóлько сидéли онú на гарантúйке. In the wintertime the weak contingent didn't work at all; they just lived on their guaranteed ration.

слезть ⊂ На мне далекó не уéдешь, / Где ся́дешь, там и слéзешь. *See* уéхать.

слепотá ⊂ курúная слепотá, 'night blindness,' a common disease in the far-northern camps. Большинствó з/к на Воркýте страдáло от курúной слепоты́. Most of the prisoners at Vorkuta suffered from night blindness. [AD]

слизнýть, pf., 'to lap up, to drink greedily.' Кóля слизнýл сивýху у вольня́жки и срáзу опьянéл. Kolja lapped up some vodka at a free employee's house and instantly became drunk. [AD]

слóво ⊂ Дал слóво — сдержú; взял обязáтельство — вы́полни. 'You gave your word—keep it; you accepted an obligation—fulfill it,' one of numerous slogans found in all barracks in camps.

СЛОН [slón], сéверные [соловéцкие, сибúрские] лагеря́ осóбого назначéния, 'SLON,' northern [Solovetsk, Siberian] camps of special designation, for mining, logging, and the like. Вчерá привезлú большóй этáп из СЛÓНа; все доходя́ги, как одúн. Yesterday a large transport was brought in from the SLON; to a man all were goners. [KK]

слóпать, лóпать   1. 'to devour, to eat.' Приéхавши из этáпа, наш дневáльный лóпал балáнду вёдрами. When our orderly arrived from the transport, he gobbled up gruel by the pail. [AD, pop.]   2. 'to beat, to eat alive.' Отвяжи́сь по-хорóшему, а то живьём слóпаю. Leave me alone or I'll eat you alive.

слю́нка, 'a knife.' Кóлька вы́тащил слю́нку и нáчал рéзать фрайерóв. Kol'ka pulled out a knife and began to cut up the pigeons.

смахну́ть, pf., 'to run away.' Иванóв стащи́л часы́ и смахну́л [смы́лся, кóгти рвал]. Ivanov swiped a watch and ran away. [AD, colloq. 'to snatch up'; D, to run someplace and return] *Also* смы́ться, кóгти рвать.

смéртная, 'death cell.' Most of the condemned are kept in these cells for 100 days, after which they are either shot or their sentences are commuted to 10- to 25-years' imprisonment. Си́доров просидéл в смéртной сто дней и пóсле э́того вы́шку замени́ли ему́ 25 годáми. Sidorov sat in a death cell for 100 days and then his death sentence was commuted to 25 years.

смéртник, 'someone sentenced to death, an occupant of a death cell.' Си́доров был смéртником в течéние ста дней. Sidorov was a prisoner on death row for 100 days. [AD]

СМЕРШ [sṃérš], смерть шпиóнам, 'SMERSH,' death to spies, a subsection of the Special Division (1942–1946), an organ of the secret police attached to the armed forces. SMERSH was in charge of interrogating ex-POW's to determine whether or not they were German spies. Вóльский был сотрýдником СМÉРШа. Vol'skij was an employee of SMERSH. [K]

смотáть ⊂ смотáть ýдочки, 'to take to one's heels, to make off.' Вáська очи́стил кварти́ру в Москвé и срáзу же смотáл ýдочки. Vas'ka cleaned out an apartment in Moscow and immediately took to his heels. [AD, pop.]

смочь ⊂ Кто когó смóжет, тот тогó и глóжет. *See* глодáть.

смы́ться. [AD, pop.] *See* смахну́ть.

собáка ⊂ вóхровская собáка   1. 'watch dog.' Крóме охрáнников две вóхровские собáки следи́ли за кáждым шáгом рабóчей колóнны, готóвые брóситься в слýчае попы́тки побéга. Besides the guards, two watch dogs followed every step of the work column, ready to leap in the event of an attempt at flight.   2. 'stool pigeon, an informer.' Э́та вóхровская соба́ка опя́ть настуча́ла на бе́дного Ивано́ва и его́ опя́ть посади́ли в изоля́тор. That stool pigeon again informed on poor Ivanov and he was placed in the isolator.

со́весть ⊂ Где ра́ньше была́ со́весть, там пизда́ вы́росла. *See* пизда́ 2.

совеща́ние ⊂ Осо́бое совеща́ние. *See* ОСО.

сожра́ть, pf., 'to get rid of, to cause to be removed (as from a job).' Кра́вченко рабо́тал каптёром в Доли́нке. Не ла́дил он с остальны́ми приду́рками уча́стка и в тече́ние четырёх ме́сяцев его́ сожра́ли. Kravčenko worked as a supply clerk in Dolinka. He couldn't get along with the other *priduroks* and in four months they got rid of him. [AD, c. pop. 'to devour']

созна́ние ⊂ Битьё определя́ет созна́ние. *See* битьё.

сока́мерник, 'a cell-mate.' Когда́ вы́грузили наш эта́п, я встре́тил в зо́не бы́вшего сока́мерника из Буты́рки. When our transport was unloaded, I came across a former cell-mate from Butyrka.

Соловки́, pl., Солове́цкие острова́, '*Solovki,*' a popular designation for *Soloveckie ostrova* (the Solovetsk Islands) of the White Sea and a notorious labor camp for political prisoners. Соловки́ бы́ли одни́м из пе́рвых лагере́й в Сове́тском Сою́зе для полити́ческих заключённых. Перебро́ска з/к на Солове́цкие острова́ производи́лась по му́рманской желе́зной доро́ге. *Solovki* was one of the first camps in the Soviet Union for political prisoners. Transportation of the prisoners to the Solovetsk Islands was by the Murmansk railroad.

со́пка ⊂ вы́везти за со́пку, 'to take to boot hill, to bury.' Тара́са вы́везли за со́пку вчера́. They took Taras to boot hill yesterday. Е́сли так иша́чить придётся, то ско́ро за со́пку вы́везут. If we have to keep working like a dog this way, we'll soon be taken to boot hill. [AD, a small, cone shaped mountain in the Far East and Siberia]

сопроводи́ловка, 'accompanying document.' Сле́дователь подписа́л сопроводи́ловку и вручи́л конво́йру. The investigator signed the accompanying document and handed it to the guard.

сорва́ться, pf., 'to escape, to run away.' Карзу́бый, как попа́л на кирпи́чный, по́нял, что ему́ пизде́ц, и реши́л сорва́ться. When he ended up at the brickmaking compound, Karzubyj knew the jig was up, and decided to run away. [AD, pop.]

‡ **сосáловка,** 'starvation conditions.' Мáсло, ребя́та, сейчáс тóлько конопля́ное. Вы дýмаете, в посёлке как? Тóже сосáловка. There's only linseed oil now, boys. How do you think things are in the free settlement? It's desperate there, too. (Олень и шалашовка) « Чем я бýду кормúть людéй? » — « А э́то пусть у тебя́ головá болúт, как с начáльником рассчúтываться ». — « Вообщé-то бригадúр прав. Тут сосáловка ». "How'll I feed the men?" "That's your headache. Figure it out with the commandant." "Actually, the gang boss is right. We're starving here." (Олень и шалашовка)

соцдóговор, социалистúческий дóговор, 'socialistic pact,' concerning competition between workers. Дáже вóхра былá свя́зана соцдóговором, а úменно, чтобы довестú до минимýма число побéгов и число берéменных заключённых. Even the camp garrison was bound by the socialistic pact, namely, to minimize the number of escapes and the number of pregnant prisoners. [AD]

соцнакоплéние, социалистúческое накоплéние, 'socialistic accumulation,' ironic term for belly fat. Смотрú на егó соцнакоплéние! Just look at his "socialistic accumulation!"

СОЭ [es-o-é], социáльно-опáсный элемéнт, 'SOÈ,' socially dangerous element, a popular camp and semiofficial designation for the politically dangerous, as opposed to the socially dangerous. В послéднем этáпе привезлú попá. Посадúли егó, как СОЭ. They brought in a priest on the last transport. He was imprisoned as an SOÈ. *Cf.* СВЭ.

СП [es-pé], социáльное происхождéние, 'SP,' social origin. Although no special provision exists, many Soviet officials, after years of devoted service, have been removed from their jobs because of their social origin. Вороты́нцев прорабóтал 10 лет начáльником лáгеря, и кáк-то дéло вы́шло, что он сын попá; сня́ли егó с рабóты и судúли за скры́тие СП. Vorotyncev served 10 years as a camp commandant, and somehow it came out that he was a priest's son. He was removed from his post and convicted for concealing his SP.

сперéть, pf., 'to steal.' Сúдоров спёр одея́ло из ИТРовского барáка. Sidorov stole a blanket from the ITR (engineering technical workers') barracks. [AD, pop.; St 143]

спецконтингéнт, специáльный контингéнт, 'special contingent,' political prisoners destined for the special camps. Банде́ровцы, вла́совцы и дома́новцы счита́лись, как спец-контингéнт. Banderites, Vlasovites, and Domanovites were regarded as a special contingent.

спецла́герь. *See* ла́герь 4.

спецларёк, специа́льный ларёк, 'special commissary,' mostly for party members and high officials. За ра́зные услу́ги женá надзира́теля ча́сто покупа́ла мне ма́сло в спецларьке́. For various favors the supervisor's wife would often buy butter for me at the special commissary.

спецнаря́д, специа́льный наря́д. *See* наря́д 5.

спецпереселéнец, специа́льный переселéнец, 'a special migrant,' the official designation for a person banished to a remote part of the Soviet Union. *See* спецпереселé-ние.

спецпереселéние, специа́льное переселéние, 'special settle-ment,' an area settled by special migrants. At different times they have been populated by peasants who refused to be collectivized, by inhabitants of Eastern Poland and the Baltic states, and, during World War II, by unreliable nationalities in the Soviet Union. Special settlers are either supervised by the secret police, or are completely administered by them. Во вре́мя второ́й мирово́й войны́, чечéнов и ингушо́в этапи́-ровали в спецпереселéния вокру́г Акмоли́нска. Пра́во их передвижéния бы́ло ограни́чено. During World War II the Chechens and the Ingush were banished to special settlements around Akmolinsk. Their freedom of movement was limited. *Cf.* переселéние.

спецпоселéние, специа́льное поселéние, 'special settlement,' an area settled by special migrants, a broader term than спецпереселéние (q.v.).

спецча́сть, специа́льная часть, 'special section,' an organ of the secret police attached to a free enterprise. This term is frequently confused with and erroneously applied to the corre-sponding organ in labor camps, the third section. Нача́льник уча́стка хода́тайствовал, чтóбы Ивано́ва расконвои́ровать — тóлько спецча́сть отказа́ла. The commandant applied to make Ivanov a trusty, but the special section refused permission. *See* трéтий.

спи́здеть. *See* спи́здить.

спи́здить, pf., 'to steal.' Варва́ра, рабо́тая в колхо́зе, спи́здила

10 килогрáммов картóшки. While working on a *kolkhoz*, Barbara stole 10 kilograms of potatoes. *Also* спúздеть.

сплáвить. [AD, pop.] *See* бáхнуть 1.

спрáвка ⊂ спрáвка об освобождéнии, 'a release certificate.' Жигáлин получúл спрáвку об освобождéнии и сухóй паёк на три дня, чтóбы доéхать до мéста назначéния. Žigalin was given a release certificate and dry rations for three days, the time required to reach his destination. [AD]

срок 1. ———— нóски, 'wearing term for clothing,' usually six months, but longer for some items (such as shoes). Clothing is supposed to last for three terms, but the quality is so bad and the amount issued so limited, it rarely lasts one term. Срок нóски для ботúнок был год. The wearing term for shoes was a year. **2.** дéтский ———— . *See* дéтский. [AD]

ссýченный ⊂ ссýченный вор. *See* сýка 1.

ссýчиться, ссýчиваться, 'to turn informer.' Кóля-Морáк ссýчился; говорáт, что начáльник режúма велéл перевестú его в ИТРовский барáк, чтóбы наблюдáть за нúми. Kolja-Morjak has become an informer; they say that the disciplinary officer ordered him transferred to the ITR (engineering technical workers') barracks in order to spy on them. [KK] *Cf.* сýка 1.

ссы́лка, 'deportation,' imposed to remove populations from their homelands and to supply labor to sparsely populated areas in poor climates. Prisoners after their release are often forced to remain in these areas, even though their sentences usually do not include deportation. Во врéмя войны́ всем освобождённым давáли ссы́лку. During the war all freed prisoners were deported. [AD]

стáвка ⊂ óчная стáвка, 'person to person confrontation during an investigation.' Пéред окончáнием слéдствия, слéдователь устрóил мне óчную стáвку с мойм бы́вшим сотрýдником, показáния котóрого бы́ли оснóвой для моегó арéста. Before the conclusion of the investigation, the interrogator arranged a confrontation with my former colleague, whose testimony was the basis for my arrest. [AD]

старшóй, 'a block warder on a floor or section of a prison.' Старшóй расстáвил надзирáтелей по постáм и пошёл с доклáдом к начáльнику тюрьмы́. The block warder posted the overseers and went to the warden with a report. [AD, pop. ᶜelder, senior'] *Cf.* корпуснóй.

статья́ 1. бытова́я ———, 'a nonpolitical article of the Soviet Criminal Code.' Согла́сно ука́зу Верхо́вного сове́та СССР, то́лько бытовы́е статьи́ подлежа́т амни́стии. According to an edict of the Supreme Soviet of the USSR, only those sentenced under nonpolitical articles are eligible for amnesty. 2. заключи́тельная ———, 'article of conclusion,' article 206 (in some republics, it carries a different number) of the Code of Criminal Procedure of RSFSR (1923), concerning the signing by the prisoner of all testimony following the investigation. Рома́н вчера́ подписа́л заключи́тельную статью́ [две́сти шесту́ю]. Yesterday Roman signed the article of conclusion [the two-hundred-sixth]. *Also* две́сти шеста́я статья́. 3. две́сти шеста́я ———. *See* meaning 2. 4. три́дцать девя́тая ———, 'article 39 of the passport statute,' which restricts employment and residence rights of former prisoners. Когда́ наш агроно́м освободи́лся, ему́ да́ли три́дцать девя́тую. When our agronomist was released, he was given the thirty-ninth.

стаха́новец, 'Stakhanovite,' in camps, someone who fulfills 200 percent of his quota, a rare occurrence. The term, taken from free life, is used interchangeably in camps with the official term, рекорди́ст. Бригади́р Воло́дя выпи́сывал ка́менщику Ивано́ву 200 проце́нтов вы́работки; по́сле десяти́ дней воспита́тель объяви́л его́ стаха́новцем и ве́чером орке́стр встре́тил его́ на ва́хте. The brigadier Volodja continued to report 200 percent output for the mason Ivanov, and in 10 days the education officer declared him a Stakhanovite and an orchestra met him at the gate. [AD]

‡ **стаха́новка,** fem. form of стаха́новец (q.v.). (Оле́нь и шала́шовка)

стациона́р, 'a small infirmary' (for 5 to 8 patients), located in each camp section. It is used for brief illness or before transfer to a hospital at a larger camp. Чипари́дзе заболе́л поно́сом и лекпо́м положи́л его́ в стациона́р. Čiparidze got diarrhea and the medic put him in the infirmary.

стёклышко ⊂ под стёклышком, 'under observation' (lit., under glass). Из материа́лов моего́ сле́дствия я по́нял, что почти́ год до моего́ аре́ста я ходи́л под стёклышком. From the materials of my investigation I learned that I was under observation for a year before my arrest.

стибрить, pf., 'to steal.' Карзубый сумел стибрить сидор у одного казаха, и мешок как в воду канул. Karzubyj managed to snatch a parcel from a Kazakh and it simply disappeared. [AD, pop.]

стирки, pl., 'cards.' Вытащи стирки; сыграем в стосс. Take out the cards; let's play stuss. [Tr; F 183; To 298; St 142, 143, стирки]

столовая ⊂ коммерческая столовая, 'commercial dining room,' where one can buy extra food in addition to the usual ration. После введения коммерческих столовых, жизнь в лагерях изменилась до неузнаваемости. After the introduction of commercial dining rooms, life in the camps changed beyond recognition. [AD]

столыпинский ⊂ столыпинский вагон, 'Stolypin car,' a railroad car for transporting prisoners, named after the pre-revolutionary Minister of the Interior, Petr Arkad'evič Stolypin (1862–1911). Although its compartments were designed for 8 prisoners, the Soviet authorities manage to pack in 25–28 prisoners. Нас этапировали в столыпинских вагонах [в вагонзаках] до Красноярска. We were transported to Krasnojarsk in Stolypin cars. *Also* вагонзак.

СТОН [stón], сибирская тюрьма особого назначения, 'STON,' Siberian prison of special designation. Вчера привезли большой этап. Много заключённых пришло из СТОНа. Yesterday a large transport was brought in. Many prisoners came from a STON. [KK]

стосс, 'stuss,' a popular card game of chance resembling faro. Давай сыграем в стосс [штос]. Let's play stuss. *Also* штос.

стояк ⊂ на стояка, 'in a standing position' (for intercourse). Встретил я Машу на пересыльном пункте во время этапа. Идти было некуда и пришлось всё сделать на стояка в коридоре. I met Maša at a transfer point during transport. There was no place to go and we had to do everything standing up in the corridor.

стрелок, 'a guard.' Машу дневальную посадили в карцер за сожительство со стрелком; стрелка сняли с работы. The barracks orderly Maša was put in the cooler for sleeping with a guard; the guard was removed from his post. [AD, a rifleman]

стрелять. *See* подстрелить.

‡ **стрёма,** 'watch.' Ще вин молодый мэнэ схопыть! Димка!

На стрёму! He's too young to catch me! Dimka, you keep watch! (Олень и шалашовка) [D; KK]

строга́ч, стро́гая изоля́ция, 'penalty isolator.' Ивано́ва посади́ли в строга́ч. Ivanov was put in the penalty isolator. [KK, a severe reprimand]

стро́йка ⊂ ста́линская стро́йка, 'Stalin construction site,' a designation for camps of special industrial importance, where prisoners were induced to work harder by bonuses. В 1948-м году́ Китла́г был объя́влен ста́линской стро́йкой; сра́зу пита́ние улу́чшилось и бы́ли введены́ зачёты. In 1948 Kitlag (the Kitoj camp) was designated a Stalin construction site; at once the food improved and bonuses were introduced. [AD]

стука́ч, 'a squealer, an informer.' Вчера́ но́чью заре́зали стукача́ в на́шем бара́ке. Last night a squealer in our barracks had his throat cut. [KK]

стуча́ть. *See* настуча́ть.

суд ⊂ ла́герный суд, 'camp court,' with jurisdiction only over prisoners. Тара́са суди́ли ла́герным судо́м и ему́ приба́вили три го́да. Taras was sentenced by the camp court and given three additional years.

су́ка 1. 'a stoolie, turncoat,' a criminal who has turned informer on his own kind, who has broken the criminal code. У́рки но́чью ухло́пали су́ку [ссу́ченного во́ра]. During the night the criminals killed a stoolie. [To 146] *Also* ссу́ченный вор. **2.** ——— ляга́вая, 'a detective informer.' Днева́льный на́шего бара́ка э́то така́я су́ка ляга́вая — ху́же ку́ма. Our barracks orderly is a detective informer—worse than the security officer. [Tr; F 179] **3.** позо́рная ——— (usually with adjective), 'a shameless bitch.' Э́та позо́рная су́ка приходи́ла на всю ночь в мужско́й бара́к. That shameless bitch would come to the men's barracks and spend the whole night. [AD, c. pop.]

сучо́к, 'rotgut vodka,' vodka of the lowest quality, thought to be manufactured from sawdust and other wood industry byproducts. Вчера́ вольня́га, сво́лочь, притащи́л буты́лку сучка́ и запроси́л втри́дорога. Yesterday a free employee, a bastard, hauled in a bottle of rotgut vodka and asked three prices for it. [AD, twig]

схавать, хавать, 'to eat voraciously.' Не́сколько блатны́х слови́ло ко́шку в рабо́чей зо́не; они́ её свари́ли и сха́вали.

Several criminals caught a cat in the work zone. They cooked it and devoured it.

СХВ [es-xa-vé], сельскохозя́йственное вреди́тельство, 'SXV,' agricultural wrecking, sabotage, a reference to article 58.7 of the Soviet Criminal Code of 1926. Пара́ши шли, что ста́рший агроно́м Карла́га был суди́м, как СХВ. The scuttlebutt was that the senior agronomist of Karlag (the Karaganda camp) was sentenced for agricultural wrecking.

схвати́ть, pf., 'to fulfill.' Дава́й схва́тим полно́рмы до обе́да. Let's fulfill half the quota before noon. [AD, to seize, grab]

счёт ⊂ лицево́й счёт, 'personal account,' opened for each prisoner at the beginning of his stay. Everything he earns is put in his account. К моме́нту освобожде́ния из ла́геря у меня́ оказа́лось каки́х-то 500 рубле́й на лицево́м счету́, и я вы́нужден был оплати́ть свой прое́зд. On my release from camp it turned out that I had some 500 rubles in my personal account and I had to pay for my own passage. [AD]

съём, 'a signal to knock off, to stop working.' Бригади́р объяви́л съём; вся брига́да начала́ собира́ться во́зле ва́хты. The brigadier gave the signal to knock off; the whole brigade began to gather near the guard shack.

сыгра́ть ⊂ сыгра́ть на роя́ле, 'to be fingerprinted' (lit., to play the piano). На сле́дующий день по́сле аре́ста меня́ вы́вели из ка́меры, чтобы сыгра́ть на роя́ле. The next day after my arrest I was taken from my cell to be fingerprinted.

ся́вка, 'small fry, petty crooks.' Из после́днего эта́па кру́пную шпану́ отпра́вили в Джезказга́н, а ся́вку к нам пригна́ли. From the last shipment the important criminals were directed to Džezkazgan and the small fry to us.

Т, т

табачóк, 'cigarette butt.' Дай хоть пососáть табачóк. Let me at least finish up the butt.

тáбельщик, 'timekeeper,' the lowest ranking employee of the coordination planning section who, in camps where the brigadier cannot go to the office, turns in the work sheets. Нáшего тáбельщика снáли с рабóты за махинáции в нарáдах. Our timekeeper was removed from his job for falsifying the work sheets. [AD]

талóн, 'meal ticket,' distributed in larger camps for cooked food. They, along with bread tickets, are picked up at the food distribution office by the brigadier for the entire brigade. At the breadcutter's or the food storage he exchanges the bread tickets for bread and gives it and the meal tickets to members of the brigade. The meal ticket is then exchanged by the prisoner at the kitchen hatch for his cooked portion. Сегóдня за одúн паёк хлéба я купúл два талóна цингóтного на барахóлке. Today I bought two tickets for the scurvy ration at the market in exchange for a share of bread. [AD]

‡ **Ташкéнт,** 'a break, a holiday (lit., Tashkent).' Ар-тúсты!! Кон-чáй Ташкéнт! Пошлú вкáлывать! OK, artists! The holiday's over! Let's get to work! (Олень и шалашовка) Таш-кéнт! Нáша бригáда на обéд послéдняя! Time out! Our gang's last for dinner. (Олень и шалашовка)

телогрéйка, 'a wadded jacket.' Ввиду́ тогó, что я не вы́полнил нóрмы за послéдний мéсяц, начáльник учáстка отказáл мне в телогрéйке пéрвого срóка. Since I hadn't fulfilled my norm for the last month, the commandant denied me a first-term wadded jacket. [AD, colloq.]

телятник, 'a cattle car,' frequently used to transport people. [AD, calf shed or one who herds calves]

темнúло, 'an obfuscator, a liar.' [AD, colloq. темнúть 'to speak obscurely']

темнúть, impf., 'to cheat.' Не темнú, знáем тебя́, как облу́п-ленного. Don't cheat. We know you thoroughly (lit., as if peeled). [AD, colloq. 'to speak obscurely']

теплу́шка, 'a heated railroad car for cattle or cargo,' used to transport people to exile when Stolypin cars are unavailable. Всех калмыко́в погрузи́ли в теплу́шки и вы́везли в Акмоли́нскую о́бласть. All Kalmyks were loaded into cattle cars and deported to the Akmolinsk district. [AD, colloq.; S 176]

това́рищ ⊂ Твои́ това́рищи в бря́нском лесу́. 'Your comrades are in the Brjansk forest,' an expression used by any official who is mistakenly addressed as "comrade," instead of as "citizen," by a prisoner. The implication is that the prisoner's comrades are the wild animals of the forest. Or it may refer to the fact that these woods were infested with bandits during the Time of Troubles. « Това́рищ сле́дователь! » — « Я тебе́ не това́рищ; твои́ това́рищи в бря́нском лесу́; обраща́йся ко мне ,,граждани́н сле́дователь" ». "Comrade interrogator!" "I'm not 'comrade' to you; your comrades are in the Brjansk forest. Address me as 'citizen interrogator.' "

товарня́к, 'a freight car or train.' Наш эта́п погрузи́ли в товарня́к и отпра́вили в Карла́г. Our transport was loaded into freight cars and shipped to Karlag (the Karaganda camp).

то́карь ⊂ то́карь по хле́бу и са́лу, 'a turner of bread and lard,' a jocular response to work-assigners, who are always looking for wood or metal turners. « Вы како́й специа́льности? » — « То́карь ». — « По мета́ллу? » — « Нет, по хле́бу и са́лу ». "What's your specialty?" "Turning." "Metal?" "No, bread and lard."

толкану́ть. [AD, pop. 'to push, incite'] *See* втри́нить 2.

ТОН [tón], тюрьма́ осо́бого назначе́ния, 'TON,' a prison of special designation. В ли́чном де́ле Си́дорова была́ поме́тка: подлежи́т отпра́вке в ТОН. In Sidorov's dossier was a special note: should be sent to a TON.

то́нкий ⊂ то́нкий, зво́нкий и прозра́чный, 'thin, shrill, and transparent,' a reference to goners, who are emaciated, have thin voices, and nearly transparent skin. Посмотри́ на э́того балти́йского моряка́; за три ме́сяца он стал то́нким, зво́нким и прозра́чным. Look at that Baltic sailor; in three months he has become thin, shrill, and transparent.

тóпать, impf., 'to leave, to run away.' Иванóв, тóпай отсю́да, покá цел. Ivanov, leave this place while you're in one piece. [AD, colloq. 'to run noisily'; AD, pop. 'to go in general']

транзи́тка, транзи́тная тюрьмá, 'transit prison,' a term seldom used, being replaced by пересы́лка. *See* перпу́нкт.

трáсса, 'road.' Нáша бригáда рабóтала ежеднéвно на трáссе. Our brigade worked every day on the road. [AD]

трепáться, impf., **1.** 'to brag, to shoot the breeze.' Пéтька, нéчего про вóлю трепáться; докажи́ чтó-нибудь в лагеря́х. Pet'ka, it's useless to brag about your life outside; prove yourself inside camp. [AD, c. pop.] **2.** ——— языкóм, 'to brag.' Вáська трéплется языкóм. Не трепи́сь языкóм. Vas'ka brags. Don't brag. [AD, pop. трепáть языкóм]

трепня́, 'chatter, twaddle.' [KK]

трéтий ⊂ трéтья часть, 'third section,' often erroneously called спецчáсть (q.v.), an office in camps representing the secret police, and supervising both the prisoners and free employees. This office has to approve all important changes in status of a prisoner, as, for example, being transported, or being made a trusty. Начáльник механизáции попáлся с каки́м-то делóм. Нóчью вы́тащили егó из кровáти и забрáли в трéтью часть. The chief of mechanization was caught in some affair or other. At night he was taken from his bed to the third section.

трибунáл ⊂ воéнный трибунáл, 'military tribunal,' where military and political prisoners are tried. Дéло по обвинéнию Си́дорова, Ивáна Петровича, пересмóтрено Воéнным трибунáлом Москóвского воéнного óкруга 21 октября́ 1953 гóда. The case concerning the charges against Sidorov, Ivan Petrovič, was reviewed by the military tribunal of the Moscow military district on 21 October 1953.

трóйка, *'troika,'* the colloquial name for the three-man commissions set up by the security organs (such as the Special Commission of the NKVD) for the quick disposal of counter-revolutionary cases through summary sentences. They are said to have been abolished in 1953 and were officially abolished by the legal reform of 1958. The term, used interchangeably with OCO (q.v.), was rarely used in camps after the beginning of World War II. Копылóва арестовáли пóсле уби́йства Ки́рова; егó суди́ла трóйка. Kopylov was arrested after the murder of Kirov; he was sentenced by a *troika*. [AD, body made up of three persons]

труд 1. индивидуа́льный ———, 'individual work,' employment according to the state of health of prisoners, granted by the health commission to prisoners with impaired health. Из-за недоста́точности се́рдца враче́бная коми́ссия « призна́ла » мне индивидуа́льный труд. Since I had a weak heart, the medical commission assigned me individual work. *Cf.* ЛФТ, ТФТ. 2. Труд — де́ло че́сти и со́вести. 'Labor is a matter of honor and conscience,' one of numerous slogans placed in camp barracks. В на́шем бара́ке висе́л плака́т, что « труд — де́ло че́сти и со́вести ». In our barracks hung a poster saying "Labor is a matter of honor and conscience."

трудколо́ния, трудова́я коло́ния, 'labor colony,' for short-term, chiefly nonpolitical prisoners, located near the larger cities. Ивано́в опозда́л три ра́за на рабо́ту. Суд приговори́л его́ к одному́ го́ду трудколо́нии [ИТК, коло́нии]. Ivanov was late to work three times. The court sentenced him to a year in a labor colony. *Also* ИТК, коло́ния.

трудотерапи́я, 'labor therapy,' used by some unscrupulous doctors and camp officials to "cure" goners, which results only in hastening their death. Нача́льник отделе́ния вме́сте с нача́льником санча́сти приду́мали трудотерапи́ю для слаборси́лки. По́сле ме́сяца мно́гих вы́везли за со́пку. The district commandant and the head of the medical office cooked up labor therapy for the weak contingent. After a month many were taken to boot hill. [AD, medical]

трудсоревнова́ние, трудово́е соревнова́ние, 'labor competition,' organized by the culture and education department to raise the о́utput of the prisoners and to inspire them to exceed their quotas by appealing to their patriotism. Воспита́тель всё вре́мя галде́л о трудсоревнова́нии, когда́ у всех то́лько хлеб был на уме́. The education officer was always shouting about labor competition, when everyone had only bread on his mind.

трусы́, pl., 'shorts.' На всё ле́то вы́дали мне то́лько одни́ трусы́. I was issued only one pair of shorts for the whole summer. [AD]

тря́почка ⊂ молча́ть в тря́почку, 'to be silent, speechless.' Работя́ги на́шего бара́ка так поколоти́ли у́рок, что после́дние молча́ли в тря́почку. The hard workers in our barracks gave the criminals such a drubbing that they were speechless. [AD; F 186]

туфта́   **1.** 'chiseling, padding,' false, inflated data used in work reports to obtain a better percentage and, hence, a better ration. Все, включа́я нача́льника отделе́ния, зна́ли, что без туфты́ [тухты́] не проживёшь. Everyone, including the commandant, knew that you couldn't last it out without chiseling. [KK]*Also* тухта́. **2.** заряди́ть туфту́, 'to chisel, to swindle, to use false data.' Бригади́р заряди́л туфту́ и вся брига́да получи́ла стаха́новский котёл в про́шлом ме́сяце. The brigadier chiseled on his work report and the whole gang received the Stakhanovite ration last month.

туфта́ч, 'a chiseler, a swindler, a cheat.' Наш бригади́р — э́то настоя́щий туфта́ч [туфти́ло]; ро́ем песо́к, а в све́дениях — гли́на. Our brigadier is a real chiseler; we dig sand, but in the reports—clay. *Also* туфти́ло.

туфти́ло. *See* туфта́ч.

туфти́ть, impf., 'to chisel, to pad, to swindle.' Нормиро́вщик наш получа́л всё вре́мя ла́пу от бригади́ра, потому́ что туфти́л всю доро́гу в по́льзу брига́ды. Our norm-setter was bribed by the brigadier, because the latter always padded his output for the benefit of the brigade.

тухта́. *See* туфта́.

ТФТ [te-ef-té], тяжёлый физи́ческий труд, 'TFT,' heavy physical work, assigned to healthy prisoners. Комиссо́вка перевела́ Ивано́ва из ЛФТ в ТФТ; наря́дчик его́ сра́зу перевёл в другу́ю брига́ду. A decision of the medical commission shifted Ivanov from LFT (light physical work) to TFT; the work-assigner immediately transferred him to another brigade. *Cf.* ЛФТ, труд 1.

тю́кнуть, pf., 'to knife, stab, cut up.' Вчера́ бригади́р наш подра́лся с одни́м блатны́м и после́дний тю́кнул бригади́ра фи́нкой. Yesterday our brigadier got into it with a criminal and the latter stabbed him with a knife. [AD, pop. 'to kill']

тюрьма́   **1.** вну́тренняя ———, 'inner prison,' prison for political prisoners, found in the larger cities. Вну́тренняя тюрьма́ [Вну́трянка], в отли́чие от о́бщей тюрьмы́, была́ совсе́м изоли́рована от нару́жного ми́ра. Unlike the general prison, the inner prison was completely isolated from the outside world. *Also* вну́трянка. **2.** о́бщая ———, 'general prison,' where criminals and political prisoners are confined together. Три дня по́сле аре́ста Ивано́ва перевели́ из о́бщей тюрьмы́ во вну́треннюю. Three days after his arrest, Ivanov was transferred from the general prison to the inner prison. **3.** пересы́льная ———, 'transit prison.' Пересы́льная тюрьма́ находи́лась в трёх киломе́трах от ста́нции. The transit prison was three kilometers from the station. **4.** Тюрьма́ и ла́герь, э́то на́ши родны́е. 'The prison and camp are kin to us,' an expression of the criminals' feelings for prisons and camps, where they feel quite at home. **5.** От тюрьмы́ и от сумы́ не зарека́йся. 'One can escape neither prison nor begging,' an expression of the inevitability of both prison and begging. [Ž, obs. ... не отрека́йся] **6.** Без тебя́ тюрьма́ пла́кать бу́дет. After you're gone, the prison will miss (lit., weep over) you,' an ironic expression directed to fellow prisoners who work too hard, or not at all. *Also* За тобо́й тюрьма́ пла́кать бу́дет. **7.** Кто в тюрьме́ не сиде́л, тот бу́дет;/ Кто отсиде́л, тот (вове́к) не забу́дет. 'He who has not been in prison will be;/ He who has been there will not (ever) forget it,' a popular commentary on the hardships of prison life and its inevitability.

тю́ря, 'bread soup,' consisting of bread soaked in boiling, salted water, more satisfying because of the increased volume. Сего́дня с утра́ я раскроши́л свою́ па́ечку и зафасова́л тю́рю с со́лью. Лу́чше пиро́жного. This morning I crumbled up my bread ration and made bread soup. It was better than pastry! [AD, a soup containing bread and onions]

тюря́га. *See* тюрьма́.

тяну́ть 1. ——— ля́мку, 'to work hard.' На лесопова́ле все з/к му́чились и тяну́ли ла́герную ля́мку. At the logging camp the prisoners suffered and worked hard. [AD, to do long, monotonous work] **2.** ——— рези́ну, 'to protract, dawdle, stretch out (needlessly).' *Cf.* рези́нщик.

тя́пнуть, pf., 'to drink.' Наш коменда́нт суме́л тя́пнуть два стака́на и хоть бы хуй. Our barracks chief could swallow two glasses of vodka and not give a fuck [i.e., show no visible effect]. [AD, pop.]

У, у

у́гол, 'suitcase.' Сего́дня эта́пом привезли́ каку́ю-то большу́ю ши́шку с заграни́чным угло́м. On the transport today they brought in some big shot with a foreign suitcase.

угро́зыск, уголо́вный ро́зыск, 'criminal investigation department.' Ивано́ва забра́ли из КПЗ в угро́зыск для допро́сов. Ivanov was taken from the KPZ (preliminary detention cell) to the criminal investigation department for questioning. [AD]

уе́хать ⊂ На мне далеко́ не уе́дешь,/ Где ся́дешь, там и сле́зешь. 'You won't ride far on me,/ Where you mount, there you will dismount,' a proverbial response to an attempt by someone to take advantage of one.

ука́зник, '*ukaznik*,' a prisoner sentenced under an ukase, an edict issued by the Presidium of the Supreme Soviet. В на́шем бара́ке бо́льше полови́ны з/к бы́ло ука́зников. In our barracks over half the prisoners were *ukazniks*. [D, lawyer, one who knows the ukases]

укра́сть ⊂ Не украдёшь, не проживёшь. 'If you don't steal, you won't make it,' an expression, heard also in free life, indicating the necessity of stealing in order to survive.

улупи́ть, улупа́ть, 'to gulp down, to stuff.' Си́доров стал таки́м доходя́гой, что по три бала́нды улупа́л враз. Sidorov became such a goner that he managed to gulp down three bowls of gruel at once.

умере́ть ⊂ Умри́ ты сего́дня, а я за́втра! *See* подо́хнуть 1.

упира́ться, impf., 'to work hard.' Ивано́в упира́лся весь срок, пока́ пиздо́й не накры́лся. Ivanov worked hard his whole term until he dropped dead.

УРБ [u-er-bé], учётно-распредели́тельное бюро́, 'URB,' registration distribution office, responsible for accepting prisoners, for distributing them in camp, for conducting prisoner counts, and, eventually, for releasing them. It also preserves the prisoners' dossiers and keeps them up to date. Во вре́мя пове́рки надзира́тель вме́сте с нача́льником УРБ обходи́ли все бара́ки и учи́тывали всех з/к. During a prisoner count the supervisor and the URB chief used to visit all the barracks and verify all the prisoners.

у́рка, 'a hardened, professional criminal.' Как привезли́ у́рок [уркага́нов, уркаче́й] на наш уча́сток, так и жи́зни не ста́ло. When they brought the criminals to our section, then life became unbearable. [Tr, also у́рок; То 61; St 142] *Also* уркага́н, урка́ч.

уркага́н. [St 142, also урка́н] *See* у́рка.

урка́ч. *See* у́рка.

УРЧ [u-er-čé], учётно-распредели́тельная часть, 'registration distribution section.' *See* УРБ.

утащи́ть, 'to steal.' Сего́дня у́рки утащи́ли паёк из рук Ивано́ва. Today the criminals stole the rations right out of Ivanov's hands. [AD, colloq.]

ухло́пать, pf., 'to kill.' У́рки но́чью ухло́пали су́ку. The criminals killed a stoolie during the night. [AD, pop.]

уча́сток 1. 'camp section,' normally the smallest administrative unit of a camp complex, containing some support facilities, such as a kitchen, an infirmary, storage areas, administrative offices, and, sometimes, a bath. It might or might not contain a compound (зо́на, q.v.). Нача́льник уча́стка [л/п, ла́герного пу́нкта, лагпу́нкта] приказа́л предоста́вить ему́ сво́дку за про́шлую неде́лю к двум часа́м дня. The camp section commandant ordered a summary of last week's operations to be brought to him by two o'clock. *Also* ла́герный пункт, лагпу́нкт, л/п. 2. ма́мский ———, 'mother section,' a special camp section for mothers and pregnant prisoners, found only in large camp systems. В лагеря́х забере́меневшие же́нщины переводи́лись на ма́мские уча́стки. In the camps, prisoners who became pregnant were transferred to special mother sections.

учётчик, 'a bookkeeper,' an employee of the coordination planning section, who measures work done, calculates percentages, and checks attendance. Под коне́ц рабо́чего дня учётчик появи́лся, чтобы изме́рить рабо́ту брига́ды. At the end of the work day the bookkeeper came to measure the brigade's work. [AD]

Ф, ф

фарт 1. 'a dashing, bold person.' Ивано́в э́то фарт-па́рень. Ivanov is a dashing guy. **2.** 'thief's wages, booty, take.' Фарт Карзу́бого был по́лный чемода́н веще́й. Karzubyj's take was a suitcase full of things. [Tr; F 180, идти на фарт 'to go out to steal'] **3.** 'happiness, luck.' Жела́ю вам фа́рта. I wish you luck. [AD, pop.; Tr]

фарто́вый ⊂ фарто́вый па́рень, 'a dashing, bold fellow.' Ва́ня, когда́ прие́хал эта́пом, был доходны́м; пото́м стал таки́м фарто́вым па́рнем, что не подходи́. When he arrived with the transport, Vanja was a goner; then he became such a dashing fellow that you couldn't get near him. [AD, pop.; Tr; F 180; St 138]

фаши́ст, 'a fascist,' a term of abuse applied to political prisoners by criminals and officials. Ах, ты фаши́ст, рабо́тать отказа́лся, искупи́ть свою́ вину́ пе́ред ро́диной не хо́чешь. Ah, you fascist! You've refused to work and don't want to expiate your guilt before the fatherland. [AD]

фе́ня ⊂ по-фе́не бо́тать. *See* бо́тать.

фера́йна. *See* хе́вра.

фило́н, 'a shirker.' Петро́ва все зна́ли, как фило́на, и брига́да так привы́кла к э́тому, что переста́ли его́ тро́гать. Everyone knew Petrov as a shirker, and the brigade was so used to it that they had stopped bothering him. [KK]

фило́нить, impf., 'to shirk, to goof off.' Джамбу́л филони́л всю доро́гу в ла́гере, то́лько э́то не спасло́ его́ от сангородка́. Džambul always goofed off in camp, but it didn't save him from the hospital-medical block. [KK]

фило́нство, 'laziness.' Ах, ты ко́нтрик, э́то фило́нство я вы́бью из тебя́. You counter-revolutionary, I'll knock the laziness out of you.

фитилёк, dim. of фити́ль (q.v.).

фити́ль, 'a goner' (lit., a candlewick). Иванов проштра́фился и его́ посла́ли на известко́вый уча́сток. За два ме́сяца из него́ получи́лся фити́ль [фитилёк]. Ivanov committed a minor infraction and was sent to a lime compound. In two months he had become a goner. [KK] *Also* фитилёк.

фо́мка, 'a jimmy,' used for breaking into houses. Но́чью фо́мкой откры́ли вещкаптёрку и утащи́ли мно́го оде́жды. During the night the clothing storage was jimmied open and a lot of clothing was stolen. [Sm; D; Tr; F 180; To 158]

фо́ня ⊂ на фо́не бо́тать. *See* бо́тать.

формуля́р, 'a dossier.' Begun by the first camp administration, the dossier accompanies the prisoner throughout his term. У Были́нского в формуля́ре была́ поме́тка: « без пра́ва перепи́ски ». In Bylinskij's dossier was the notation: "without the right of correspondence." [D]

фо́рса, 'pomposity.' Не ры́пайся, а то фо́рсу наждако́м счищу. Don't be pushy, or I'll remove your pomposity with emery paper. [AD, pop. форс]

форсу́н, 'a braggart.' Все в бара́ке зна́ли, что Алёша форсу́н, то́лько интере́сно бы́ло всем слу́шать его́ расска́зы о во́ле. Everyone in the barracks knew that Aleša was a braggart, but they liked to listen to his stories about free life. [AD, pop. 'a show-off'; D]

форт ⊂ бе́гать по фо́ртам, 'to be a burglar,' specifically, to enter apartments through a small casement window (фо́рточка). Са́ша всю жизнь бе́гал по фо́ртам. All his life Saša was a burglar. [Sm, форточничать; To 343]

фо́рточка 1. 'a small casement window.' [AD] *Cf.* форт, фо́рточник. **2.** откидна́я ———. *See* корму́шка.

фо́рточник, 'a burglar,' who enters apartments through a small casement window (фо́рточка). Са́ша всю жизнь был фо́рточником [око́нщиком], то́лько без сча́стья. Бо́льше просиде́л в тюрьме́, чем на во́ле. Saša was a burglar all his life, but without success. He spent more time in prison than at liberty. [KK] *Also* око́нщик.

фра́йер, 'a pigeon, a dupe,' a political or a nonpolitical prisoner unused to prison or camp ways. С после́дним эта́пом почти́ одни́ фрайера́ при́были. The last transport consisted almost entirely of pigeons. [Tr, also фра́ер; F 180; To 106, also фра́вер, фрайгер]

фра́йерша, fem. form of фра́йер (q.v.). [To 107, фра́верша]

фриц, 'a Kraut, a Fritz,' derog. name for a German, also applied to Russians as a term of abuse. Арбýзов, чего́ согнýлся, как фриц под Москво́й; дава́й рабо́тать. Arbuzov, why have you folded up like the Krauts at Moscow? Let's get on with the work.

фуганýть, pf., 'to slug, hit, beat.' Оди́н фра́йер приста́л ко мне, что́бы я емý вернýл его́ сапоги́, но и я его́ фуганýл в ро́жу. A pigeon begged me to return his shoes, but I just slugged him in the face.

футля́р, 'a louver.' Все о́кна внýтренних тю́рем в таки́х футля́рах; в ка́меру то́лько полусве́т проника́ет. All windows of the inner prison are covered with louvers; only twilight penetrates the cell. [AD, box, chest] *Also* намо́рдник, козырьки́.

X, x

хаба́р, 'a bribe.' Ко́лька су́нул хаба́р нача́льнику коло́нны и тот поста́вил его́ ночны́м днева́льным. Kol'ka slipped the column chief a bribe and was made a night orderly. [AD, pop. obs.]

хаба́рник, 'a fixer, a bribe-taker.' Наш бригади́р был большо́й хаба́рник; всего́ мо́жно бы́ло у него́ доби́ться за ла́пу. Our brigadier was a great fixer; you could get anything from him for a bribe. [D]

ха́вало, 'mug, snout, trap, face.' Закро́й ха́вало, а то приду́шу́. Shut your trap, or I'll strangle you.

ха́вать. *See* сха́вать.

ха́зерлах, indecl., 'a gold coin.' Ивано́в рассказа́л нам, что НКВД обнару́жило у него́ 50 ха́зерлах [кру́гленьких]. Ivanov told us that the NKVD discovered 50 gold coins on him. *Also* кру́гленькая.

хала́тность, 'negligence,' a reference to articles 111 and 112 of the Soviet Criminal Code of 1926, under which many people were imprisoned for the slightest misstep. « Ивано́в, за что тебя́ посади́ли? » — « За хала́тность ». — « А в чём де́ло? » — « Кобы́лу укра́л, а жеребёнка оста́вил ». "Ivanov, what were you imprisoned for?" "For negligence." "What precisely?" "I stole a mare, but left the foal behind." [AD]

халту́ра, 'an extra job.' [AD, colloq.] *Cf.* подхалту́рить.

халту́рить, impf., **1.** 'to cheat, finagle, pad.' Че́стным трудо́м нельзя́ бы́ло получи́ть прили́чную вы́работку; ка́ждый стара́лся халту́рить, как мог. With decent work one couldn't earn a decent output; everyone tried to cheat as much as he could. [AD, colloq. 'to work carelessly'] **2.** *See* подхалту́рить.

халя́ва, 'slut, whore.' Со́нька, э́та халя́ва из шесто́го же́нского бара́ка, опя́ть притащи́лась в мужску́ю зо́ну. Son'ka, that slut from the sixth female barracks, has come to the men's compound again. [D]

хамса́. *See* камса́.

хана́, 'the end.' В 1946-м году́ о́пер посади́л меня́ в изоля́тор и я поду́мал, что мне хана́. In 1946 the security officer put me in the isolator, and I thought it was the end of me.

хапо́к ⊂ на хапо́к, 'by swiping.' Карзу́бый пыта́лся на хапо́к отня́ть па́йку у инвали́да Моро́зова, но бригади́р накры́л его́ и дал ему́ отбивны́е по рёбрам. Karzubyj tried to swipe the invalid Morozov's bread ration, but our gang boss caught him and gave him a very severe beating. [AD, pop. хап 'steal, swipe']

харби́нец, 'Harbinite,' a general name for prisoners from Manchuria after 1945, many of whom were former White Guards. В 1948-м году́ привезли́ эта́п харби́нцев. Большинство́ из них — бы́вшие белогварде́йцы. In 1948 a transport of Harbinites was brought in. Most of them were former White Guards.

ха́ря, 'face, mug.' Посмотри́ на э́ту ха́рю; ведь ему́ на лбу́ напи́сано « иша́чить ». Look at this ugly mug; "work like a dog" is writ large on his face. [AD, c. pop.]

ха́халь. [D] *See* ёба́рь.

‡ **ха́ять,** impf., 'to worry, to concern oneself.' Зря лите́йщиков не хай! Не хай! Тут я смотрю́! Я не допущу́! Don't bother the foundrymen for nothing! Keep out of it. I'm in charge here! I won't allow it. (Оле́нь и шалашо́вка) [D]

хе́вра, 'a gang of criminals.' Вчера́ гру́ппа у́рок собрала́сь, что́бы заплани́ровать обрабо́тку продкапте́рки, и всю хе́вру [бра́шку, фера́йну] накры́л уполномо́ченный. Yesterday a group of criminals gathered to plan the food storage job and the security officer discovered the whole gang. [Tr; To 54] *Also* бра́шка, фера́йна.

хер 1. 'prick, penis.' Ма́ша—э́то така́я шваль; сама́ напра́шивается на на́ры, сама́ на хер ле́зет. Maša is such an animal; she invites herself onto the bed boards and crawls onto your prick herself. [D] **2.** ——— моржо́вый, 'a walrus's prick,' a derogatory characterization of someone who is unable to adapt to camp life. Э́тот хер моржо́вый до́лго не протя́нет в лагеря́х; он да́же не зна́ет, как поматери́ться. That walrus's prick won't last long in camps; he doesn't even know how to curse. [S 74] **3.** На хи́трую жо́пу, хер винто́м. *See* жо́па.

хиля́ть, impf., 'to pass for, to pretend to be.' Наш бригади́р на во́ле был шахтёром. В ла́гере он наблаты́кался и хиля́л под блатно́го. Our gang boss was a miner on the outside. In the camp he soaked up criminal ways and passed for a criminal.

хипе́сница, 'a whore, a prostitute who robs her clients.' Ма́ша на во́ле была́ хипе́сницей [хупе́сницей]. In free life Maša was a client-robbing whore. *Also* хупе́сница. [Tr, хи́песница; To 484]

хи́трый ⊂ хи́трый до́мик, 'security office.' Я пыта́лся спла́вить казённый матра́ц вольня́жке и накры́лся; меня́ потащи́ли в хи́трый до́мик на допро́с. I tried to sell a government mattress to a free employee and was caught in the act. I was dragged to the security office for interrogation.

хлеба́ло, 'face.' Уйди́ по-хоро́шему, а то су́ну в хлеба́ло, что и родна́я не узна́ет. You better get out of here, or I'll work your face over so that your own mother won't know you. [D, mouth; St 143, закро́й хлебало 'shut up']

хлеборе́з, 'the breadcutter'. С рабо́ты я пря́мо в каптёрку ходи́л помога́ть хлеборе́зу [хлеборе́зчику]. From work I used to go straight to the food storage to help the breadcutter. *Also* хлеборе́зчик.

хлеборе́зка, 'the breadcutter's,' the place where every prisoner dreams of working. Мой сосе́д познако́мился с одни́м из хлеборе́зки, и но́чью ходи́л помога́ть ему́ хлеб ре́зать. My neighbor met someone from the breadcutter's and at night would go to help him cut bread. [AD, machine for cutting bread; colloq. 'a woman who cuts bread']

хлеборе́зчик. *See* хлеборе́з.

хло́пнуть, pf., 'to shoot.' Из мои́х однодѐльцев двух хло́пнули, а остальны́м да́ли по черво́нцу. Two of my accomplices were shot and the others were given ten years each. [AD, pop.]

хозрасчёт, хозя́йственный расчёт, 'economic accounting,' a method of payment to prisoners introduced in 1947–1948, in response to slave labor charges from abroad. В лагеря́х в европе́йской ча́сти Сове́тского Сою́за ввели́ хозрасчёт в 1947-м году́, в сиби́рских лагеря́х то́лько в 1948-м году́. Economic accounting was introduced in camps in the European part of the Soviet Union in 1947, but in the Siberian camps only in 1948. [AD]

холу́й ⊂ холу́й холуём погоня́ет, 'one slave will drive another,' an expression used to characterize the camp system which forces prisoners to drive one another to work. В сове́тских лагеря́х холу́й холуём погоня́ет так, что никуда́ не де́нешься. In Soviet camps one slave will drive another so that you can't hide from work. [AD, pop. obs.]

хомута́ть. *See* нахомута́ть.

хрено́вина, 'annoying crap,' stupid, annoying details. В лагеря́х не обраща́й внима́ния на хрено́вины, а то страда́ть бу́дешь всю доро́гу. Pay no attention to the annoying crap in camps or you'll suffer the whole time. [KK]

христо́сик, 'a Christer,' a name applied to members of various Christian sects who openly defy Soviet authority in camps and who are cruelly suppressed. The Christians are generally admired for their stand by both criminals and political prisoners. В на́шем бара́ке жи́ло два христо́сика. Они́ че́стно рабо́тали, то́лько призна́ть Сове́тскую власть не хоте́ли. Two Christers lived in our barracks. They worked honestly, but did not want to acknowledge Soviet power.

хро́ник, 'a chronically sick person,' considered incurable. Such prisoners cannot be assigned to a rehabilitation point, meant only for those who can be restored to working condition. Most of the chronically ill are kept in special barracks until they die. Для хро́ников вы́делили оди́н бара́к. Их на рабо́ту не гоня́ли — то́лько сиде́ли на гаранти́йке. One barracks was set aside for the chronically sick. They weren't sent out to work—they just lived there on their guaranteed ration. [AD, colloq.]

хрю́кать по-фе́не [на фо́не]. *See* бо́тать.

хуй ⊂ хоть бы хуй, 'not give a fuck, couldn't care less.' Нача́льник режи́ма предупреди́л на́шего бригади́ра, что, е́сли не порвёт с Ма́шей, то его́ в зо́ну поса́дит, а бригади́р хоть бы хуй. The disciplinary officer warned our brigadier that if he didn't break off with Maša, he would be put in the guarded zone, but the brigadier didn't give a fuck. [D, хуй 'prick, penis']

хупе́сница. *See* хипе́сница.

Ц, ц

цап-цара́п, 'a heist, a theft.' Оди́н Каза́х в на́шем бара́ке получи́л посы́лку с кишмишо́м; дава́й сде́лаем цап-цара́п. One of the Kazakhs in our barracks received a package of currants; let's swipe it. [AD, colloq. conj. used as predicate 'grabbed, took']

цара́пнуть, цара́пать, 'to seize, to grab.' Ко́лька цара́пнул хлеб из рук доходя́ги, кото́рый проголода́л весь день. Kol'ka grabbed the bread out of the hands of a goner, who had gone hungry all day. [D]

цветно́й, 'a "colored" criminal.' This term refers to the two subgroups of the organized criminal world, кра́сненькие, 'the reds' and бе́ленькие, 'the whites.' *See* блатно́й 1.

цвето́чек ⊂ Это то́лько цвето́чки, а я́годки впереди́. 'These are only flowerets, the (little) berries lie ahead,' a proverb frequently heard in camps. It means that the worst is still to come. [Ž]

це́лка 1. 'a virgin,' a derogatory name for a person who pretends to be honest. Посмотри́ како́й це́лкой [це́лочкой] он притворя́ется; вчера́ то́лько лупи́л доходя́гу до сме́рти. See what a virgin he's pretending to be; but yesterday he beat a goner to death. [D; Tr, prostitute not registered with police] *Also* це́лочка. **2.** сиде́ть за це́лку, 'to do time for rape.' « Петро́в, за что посади́ли? » — « За це́лку ». "Petrov, what are you doing time for?" "For rape."

це́лочка 1. dim. of це́лка 1 (q.v.). **2.** расколо́ться, как ———, 'to break like a hymen,' a frequently used phrase to describe one's giving in under the strain of the interrogation. Си́доров до́лго держа́лся на сле́дствии, не сдава́ясь нажи́му сле́дственных о́рганов; одна́ко по́сле шести́ ме́сяцев он расколо́лся, как це́лочка. During the investigation Sidorov held his ground for a long time without giving in to the pressure of the interrogators; after six months, however, he broke like a hymen.

ЦТРМ [це-те-ер-е́м], центра́льная техни́чески-ремо́нтная мастерска́я, 'CTRM,' central technical repair shop, located in each agricultural compound to repair tractors and other machinery. ЦТРМ на́шего отделе́ния находи́лось в двадцати́ киломе́трах от тра́кторной брига́ды. The CTRM of our district was 20 kilometers from the tractor brigade.

цы́рлах ⊂ на цы́рлах, 'on tiptoe.' Карзу́бый стал шестёркой на́шего бригади́ра; он стоя́л на цы́рлах пе́ред ним, гото́вый испо́лнить вся́кое его́ жела́ние. Karzubyj became our brigadier's lackey; he tiptoed around him, ready to fulfill his every desire. [Tr, ци́рлих (German, *zierlich*), a type of robbery in which someone enters a hotel room very quietly]

Ч, ч

ча́пать. *See* прича́пать.

Чека́, indecl., according to K., but frequently decl. in colloq. speech, Чрезвыча́йная коми́ссия по борьбе́ с контрреволю́цией и сабота́жем, 'Cheka,' extraordinary commission for the suppression of counter-revolution and sabotage (1917–1922), the name of the Soviet secret police agency which organized and first managed prison camps. The agency underwent a number of reorganizations and name changes, becoming subsequently ГПУ (February to December, 1922), ОГПУ (1922–1934), НКВД (1934–1943), НКГБ (1943–1946), МГБ (1946–1953), МВД (1953), and КГБ (1953–). Сосе́д донёс, что Соколо́в был офице́ром в ца́рской а́рмии, и его́ сра́зу же посади́ли по распоряже́нию Чека́ [ЧК]. A neighbour denounced Sokolov as a former tsarist officer and he was immediately imprisoned by an order of the Cheka. [AD, colloq.] *Also* ЧК.

чеки́ст 1. 'hangman.' Коменда́нт на́шей зо́ны вёл себя́, как настоя́щий чеки́ст. За ничто́ сажа́л заключённых в БУР. The barracks chief in our compound behaved like a real hangman. He would put prisoners in the punishment block for nothing at all. **2.** 'Chekist,' an employee of the secret police, a term still used although the Cheka was reorganized and renamed in 1922. *Cf.* Чека́. [AD, an employee of Cheka]

чеку́ша, 'a female thief.' Ко́стя нам рассказа́л, что у него́ жена́ чеку́ша и вме́сте рабо́тали на во́ле. Kostja told us that his wife was a thief and that they worked together on the outside.

челове́к ⊂ **1.** Был бы челове́к, а де́ло найдётся. 'Provided we've got the man, we can find a charge for him,' an expression describing the ease with which a person may be charged, and its inevitability. [Ž, Была́ бы спина́, найдётся и вина́] **2.** Челове́к до́лжен то́лько существова́ть, а преступле́ние найдётся. 'You need only exist, and a crime will be found,' a frequent response to a prisoner who wonders what he will be charged with. Вновь аресто́ванный волну́ется. Каку́ю статью́ мо́гут ему́ пришй́ть? Ему́ отвеча́ют: « Ты до́лжен то́лько существова́ть, а преступле́ние найдётся ». The newly arrested prisoner was agitated. What provision could they pin on him? They answered him, "You have only to exist, and a crime will be found for you."

че́рви, pl. ⊂ с черве́й ходи́ть, 'to fawn on' (lit., to lead with hearts). Ты мне с черве́й не ходи́, режь пря́мо! Don't fawn on me, speak up! [AD, hearts (in cards)]

черво́нец 1. 'a ten-year stretch, a ten-year term.' Из мои́х однодѐльцев двум да́ли по черво́нцу. Two of my accomplices were each given a ten-year stretch. [AD, 10-ruble note, 1922–1947] **2.** меня́ть ———, 'to serve a ten-year stretch' (lit., to change a 10-ruble note). « Гей, Ва́ня, ско́лько тебе́ втри́нили? » — « Чепуха́, меня́ю черво́нец ». "Hi, Vanja! What's your sentence?" "A trifle. I'm serving a ten-year stretch."

черну́ха, 'a lie, a false front.' Пото́м он сиде́л, откры́в для черну́хи спра́вочник, и погля́дывал, что де́лается с его́ листо́м да́льше. Then he sat down, opened a reference book for the sake of appearances, and looked to see what would happen to the sheet next. (В круге первом)

черну́шник, 'a liar, cheater.'

черпа́к ⊂ **1.** черпако́м по голове́, 'a ladle over your head,' a frequent response of the cook to prisoners who ask for second helpings. Убира́йся со свои́м котелко́м, а то полу́чишь черпако́м по голове́. Get out of here with your kettle, or you'll get a ladle over your head. **2.** Прокуро́р медве́дь, а хозя́ин черпа́к. *See* прокуро́р.

чеса́ть 1. 'to run.' Бригади́р сказа́л Жу́кову: « Чеши́ в ба́ню, а то у́жина не полу́чишь ». The brigadier said to Žukov, "Run to the bathhouse, or you won't get any supper." [AD, pop.; D, to go] **2.** 'to chew out, to light into, to scold harshly.' Помо́щник бригади́ра опозда́л на развод; бригади́р дава́й его́ чеса́ть для блези́ру. The brigadier's deputy was late for the march off to work; the brigadier lit into him as a matter of form.

честня́га, че́стный вор, 'a criminal covered by the code.' *Cf.* зако́н 1.

четверта́к. [AD, obs. '25 kopeks'] *See* четвертно́й.

четвертно́й, 'a 25-year stretch, a 25-year term.' Кли́мов четвертно́й [четверта́к] себе́ отхвати́л. Klimov was sentenced to a 25-year stretch. [AD, obs. '25 rubles'] *Also* четверта́к.

чечётка, 'a tap dance,' done by criminals in cells and barracks for exercise. Чечётка была любимым танцем преступного мира, в особенности в тюрьме и изоляторах. The tap dance was the favorite dance of the criminals, especially in prison and in isolators. [AD]

ЧИС [čís], часть интендантского снабжения, 'ČIS,' a section of commissary supply. В большинстве лагерей ЧИС состоял из двух отделов: пищеблока и вещблока. In most of the camps the ČIS was made up of two sections, the food and the clothing sections.

чистка ⊂ Большая [Великая] чистка, 'the Great Purge' (1936–1938). Сидоров попал в лагеря во время Большой [Великой] чистки. Sidorov was sent to labor camps during the Great Purge.

чифир, '*čifir*, a narcotic brewed from tannin and caffein.' Блатные зафасовали пачку чая и заварили крепкий чифир. Сидя на корточках они попивали по ложке и им всё море было по колено. The criminals obtained a package of tea and brewed up a strong *čifir*. Squatting on their heels, they sipped the brew with a teaspoon and got high.

чифирист, 'one who gets high on чифир (q.v.).'

‡ **чихня,** 'a trifle, nonsense.' А ты Гурвичу с охраной труда голову морочишь. Чихня это всё. Не твоё дело. And you're pestering Gurvič about some labor safety regulations. It's a lot of nonsense. It's none of your business. (Олень и шалашовка)

ЧК. *See* Чека.

членовредительство, 'self-mutilation,' done in order to avoid hard labor. It was considered sabotage during the war, and was punished under article 58.14 of the Soviet Criminal Code of 1926. Всякое членовредительство считалось саботажем во время войны и судилось по 58.14. Self-mutilation was considered sabotage during the war and was tried under article 58.14. [AD]

чокнутый, 'a person with a screw loose, a somewhat odd, or crazy, person.' Смотри, этот доходяга когда-то был председателем облисполкома, а теперь он немножко чокнутый. Look, that goner was once the chairman of a district executive committee, and now he has some of his screws loose.

ЧОС [čós], часть особого снабжения, 'ČOS,' section of special supply, a division of the department of special supply, which supplies the camps and free population with food, clothing, and the like. Вещстóл поéхал в ЧОС, чтóбы получи́ть наря́д на телогрéйки для трактори́стов. The clothing clerk went to the ČOS to pick up an order for jackets for the tractor operators.

ЧСВН [če-se-ve-én], член семьи́ врагá нарóда, 'ČSVN,' a member of the family of an enemy of the people. Дочь Тухачéвского былá посáжена в мари́йские лагеря́, как ЧСВН. Tuxačevskij's daughter was put in the Mariinsk camps as a ČSVN.

ЧСИРовка [če-se-írafka], член семьи́ измéнника рóдине, 'ČSIR,' a female member of a traitor's family. Женá Гамáрника сидéла, как ЧСИРовка в Карлáге. Gamarnik's wife served time in Karlag (the Karaganda camp) as a ČSIR.

ЧТЗ [če-te-zé], Челя́бинский трáкторный завóд, 'ČTZ,' Čeljabinsk tractor plant, a main tire producer in the Soviet Union. In camps, a ČTZ is a handmade sandal with a rubber tire sole. Óбуви совершéнно нé было в лагеря́х; з/к обувáлись в ЧТЗ. There was absolutely no footwear in camps; the prisoners were shod in ČTZ. [K]

чумá, 'a swindler.' Ивáнов э́то настоя́щая чумá; с ним лýчше делóв не имéть. Ivanov is a real swindler; better have no dealings with him. [AD, plague]

чумáзый, 'a tractor operator.' Сегóдня чумáзые вернýлись с сенокóса. Today the tractor operators returned from mowing. [AD, colloq. 'dirty']

чу́ни, pl., 'rubber overshoes.' Чу́ни — э́то назвáние галóшей, котóрые надевáлись на вáтные чулки́ и завя́зывались верёвками. Čuni is the name of the rubber overshoes which were put on over cotton socks and fastened with strings. [AD, prov.]

Ш, ш

шабáш, 'finished,' often used by brigadiers to signal the end of work. Ребя́та, шабáш! Давáй на вáхту. We're done, fellows! Let's go to the guard shack. [AD, pop.]

шакáл, 'a jackal, a scavenger.' От э́того шакáла жи́зни нет; он ужé все помóйки перерьíл. There's no peace from that jackal; he's already dug through all the trash heaps. [AD]

шакáлить. *See* пошакáлить.

шалашóвка, 'a whore.' Смотри́, э́та шалашóвка опя́ть полéзла в мужску́ю зóну. Look, that whore has crawled into the men's compound again. *Also* шалошóвка.

шалмáн, 'a den.' Барáк малолéток э́то был настоя́щий шалмáн; все избегáли егó, как огня́. The teenagers' barracks was a real den; everyone avoided it like fire. [AD, c. pop. 'a cheap tavern']

шалошóвка. *See* шалашóвка.

шáмать. *See* пошáмать.

шамóвка, 'food.' В Карлáге, дáже во врéмя войньí, былá хорóшая шамóвка [гужóвка]. Even during the war there was good food at Karlag (the Karaganda camp). [AD, c. pop.] *Also* гужóвка.

‡ **шарáшка,** 'šaraška,' a special prison and research institute, staffed by prisoners who are trained specialists and technicians, and where living conditions are vastly superior to ordinary prisons and camps. Зэ́ки шарáшки в то врéмя ещё не наедáлись, и борьбá за пять грáммов муки́ воспринимáлась острéй, чем междунарóдные собы́тия. The šaraška zeks at that time did not get their fill to eat, and the struggle for five grams of flour was of much greater interest than international affairs. (В круге пéрвом) [Fraz., шарашкина контóра 'an unreliable, untrustworthy enterprise or organization']

шáрики, pl., 'brain.' На негó надéяться нельзя́, у негó шáрики не рабóтают. It's impossible to rely on him, his brain doesn't work.

шестери́ть, 'to serve as a lackey.' Ефи́м шестери́л на́шему бригади́ру. Efim served as a lackey to our brigadier. [D, to run back and forth frequently]

шестёрка, 'a criminal's lackey,' held in contempt by other prisoners. Every "self-respecting" criminal tries to have one or more lackeys. Ефи́м был шестёркой на́шего бригади́ра бо́льше го́да; чи́стил боти́нки, стира́л портя́нки и чини́л оде́жду бригади́ра. Efim was our brigadier's lackey for more than a year; he cleaned the shoes, washed the foot cloths, and repaired the clothing of the brigadier. [S 75, waiter]

ше́я ⊂ Была́ бы ше́я, а ярмо́ найдётся. 'If you have a neck, a yoke will be found for it,' an ironic response of camp veterans to new arrivals who express concern about the work that will be assigned to them. [Ž, ... а хомут найдётся]

шизо́, indecl., штрафно́й изоля́тор, 'a penalty isolator,' under a special commandant, for prisoners being interrogated for crimes committed in camp. Все зна́ли, что Ивано́ва забра́ли в шизо́, потому́ что вну́тренник настуча́л на него́. Everyone knew that Ivanov had been taken to the penalty isolator because a prisoner guard squealed on him.

ширма́ч, '*širmač*,' a thief who carries out his work under the cover of a regular job. Наш паха́н на во́ле был ширмачём; рабо́тал успе́шно под прикры́тием. In free life our brigadier was a *širmač*; he worked successfully under cover. [Tr; To 2; St 133, all with definition 'pickpocket']

ши́шка, 'a big shot, an influential person.' Вчера́ кака́я-то больша́я ши́шка инспекти́ровала на́шу зо́ну. Some big shot inspected our compound yesterday. [AD, pop.]

шка́ры, pl., 'pants.' Дава́й махнёмся шка́рами; дам в прида́чу два пайка́ хле́ба. Let's trade pants; I'll give you two shares of bread to boot. [Tr; F 183; To 484, also шке́ры]

шкет, 'an apprentice criminal.' Наш паха́н взял себе́ шке́та в шестёрки. Our ringleader took on an apprentice as a lackey. [AD, pop. 'boy'; F 180]

шко́да, 'a pest, a mischief-maker.' Карзу́бый э́то тако́й шко́да [шко́дник]; где ни поя́вится, непреме́нно что́-то натвори́т. Karzubyj is such a pest; wherever he turns up, he constantly makes a mess of things. [AD, pop.] *Also* шко́дник.

шко́дник. *See* шко́да.

шко́дничать. *See* нашко́дничать.

шкýра ⊂ Былá бы кость, а шкýра нарастёт. *See* кость.

шлёпка, 'execution by shooting.' В 1937-м годý мнóгие высоко-поста́вленные ли́ца зна́ли, что их ожида́ет ве́рная шлёпка, и поэ́тому предпочита́ли поко́нчить жизнь самоуби́йством. In 1937 many high-ranking officials knew that they couldn't escape being shot and therefore preferred to commit suicide. [D, a slap]

шлёпнуть, pf., 'to execute by shooting.' Говоря́т, что всю верхýшку из 1937 гóда шлёпнули. It is said that the entire ruling clique of 1937 was executed. [AD, pop.]

шлю́нка, 'a watery camp soup.'

шмон, 'a frisk, a search.' Пéред Октя́брьскими пра́здниками вóхра производи́ла тща́тельный шмон во всех бара́ках. Before the October celebrations the camp garrison conducted a thorough frisk in all barracks. [KK]

шмона́ть. *See* прошмона́ть, прошмони́ть.

‡ **шмони́ть.** *See* прошмона́ть, прошмони́ть.

‡ **шмоня́ть.** *See* прошмона́ть, прошмони́ть.

шмóтки, pl. *See* мана́тки.

шни́фер. [Tr, housebreaker; To 22] *See* медвежа́тник 1.

шпáер. *See* шпа́лер.

шпáлер, 'a revolver.' Заряди́вшись, нача́льник режи́ма зашёл со шпа́лером [шпа́ером] в зóну. The drunken disciplinary officer entered the compound with a revolver. *Also* шпа́ер. [F 183; To 173; St 140, all шпа́лер; St 140, *also* шпа́ер]

шпана́, coll., 'young thugs,' used by hardened criminals for young, beginning criminals. Жи́зни нé было от шпаны́; отнима́ли послéднюю крóшку табакý. There was no respite from the young thugs; they would take your last crumb of tobacco. [AD, c. pop. 'hooligans'; Tr; F 181; To 141, faceless mass of prisoners; aLi 68, not belonging to thieves' group]

шпа́ненька. *See* шпаню́га.

шпаню́га, 'a young thug,' a term used by hardened criminals. Надзира́тель посади́л однó шпаню́гу [шпаня́гу, шпа́-неньку] в изоля́тор. The overseer put a young thug in the isolator. *Also* шпаня́га, шпа́ненька.

шпаня́га. *See* шпаню́га.

шпа́рщик ⊂ шпа́рщик клопóв, 'bug steamer,' a prisoner from the medical section, whose duty is to kill bugs in the barracks.

Нача́льник санча́сти назна́чил Ивано́ва шпа́рщиком кло-по́в. The head of the medical office made Ivanov a bug steamer.

шпик, 'a spy, an informer.' Все говори́ли, что наш д穓дева́льный шпик; з/к избега́ли его́, как огня́. Everyone said our barracks orderly was a spy; the prisoners shunned him like fire. [AD, colloq.]

штимп, 'a gull, a pigeon,' a criminals' derogatory name for a prisoner who is not one of their own kind. В на́шем бара́ке прожива́ло не́сколько блатны́х; все остальны́е бы́ли одни́ шти́мпы. Only a few professional criminals lived in our barracks; all the rest were gulls. [St 135, victim] *Also* штымп.

штос. [AD] *See* стосс.

штрафизоля́тор, штрафно́й изоля́тор, 'penalty isolator.' Стрелки́ пойма́ли беглецо́в и посади́ли их в штрафизоля́тор. The guards caught the escapees and put them in the penalty isolator.

штрафни́к, 'one who breaks a camp rule.' Китла́г отпра́вил всех штрафнико́в в Бра́тск. Kitlag (the Kitoj camp) sent all those convicted of breaking camp rules to Bratsk. [AD, colloq.]

штрафня́к, штрафно́й ла́герь. *See* ла́герь 9.

штурмовщи́на, 'rush-work tactics,' an all-out effort the last few days of the month to improve the work output. В после́дние не́сколько дней ме́сяца наш бригади́р применя́ет штурмовщи́ну. In the last few days of the month our brigadier resorts to rush-work tactics. [AD, colloq.]

штымп. *See* штимп.

шура́к, ' "brother-in-law," ' a jocular term for the relationship between two men who have had sexual relations with the same woman. Здоро́в, шура́к [своя́к], я ничу́ть не обижа́юсь; ведь Ма́ша сама́ призна́лась. Hi, brother-in-law. I'm not sore; after all, Maša herself confessed. [D, wife's brother] *Also* своя́к.

шурану́ть, pf. *See* шуруди́ть.

шуруди́ть, pf., 'to mug, to beat up and rob.' Вчера́ мы шуруди́ли [пошуруди́ли, шурану́ли] ко́нтриков и унесли́ два угла́, по́лных веще́й. Yesterday we mugged the counter-revolutionaries and carried away two suitcases full of things. *Also* пошуруди́ть, шурану́ть.

шухер 1. 'a fight.' Блатны́е ворва́лись в бара́к ко́нтриков и там шу́хер начался́. The criminals burst into the barracks of the counter-revolutionaries and a fight began. [Tr, a cry at a discovered theft; F 183, search; To 372, noise] 2. *See* ата́нде 1.

Э, э

этáп, 'transport, shipment of prisoners.' Из сéверных лагерéй отпрáвили этáп в Карагандý. A transport of prisoners was sent from the northern camps to Karaganda. [AD]

этапи́ровать, 'to transport, to ship prisoners.' В 1943-м годý меня́ этапи́ровали из Актю́бинска в Ни́жний Таги́л. In 1943 I was transported from Aktjubinsk to Nižnij Tagil.

‡ **этáпник,** 'a member of a transport.' По мéре тогó, как сержáнт выкли́кивает, этáпники прохóдят óбыск и перехóдят налéво. As the sergeant calls out their names, the prisoners from the transport undergo a search and go over to the left (of the stage). (Олень и шалашовка)

Ю, ю

ю́шка   1. 'gruel,' not quite so derogatory a term as бала́нда, лю́ра (qq.v.). По́вар сего́дня раздава́л обе́д, одну́ ю́шку. Today the cook served dinner, only watery gruel.   **2.** 'blood.' Бригади́р пусти́л ему́ ю́шку. The gang boss hit him till he bled. [D, fish soup; KK, soup, blood]

Я, я

я́годка ⊂ Э́то то́лько цвето́чки, а я́годки впереди́. *See* цвето́чек.

язы́чник, 'a chatterbox.' [AD, pop.] *See* болту́н.

я́ма, 'a fence, a dealer in stolen goods.'

ярмо́ ⊂ Была́ бы ше́я, а ярмо́ найдётся. *See* ше́я.

я́сли ⊂ де́тские я́сли, pl., 'nursery,' located outside camps, for children born in camps and for free children. Camp mothers are taken to their children several times a day. Днева́льная Ма́ша родила́ ребёнка; ребёнка сра́зу забра́ли в де́тские я́сли, а её под конво́ем води́ли корми́ть ребёнка. The barracks orderly Maša gave birth to a child. The child was immediately taken to the nursery and she was taken under escort to feed it. [AD]

я́щик **1.** за мя́гкое ме́сто и в я́щик. *See* конве́рт 1.   **2.** за ши́ворот и в я́щик. *See* конве́рт 2.